COOKING from the
HEART of SPAIN

Also by Janet Mendel

COOKING *from the* HEART *of* SPAIN

❖

FOOD OF LA MANCHA

JANET MENDEL

FRANCES LINCOLN LIMITED
PUBLISHERS

Frances Lincoln Ltd
4 Torriano Mews
Torriano Avenue
London NW5 2RZ
www.franceslincoln.com

Cooking from the Heart of Spain: Food of La Mancha
Copyright © Frances Lincoln 2008
Text copyright © Janet Mendel 2006, 2008
Jacket images copyright © Luca Pioltelli

First Frances Lincoln edition: 2008
First published in hardback in the United States of America
by HarperCollins Publishers Ltd
Portions of this book have appeared in somewhat different form in *Foods from
Spain News, Spain Goumetoar* and *Living Spain.*
Translations of extracts of *Don Quijote de la Mancha* by Miguel de Cervantes are
by the author.

Designed by William Ruoto
Map by Gordon Studio
Glossary compiled by Delora Jones

A catalogue record for this book is available from the British Library.

ISBN 978-0-7112-2873-3

Printed and bound in China

9 8 7 6 5 4 3 2 1

To Luella

La mejor salsa del mundo es la hambre.

Hunger is the best sauce.

—MIGUEL DE CERVANTES

❖ CONTENTS

❖ Acknowledgements

Many thanks to Amanda Clark and Donna Ellefson, two good friends who joined me on my culinary travels in La Mancha and helped me so much in sourcing ingredients in the United States in preparation for the American edition of this book. I really could not have put these recipes together without them.

I want to thank photographer Jean Dominique Dallet, who let me ride shotgun on his forays through La Mancha. He was a good guide on the Quixote trail.

Thanks to Donna Daniels Gelb and Marlene Parrish, who helped with recipe testing. Thanks, too, to Robert Wolke, for consulting on the science; to writer Gerry Dawes for contacts in the wine world; and to Ed Owen of Madrid, journalist, my personal tapa guide.

Many more assisted me along the way as I collected recipes and stories in La Mancha. I especially would like to thank the following:

Sisters Maria Victoria and Blanca Morras of Monasterio San Benito, Clarisas-Franciscan nuns in El Toboso (Toledo) who shared recipes for convent sweets.

José Rosell Villasevil, president: Sociedad Cervantina, Toledo.

Dionisio de Nova of Bodegas Dionisos, Valdepeñas (Ciudad Real).

Javier Alegria, El Tablazo, Villalba de la Sierra (Cuenca).

Manuela Sevilla Mompó, librarian, Quintanar de la Orden (Toledo), and her mother, Francisca Mompó.

Carlos Falcó, Marqués de Griñón, winemaker, Malpica de Tajo (Toledo).

Iñigo Valdenebro, producer of extra virgin olive oil, Toledo.

Roberto Arcos, knife maker, Albacete.

Pepe Expósito, knife maker, Albacete.

Pedro Condés Torres, director, Manchego Cheese Board, Valdepeñas (Ciudad Real).

Pilar Martínez, Azafrán Bealar, Motilla del Palancar (Cuenca).

Ana Beatriz Callejas, Saffron Board of La Mancha, Camuñas (Toledo).

Juan Pacheco Parra, president, Garlic Cooperative, Las Pedroñeras (Cuenca).

Adolfo Muñoz, Restaurante Adolfo, Toledo.

Manuel de la Osa, Restaurante Las Rejas, Las Pedroñeras (Cuenca).

Ian Gibson, author, Madrid.

Juan Carlos Palomino, Taller Gastronómico, Los Yébenes (Toledo).

Apelio García Sánchez-Horneros, Los Yébenes (Toledo).

Amelia Moreno Rosilla and David Cohn, Quintanar de la Orden (Toledo).

Samuel del Coso Román, Sephardic Center, Toledo.

I am indebted to several cookbooks in the Spanish language that pointed the way in my recipe gathering. Some are noted in specific recipes. All are listed in the bibliography at the end of this book.

Many thanks to my agent, Fred Hill, for finding just the right place for my work. Thanks to Susan Friedland, formerly of HarperCollins, the editor who started me on this book.

And *mil gracias* to Harriet Bell, my editor at William Morrow, who edited the book with taste and saw it through to fruition. Thanks to editorial assistant Lucy Baker; Chris Benton, for careful copyediting; Luca Pioltelli, who took the jacket photograph; Don Harris of La Tienda, who provided the foods for the photograph; and Bill Ruoto, for putting together a handsome book.

Special thanks to my good friends Harry and Charlotte Gordon, who not only shared many Manchegan meals and wines with me but contributed to the book by designing the map of La Mancha.

MADRID

GUADALAJARA

ARAGÓN

Villalba
de la Sierra

TOLEDO

CUENCA

Río Júcar

CASTILLA

Campillo
de Altobuey

Los
Yébenes

El Toboso

Las
Pedroñeras

LA

VALENCIA

Alcázar
de San Juan

CIUDAD REAL

MANCHA

ALBACETE

Almagro

La Solana

Valdepeñas

ANDALUCÍA

MURCIA

La Mancha,
the Heart of Spain

Against wide open spaces and big skies, shepherds move flocks of sheep across stubbled fields. Windmills appear on ridge tops like a line of cavalry. The occasional castle with its mediaeval battlements looks for all the world like a movie set from *El Cid*. In the autumn, Spain's central *meseta,* high plateau land, surprises with bursts of colour – russet leaves of vineyards, poplar trees by riverbanks spangled with golden leaves, sweet green of new wheat springing up. Ploughed earth is a strong mineral red. Sunsets above the vast plains streak the sky with violet, pink and periwinkle. Ruffled by wind, the leaves of olive trees shimmer silvery green.

I first visited La Mancha in the autumn to write an article about saffron, the aromatic spice grown in Spain's central region. I discovered a region of contrasts, old and new, brilliant colour, savoury food, delectable sweets.

In the saffron fields I followed the pickers down the rows as they filled their baskets with tiny saffron crocuses. Later I sat with the women who opened the petals and pulled out the stigma – three orange-red wisps – which, dried, becomes the spice we know. While they worked, they told me about traditional dishes cooked with saffron, which I later tasted in a local tavern.

From there I travelled to the hilltop town of Alarcón, where I stayed in an eighth-century fortress (now a hotel belonging to the national network of paradors) and dined on succulent baby lamb roasted in a wood-fired oven. The meat, redolent of wild herbs that fuelled the fire, was meltingly tender. At the nearby Roman ruins of Valera, I found saffron flowers popping up between the foundations of walls built in the first century. Stopping in a small village for a bite to eat, I encountered a weekly street market set up in the central plaza. A gypsy woman selling snails from a wheelbarrow told me how to cook them.

At country *ventas,* the sort of roadside eateries where Don Quixote had his mix-ups, I sampled rustic country stews, hearty garlic soups, big, satisfying salads and splendid vegetable dishes such as *pisto,* the forerunner of ratatouille.

I love these foods that frankly reveal their roots in the local soil – sausages made on a local farm, bread baked daily from wheat ground at a nearby mill, cheese made from the milk of sheep that graze springtime pastures, wine lovingly made from the grapes of the region and aged in caves hacked from the limestone earth. It is ancient, yet it is fresh.

While the straightforward simplicity of this food is so appealing, I also thrill to the innovation of a new generation of chefs and winemakers in La Mancha, the *vanguardistas* of twenty-first-century cuisine. Who ever would have imagined Syrah varietal wines in the middle of La Mancha? (They are marvellous!) What would Sancho Panza have thought about cold jellied garlic soup topped with foam of pimentón? (I bet he would have chuckled heartily.) While salt cod is very old stuff in La Mancha, it surely has a new lease of life as interpreted today in several of La Mancha's finest restaurants. And I love the nerve of a chef who dares to match plebeian beans, cooked to a creamy smoothness with saffron, and seared foie gras, which, when cut, releases its juices into the beans.

On subsequent visits to La Mancha, I joined a master confectioner of almond marzipan in his Toledo *obrador* and spent a day with a shepherd and maker of artisanal Manchego cheese. I ate trout pulled from cold streams in Cuenca and partridge taken in the hills of Toledo. I sampled La Mancha in all seasons, squelching through mud in asparagus fields to cut spring's first spears and sweating in the vineyards of Valdepeñas during the late-summer *vendimia,* grape harvest. I savoured every minute of it.

❧ THE LIE OF THE LAND

La Mancha is an upland plateau in the very centre of Spain. The Arabs who conquered most of Spain in the eighth century called it Al-Manchara, meaning 'arid land'. Known as Moors, they took over towns and strongholds previously held by Visigoths and Romans before them (the city of Toledo, the Roman Toletum, was founded in 190 B.C.). The conquering Moors left an indelible mark on culture, architecture and, of course, cooking.

The Arabs, who came from the crossroads of the great spice routes to the East, brought to Spain a treasure chest of aromatics – cinnamon, nutmeg, pepper, aniseed, sesame, cumin, coriander, ginger, caraway, saffron. They introduced the cultivation of almonds, aubergine, bitter oranges, pomegranates, rice and sugarcane. They extended the olive groves, which had been planted by the Romans, and devised complex irrigation systems.

In those mediaeval times, Jewish communities also resided in central Spain. Legend relates that the Hebrew peoples had lived in Spain since the time of King Solomon and the voyages of the Phoenician traders. What is certain is that communities of Jews existed in what is now Spain from the first century, during the time of the Roman Empire. They called their country Sepharad. During periods of benevolent Moorish rule, Spain's Jews enjoyed a 'golden age', participating at court as doctors, linguists and diplomats.

During several centuries of Reconquest, as successive Christian kings struggled to take back land lost to the Moors, La Mancha was the battlefield. Military-religious orders, such as the Knights of Calatrava, Knights of San Juan and Knights of Santiago, moved into the region, building fortifications – castles – to secure fiefdoms wrested from the Moors. Thus La Mancha acquired its other name – Castilla, or Castile, meaning 'castle'. By the end of the twelfth century, Christian rulers had regained much of La Mancha, whereas in the south of Spain, in Andalucía, the last Moorish king was not routed until 1492.

After the Reconquest and until the fateful year of 1492, when Jewish and Muslim inhabitants were forced to convert to the Catholic Church or else were expelled from Spain, La Mancha enjoyed several centuries of fitful *convivencia*, fairly peaceful co-existence among Moors, Jews and Christians. The Islamic culture contributed hugely to architecture, literature, science and medicine, agriculture and the culinary arts. This influence deeply imbues Spanish cookery, which, beneath its sturdy simplicity, wafts an aroma of refinement, of a delicate complexity left from those mediaeval times – savoury dishes with subtle sweet and sour flavours, crushed almonds for richness, lavish pastries spiked with cinnamon, saffron, rose water.

The sixteenth century ushered in Spain's Golden Age, when conquistadors brought glory and riches to Spanish shores – along with new foods from a new world, such as chocolate, beans, peppers, potatoes, squash and, eventually, tomatoes. Carlos V, who ascended the Spanish throne in 1519 and became Holy Roman Emperor as well, made Toledo his imperial capital. This king expanded Spain's influence throughout Europe, bringing under a single crown most of Spain, the Hapsburg domains of Austria, parts of Italy, the Spanish colonies in America, parts of France, Belgium and the Netherlands. When he abdicated in 1556, his son, Felipe II, succeeded him and later moved the capital to Madrid.

It was during the second half of this century that Miguel de Cervantes Saavedra, born in the town of Alcalá de Henares near Madrid, came of age. By 1592, a hundred years after Columbus's first voyage and the discovery of the Americas, Cervantes' writing career was beginning to flourish (he was earlier an enlisted soldier, a prisoner captured by Barbary pirates, and a government quatermaster officer). During his lifetime, there were amazing exploits by Spanish explorers in the Americas. Cervantes himself unsuccessfully petitioned the Council of the Indies for a post in the West Indies. Cervantes' most famous work, *Don Quijote de La Mancha,* was first published in 1605.

En un lugar de la Mancha, de cuyo nombre no quiero acordarme, no ha mucho tiempo que vivía un hidalgo de los de lanza en astillero, adarga antigua, rocín flaco y galgo corredor. Una olla de algo más vaca que carnero, salpicón las más noches, duelos y quebrantos los sábados, lentejas los viernes, y algún palomino de añadidura los domingos, consumían las tres partes de su hacienda. . . . Frisaba la edad de nuestro hidalgo con los cincuenta años: era de complexión recia, seco de carnes, enjuto de rostro, gran madrugador y amigo de la caza.

In a certain place in La Mancha, whose name I don't wish to remember, there lived not so long ago a gentleman of the landed gentry, the sort who kept a lance in the rack, an old shield, a thin nag and a racing greyhound. An olla – boiled dinner – with somewhat more beef than mutton, salpicón – leftovers – on most nights, duelos y quebrantos – eggs and brains – on Saturdays, lentils on Fridays and some squab on Sundays for good measure, used up three-quarters of his income. . . . Our gentleman was getting on for fifty: he was of robust constitution, lean, gaunt-faced, an early riser and aficionado of hunting.

It was four hundred years ago that Don Quixote sallied forth from his La Mancha village in search of adventure. Wearing a rusty suit of armour and a dented helmet, he partook of a meagre meal of salt cod at a roadside inn and was unceremoniously beknighted by the innkeeper with a thwack on the shoulder.

The story opens with a description of what Don Quixote ate most days of the week. Throughout the book, Cervantes feeds us morsels about life and food at the end of the sixteenth century. Don Quixote proves an excellent guide to the foods and cooking of present-day La Mancha, for the lie of the land has changed very little.

❧ LA MANCHA TODAY

Modern-day La Mancha belongs to the autonomous region of Castilla–La Mancha, situated in central Spain, which has its seat of government in the enchanting city of Toledo. The culture of Castilla–La Mancha falls somewhere between the austerity of Aragón and Old Castile and the flamboyance of Andalucía.

Castilla–La Mancha incorporates the provinces of Toledo, Ciudad Real, Cuenca, Albacete and Guadalajara (all with provincial capital cities of the same names). These provinces border on every other region of Spain, with the exception of two archipelagos, Catalonia, La Rioja, Navarra, and those bordering the northern Bay of Biscay. La Mancha, an inland region, has no seaport but – surprise! – is famous for its seafood.

Ciudad Real in the south shares some traditional dishes with adjoining Córdoba and Jaén. Toledo on the west borders Extremadura, land of the conquistadors. Rough *dehesa*, scrubland, of holm oaks and low stone walls, extends from one region into the next. Iberico pigs thrive here, fattening on the acorns. The *accidentado* – rough – terrain of the Montes de Toledo shelters partridge and other game.

To the north, Castilla–La Mancha touches the frontier of Old Castile (now Castilla y León). The food, grave and simple like the land, seems ancient – shepherds' stews whose recipes are almost biblical; ham and sausages cured as they have been for centuries; fresh trout from fast-flowing mountain streams.

Cuenca in the east makes an abrupt transition into Aragón and the Levant of Valencia. Albacete, once part of the kingdom of Murcia, continues to share with that Mediterranean region in the cultivation of paella rice.

Madrid también es La Mancha – Madrid is La Mancha too. Long before it was the capital of a united Spain, Madrid was a dusty town on the La Mancha plateau, a crossroads for migrating flocks of sheep. The food of this vibrant and cosmopolitan city, which today encompasses flavours from every region of Spain and the world, reveals its rustic past in favourite tapa bar foods and wines.

I have lived in Spain for many years and love its food from the inside out. La Mancha, for me, is the 'real' Spain – not Andalucía, not Catalonia, not Basque, not Galicia, nor Asturias. This is Spanish cooking true to its roots and enticing in its future. The heart of Spain.

✕ USING THESE RECIPES

Most dishes included in this book are authentic and traditional. Some recipes I have modified to make them either more user-friendly or more healthful (less lard, more olive oil). Where ingredients may be hard to come by for British cooks, I suggest alternatives. A few recipes are examples of creative ways to use typical Manchegan products. Some are my own invention; others have been adapted from dishes presented by modern-day chefs. An example is saffron ice cream, which incorporates La Mancha saffron in a non-traditional dessert.

Here is a glossary of ingredients and utensils used in the recipes. For sources, see the list at the end of the book.

CAZUELA   A cazuela is an earthenware casserole, glazed on the inside, unglazed on the outside bottom, that can be used on top of the stove and in the oven. It is much used in Spanish cookery, though a heavy frying pan, sauté pan or enamelled cast-iron casserole can be used instead. Cazuelas come in many widths, though they generally are not very deep (for example, a 25cm/10in cazuela is 7.5cm/3in deep). Big ones are heavy and not easy to manoeuvre in and out of the oven. Small ones, *cazuelitas,* are perfect for individual servings.

The advantage of cazuela cooking is that earthenware holds a slow, steady heat, letting food cook gently and evenly. It's even possible to sauté or brown foods in a cazuela, by adding enough oil to cover the bottom surface, slowly heating it until very hot, and adding food to be browned without crowding.

When purchasing a new cazuela, soak it in water for twenty-four hours to help leach out the raw clay taste, though frequent use is the best method of curing. Don't heat a cazuela empty and take care not to set a hot one down on a very cold surface or it will crack.

CHILLI (*GUINDILLA*)   Hot chilli peppers are used sparingly in Spanish cooking. Mild green pickled chillies, much like peperoncini, are a favourite accompaniment to bean dishes. Dried red chillies of medium hotness, such as cayenne, are sliced or finely chopped to add to some dishes. The best substitute is dried chilli flakes.

CHORIZO   This is the most emblematic sausage in all of Spain. Made of chopped pork and pork fat and seasoned with garlic and pimentón (paprika), it is dry-cured, not smoked. Spanish chorizo is ready to eat without cooking (unlike Mexican chorizo, which is a raw sausage). In Spain chorizo is produced in two types – a hard sausage that is sliced for cold cuts and a softer sausage with more fat content that is tied off in short links, best for stewing with beans and lentils. Spanish chorizo is available in the UK in most supermarkets.

DENOMINACIÓN DE ORIGEN, DO   These initials stand for 'denomination of origin', designating wines and foods that have protected status guaranteeing their geographic home and their quality. Castilla–La Mancha presently has eight wine DOs (see page 349), plus DO Aceite de los Montes de Toledo (olive oil), DO Queso Manchego (cheese), DO Cordero Manchego (lamb), DO Ajo Morado de Las Pedroñeras (garlic), DO Melón de la Mancha, DO Miel de la Alcarria (honey), DO Berenejena de Almagro (pickled aubergine) and DO Azafrán de la Mancha (saffron).

HAM   See Serrano Ham.

MORTAR AND PESTLE   When a recipe calls for freshly ground black pepper, you probably reach for the pepper mill. The traditional Spanish method calls for freshly grinding spices in a small mortar, usually a brass *almirez*. You can use any small stone mortar. Put the saffron in first and crush it to a powder. Then add small, whole spices such as peppercorns, cloves and cumin seed. Continue with any dried herbs and finish the blend with soft items such as garlic cloves. Last, dilute the mixture with water, stock or wine before stirring it into the food.

OLIVE OIL   Use olive oil from Spain for the recipes in this book. Choose extra virgin olive oil for sautéing, for salads, for gazpacho and in other recipes where the oil is not cooked (for instance, drizzled over grilled fish, cooked vegetables, baked potato). For deep-frying, when a large quantity of oil is required, use either extra virgin olive oil (preferably of a varietal such as Picual that is stable at high heat) or one labelled simply *olive oil*. The latter is refined olive oil to which some virgin oil is added for flavour. It is much less expensive than extra virgin oil.

There are some 27 million olive trees in Castilla–La Mancha, which is the second-largest producer of olive oil, after Andalucía, in Spain. Spain has seven protected olive oil denominations of origin, one of which, Montes de Toledo, is in Castilla–La Mancha. DO Montes de Toledo oil is produced from the Cornicabra olive variety, which makes a fresh, fruity oil with aromas of apple and almond and a lovely, buttery texture. (More about olive oil on page 273.)

PIMENTÓN, PIMENTÓN DE LA VERA, SMOKED PIMENTÓN   Pimentón is Spanish paprika. It is produced in two regions, in eastern Spain, where a hot, dry Mediterranean climate allows the peppers to be sun-dried, and also in western Spain in the La Vera region of Extremadura, where the peppers are smoke-dried for 10 to 15 days over smouldering chunks of wild holm oak. The slow smoking fixes the natural carotenoid pigments of the peppers, producing an intensely red spice. It also adds an ineffable natural smokiness that complements many foods. After drying, the peppers are ground to a powder.

Pimentón is produced from the *Capsicum annuum* pepper, the chilli pepper discovered by Columbus on his first trip to the New World. Columbus carried peppers and other New World plants back to Spain, where they were cultivated by monks in various abbeys. The Hieronymite monks at the Yuste monastery in La Vera were the first to dry the peppers and use the powder as a flavouring and food preservative.

Emperor Charles V, when he abdicated the Spanish throne in 1555 and retired to the Yuste monastery, got to like the spice (he was a notorious gourmand) and recommended it to his sister, Queen Mary of Hungary. That's where it became known as *paprika*, from the Serbo-Croatian word for 'pepper'.

Spanish pimentón, smoked or unsmoked, comes in three flavours – *dulce,* sweet; *agridulce,* bittersweet; and *picante,* spicy-hot. Each is made from a different subspecies of pepper. Sweet pimentón, smoked or unsmoked, is the most versatile, while the bittersweet adds complexity to a dish. The spicy-hot is packed with flavour and not fiery. Cayenne can be substituted for hot pimentón.

In Spain, the lion's share of pimentón goes to the sausage-making industry. The most emblematic Spanish sausage, garlicky chorizo, is coloured and flavoured with it. Pimentón is widely used in home cooking, too, and not just sprinkled for colour, but in heaping spoonfuls. Use smoked pimentón with discretion, however, as its earthy, smoky aroma can overwhelm delicate flavours.

Stir pimentón into a little water and blend it to a smooth paste before adding it to a sauce. Or stir it into hot oil in a sauté and immediately add liquid so that the pimentón doesn't scorch. If using pimentón on barbecued food, add it during the last few minutes of grilling so that it doesn't burn. If a recipe calls for smoked pimentón, ordinary pimentón or paprika can be substituted. Sources are listed at the back of this book.

RICE   Spanish rice, used for paella and other rice recipes, is a round, medium-short grain. This variety of rice soaks up the flavours of the foods that are cooked with it – olive oil, garlic, chicken, rabbit, meat. It can be cooked dry, as for paella; *meloso,* juicy; or *caldoso,* soupy. Part of the growing region for Denominación de Origen Calasparra rice is situated in the valleys of the Mundo and Segura rivers, in the south-east of Albacete province, bordering Murcia. Bomba is one of three varieties of rice cultivated there. It is especially valued for cooking in soupy rice dishes, because it doesn't 'flower', or open up and become mushy. If Spanish rice is not available, substitute another medium-short-grain rice such as Arborio. When rice is cooked as a side dish or salad (not in a casserole with other ingredients), use your favourite long-grain rice instead.

SAFFRON   (More about saffron on page 160.) Look for saffron with the DO of La Mancha seal. Any other saffron may be imported from other countries. Spanish saffron is usually sold in threads (not powdered) by gram measures. One gram is a sufficient quantity for about six recipes of paella, risotto, or chicken in saffron-almond sauce. There is no substitute for saffron. Although in Spain artificial yellow colouring is frequently used in place of pricey saffron (especially in paellas served up to tourists), no other yellow spice can take the place of sensuous saffron.

It's not easy to measure strands of saffron. In this book, ¼ teaspoon or ½ teaspoon means lightly filling the spoon, tamping the threads down slightly without crushing the saffron. One half teaspoon equals about sixty filaments.

For use in cooking, when you want to extract the full flavour and colour of the saffron, first crush it in a small mortar. Perfectly dry saffron will crumble easily. If you don't have a mortar and pestle, use the end of a knife handle to crush the saffron in a teacup. It doesn't need to be totally pulverised.

Add enough liquid – wine or hot water, milk, or stock – to cover the crushed saffron. Let it infuse for at least 10 minutes and up to 45 minutes. Stir the crushed saffron and liquid into a sauce towards the end of cooking time so that the aroma doesn't dissipate in long cooking. On the other hand, if you want the golden colour to permeate the cooking food, such as for paella and some potato dishes, add the saffron infusion at the very beginning of the cooking time. Saffron can be purchased in many supermarkets and from the sources listed at the back of the book.

SALT COD (*BACALAO*)   Unless otherwise noted in a recipe, salt cod needs to be soaked for at least 24 hours to remove the salt and rehydrate the dried flesh before being incorporated in a recipe. Wash the salt cod in running water. Place in a bowl and cover with cold water. Cover the bowl and refrigerate for 6 hours. Drain, rinse the cod, and cover with fresh water. Change the water once or twice more. After draining, squeeze the cod gently to express moisture. It is now ready to be cooked according to the recipe.

Fresh cod can be substituted for salt cod in recipes, although it will contribute a very different flavour and texture.

SERRANO HAM; IBERICO HAM (*JAMÓN SERRANO*)   This is a salt-cured ham from Spain that is typically sliced paper-thin (like parma ham) and served as a tapa with wine or Sherry. It is not smoked or cooked. *Serrano* means 'mountain': these hams traditionally were cured in highland regions where temperatures and humidity enhanced the curing process. They are now produced in modern processing plants with temperature controls, allowing stable year-round conditions for curing. Castilla–La Mancha is the country's largest producer of serrano ham.

Serrano ham is exported to the UK and can be found in good supermarkets and at speciality shops. (See Sources.)

When the ham comes from a pig of the Iberico breed, a small, brown pig native to western Spain, it is called *jamón ibérico,* Iberico ham, or *pata negra,* 'black foot', because it has a black hoof. These pigs roam the *dehesas,* rough pastureland forested with wild oaks, gobbling acorns and wild grasses. Their meat makes the best ham in the world, sweet, nutty, succulent.

Diced serrano ham or scraps of the ham's fat (*tocino*) are used in cooked dishes, almost like a seasoning. They are especially good sautéed with vegetables, omelettes, mushrooms and prawns. Chunks of ham bone add flavour to a pot of beans or lentils. If serrano ham is not available, use unsmoked bacon or lean pancetta in cooked recipes, fatty bacon in place of *tocino.* In salads, sandwiches and croquettes, unsmoked cooked ham could substitute for serrano.

Slice serrano ham immediately before serving. Use a very sharp slicing knife with a long, flexible blade to slice from a whole ham. Cut lengthwise pieces, with the grain, as thinly as possible. (Special racks that clamp the ham tightly make slicing easier.) Presliced, vacuum-packed serrano ham should be brought to room temperature before the packet is opened.

STOCK In recipes that call for chicken stock, use home-made stock (page 94) or fresh chicken stock from the supermarket. For fish stock use home-made stock (page 135) or water.

VINEGAR White wine vinegar is the most widely used in Spanish cooking. Red wine vinegar may be substituted if the colour doesn't matter. Sherry vinegar is more mellow (from maturing), but also more acidic than normal wine vinegar.

Note on Measurements

In this edition of *Cooking from the Heart of Spain*, measurements have been converted for the UK market. Rather than sticking rigidly to one or other system, the conversions have been made according to what it is felt will be most useful to the cook. Thus, for dry weights usually only metric measurements have been thought necessary; for volume, an imperial or tablespoon equivalent has been given in addition to the metric measurement; for linear measures, both metric and imperial have been given.

Useful Equivalents

3 medium potatoes = about 700g/1½lb

1 medium onion = about 120g/¼lb

1 large pepper = about 230g/½lb

2 medium tomatoes = about 300–350g/¾lb

1 medium leek = about 100g/¼lb

1 medium carrot = about 100g/¼lb

1 medium garlic clove = 1 teaspoon chopped garlic

1 cup coarsely grated cheese (not packed) = 85g/3oz

½ cup diced ham or bacon = 85g/3oz

Tapas, Starters *and* Salads

From a working-class tavern in an agricultural village in the middle of La Mancha, where the lamb fried with whole garlic cloves is unconscionably good, to a trendy wine bar in upmarket Madrid, where lollipops of quails' legs accompany the reserva wines, tapa bars provide the best possible introduction to Spanish cuisine, both traditional and *vanguardista*. What a wonderful assortment of food! Hot dishes and cold ones, fresh and raw or crispy and fried, flavours both simple and exotic, old and new.

I have grouped tapas, starters, and salads together because there is much crossover between them. Many salads, such as Tomato-Tuna Salad, appear at tapa bars, while some tapas, such as Manchego Cheese and Potato Croquettes or Partridge and Chicken Pâté, serve nicely as starters or, accompanied by a salad, as a whole lunch.

Some favourite tapas require no recipe. Serrano ham is simply sliced paper-thin from a whole ham. Olives are dipped from a jug. Aged Manchego cheese is sliced and served with bread. Almonds are heaped in a bowl. If you are preparing a tapa party, be sure to include some of these.

Throughout this book are many more recipes for dishes that might also be served in a typical tapa bar. For example, the Spanish Potato Tortilla in the next chapter, Codfish Balls with Walnuts in the fish chapter or Spiced Pork Loin in Confit in the meat chapter can be served in small portions as a tapa. Similarly, recipes in other chapters – in particular those for vegetable dishes – are frequently served as starters.

Tapas were invented to go with wine. In the taverns of La Mancha and Madrid, red wine is the preferred drink with tapa foods. (See page 347 for more about the wines of La Mancha.) But equally acceptable are white wine, fino Sherry and beer.

THYME-MARINATED OLIVES

Aceitunas con Aliño de Tomillo

At a small inn in Los Yébenes in the Montes de Toledo, I was served two different sorts of home-cured olives, both prepared by Carmen Sánchez. The olives in one dish were green; those in the second were almost black. Both were of the same variety, cornicabra, an oval olive with a curved tip, the same olive that is pressed for the region's extra virgin oil. And both had been picked green. Carmen explained that one batch had been prepared in a soda-lye solution and the other had been soaked for two months in only water. The soda-lye fixes the green colour and sweetens whole olives in only twenty-four hours. They are then washed thoroughly and placed in seasoned brine. The dark olives had been sliced to the pit – Carmen showed me a little gadget with four thin blades for incising the olives, one by one – then soaked in frequent changes of water for two months until all the bitterness was removed. Then the olives were placed in the flavoured brine. Carmen used thyme and garlic to flavour the brine.

Give ordinary bottled olives a home-cured flavour by marinating them with thyme, garlic and lemon.

MAKES 450ML / ¾ PINT

450ml / ¾ pint drained, bottled manzanilla olives	1 tablespoon salt
½ teaspoon dried thyme	2 garlic cloves, slivered
1 bay leaf	½ lemon, sliced
2 teaspoons wine vinegar	1 fresh thyme sprig (optional)

Rinse the olives and soak them in water for 1 hour. Drain again.

Combine 700ml / 1¼ pints water in a saucepan with the thyme, bay leaf, vinegar and salt. Bring to the boil. Remove from the heat and allow to cool. Strain the liquid into a 1-litre non-reactive glass jar. Add the drained olives, garlic, lemon, and thyme sprig if you're using it. Combine well. Cover tightly and allow to marinate, refrigerated, for 7 days.

Store the olives in the refrigerator for up to 2 months.

TOASTED NUTS *and* SEEDS

Cañamones

La Cocina del Quijote (The Cuisine of the Quixote) by Lorenzo Díaz, an authentic Manchego, is a book about the traditional dishes of the region, many of which were known in Don Quixote's era. The author tells of a special treat that he enjoyed as a child, *cañamones*, handfuls of toasted seeds and nuts. *Cañamones* are hemp seeds, but they were mixed with wheat grains, dried chestnuts and nuts. Here is one version – without hemp seeds, but including sunflower seeds, which are famous in the province of Cuenca. Walnuts, pine nuts, linseeds, chestnuts, figs and raisins could be added as well, but do not fry the chestnuts, figs or raisins.

MAKES 1.2 LITRES/2 PINTS

170g dried chickpeas, soaked overnight

175g wheat grains, soaked overnight

4 tablespoons olive oil

130g hazelnuts

130g almonds

135g sunflower seeds

½ teaspoon aniseeds

1 teaspoon coarse salt

Drain the chickpeas and wheat grains and pat dry. Heat the oil in a deep frying pan. Fry the chickpeas over medium-high heat until golden brown and crisped, 5 minutes. Skim them out and drain on kitchen paper.

Fry the wheat grains until golden, 2 minutes. Tilt the pan so oil drains to one side and skim out the wheat. Drain.

Continue frying the hazelnuts and almonds, each for about 1 minute. Pour off the remaining oil and toast the sunflower seeds with the aniseeds in the same frying pan, about 1 minute.

Combine all the toasted seeds and nuts and sprinkle with salt. When completely cool, store in an airtight container. Keeps for up to 2 weeks in the refrigerator.

CRISP-FRIED PASTIES *with* TUNA FILLING

Empanadillas de Atún

I once made hundreds of these little pasties for a big party, stashing them in the freezer a week before the event. Happily, I had help in the kitchen when it came time to fry them. Served hot and crisp, the pasties just flew off the trays, disappearing within minutes.

The tuna filling is both delicious and convenient, but chicken, fish, minced beef and pork are other good choices. In Toledo, empanadillas are filled with thin slices of fried pork fillet in tomato sauce.

❧ MAKES FIFTY-SIX 7.5CM/3IN PASTIES OR FORTY 9CM/3½IN PASTIES

FOR THE DOUGH

300g plain flour, plus flour for the board

1 teaspoon salt

¼ teaspoon fennel seeds, coarsely ground

120g cold unsalted butter, cut into 5mm/¼in pieces

100ml/6 tablespoons cold dry white wine

FOR THE FILLING

150g drained tinned tuna

4 tablespoons Tomato Sauce, home-made (page 26) or ready-made passata

1 hard-boiled egg, chopped

1 tablespoon chopped fresh flat-leaf parsley

1 tablespoon brandy

75g finely chopped manzanilla or pimiento-stuffed olives

2 tablespoons finely chopped onion

Salt and freshly ground black pepper

1 teaspoon wine vinegar or fresh lemon juice

Pinch of cayenne

Olive or vegetable oil for deep-frying

Combine the flour, salt and fennel seeds in a food processor. Add the butter and pulse until the mixture resembles coarse meal. Add the wine and process for 30 seconds, until the flour begins to clump.

Turn the dough out onto a lightly floured board. Push it together into a ball, then stretch it once, twice, then press it into a ball again. Cover with clingfilm and refrigerate for at least 2 and up to 24 hours.

Combine all the filling ingredients in a bowl, taste, and add more salt, vinegar or cayenne if necessary. It should be strongly seasoned.

Divide the ball of dough in half. Keep one half refrigerated and place the other half on a lightly floured board. Pat it down with the rolling pin until it is slightly softened and flattened enough to start rolling. Roll the dough out as thinly as possible, sprinkling board and rolling pin with flour as needed.

Use a pastry cutter to cut 7.5cm/3in, 9cm/3½in, or larger circles. Gather up scraps, press them together and refrigerate. Place a spoonful of the filling on the bottom half of each round of dough. Dip a finger in water and moisten the edges of the bottom half. Fold the top half of the circle over the filling and press the edges together. Use the flat end of a knife handle to crimp the edges. Place each empanadilla, as filled, onto a tray.

When all of the circles are filled and sealed, roll out the second half of the dough in the same manner. Cut circles, fill and seal the empanadillas. Then roll out the remaining scraps of dough, cut circles, and fill.

Heat the oil in a deep pan to a depth of at least 2.5cm/1in, or in a deep fryer, until shimmering but not smoking (about 180°C/360°F). Fry the empanadillas, a few at a time, until they are golden brown, 5 to 6 minutes. Remove with a skimmer and drain on kitchen paper. Continue frying the remaining empanadillas. Serve hot or at room temperature.

NOTE: *To freeze uncooked pasties, place them in a single layer on a tray in the freezer until frozen. Then pack them in layers separated with clingfilm in a covered freezer container. Remove them from the freezer about 15 minutes before frying. Fry them without defrosting, allowing about 2 minutes more time in the hot oil.*

The pasties can be fried up to 2 hours in advance of serving and reheated in a 200°C/180°C fan/GM6 oven for 5 minutes.

VARIATION: *To bake the pasties, preheat the oven to 190°C/170°C fan/ GM5, and place the pasties on an ungreased baking sheet. Brush the tops with beaten egg and bake until golden, 20 to 25 minutes.*

PUFFY PRAWN FRITTERS

Buñuelos de Gambas

Serve these tasty fritters with drinks. They are best hot out of the oil.

MAKES **20** FRITTERS

65g plain flour

½ teaspoon baking powder

Pinch of celery seeds

Pinch of cayenne

4 tablespoons finely chopped green garlic shoots
or spring onions

2 tablespoons chopped fresh parsley

1 egg, separated

4 tablespoons lager

250g chopped peeled prawns

½ teaspoon salt

About 450ml / ¾ pint olive oil for deep-frying

Combine the flour, baking powder, celery seeds and cayenne in a bowl. Stir in the chopped garlic shoots or spring onions, parsley, egg yolk and lager to make a paste.

Shortly before frying the fritters, stir the prawns into the batter. Beat the egg white until stiff. Beat in the salt. Fold the egg white into the batter.

Heat the oil to a depth of about 2.5cm/1in in a deep frying pan until shimmering. Drop heaping teaspoons of the prawn batter into the oil and fry, turning once, until golden on both sides, 2 to 3 minutes.

Drain on kitchen paper and serve immediately.

TAPA HOPPING IN MADRID

It was just about 8 P.M. when three of us walked into our first tapa bar, the nineteenth-century Taberna de Antonio Sánchez in the old section of Lavapies of Madrid. We ordered red wine from Valdepeñas and the house tapa, *morcilla,* blood sausage, with pine nuts and raisins. In Madrid, 8 P.M. is a good hour to start out on a tapa crawl – early, with shops just closing and supper still a couple of hours away.

We moved on to Cava Baja, Madrid's best-known tapa street. At Lucio's adjunct, we enjoyed eggs scrambled with potatoes and ham. Yes, scrambled eggs. That simple.

Another couple joined our group. We moved along to La Carta, where the *pincho,* tomato, cheese and anchovy speared on a cocktail stick, was served free with our glasses of red wine. We ordered *revuelto de habitas,* tiny broad beans sautéed with ham.

By the time we got to La Casa del Abuelo, yet another couple joined the group. We were speaking English, Spanish and French. The *gambas al ajillo,* prawns sizzled with garlic, were delicious. We passed right by Café Brava, home of the famous *patatas brava,* crisp-fried cubes of potato in a spicy sauce. At Freiduria de Gallinejas, which specialises in offal, I had to try a La Mancha speciality, *zarajos,* lamb tripe twisted round grapevine skewers and roasted. It was tender and delicious.

At 1 A.M., in the Plaza de Santa Ana, we flagged taxis to go home. By that hour tapa bars were closed, but thousands of young people thronged the plaza. The night was young. But we weren't.

Madrid, one of the world's great capital cities, may not be where the tapa custom originated (that would be in the wine bars of Andalucía). But it's where tapas consolidated as an expression of social, cultural, artistic and culinary life. Today, life in Madrid would not be the same without the convivial rituals of the *tapeo,* the meeting and greeting, eating and imbibing. Part of the attraction of the *tapeo* is the *paseo* and the *movida.* It is a movable feast – you stop at one bar to taste its speciality, then stroll up the street to another, around the corner for a third round. Then you bump into another group of friends and move on to a different locale. The movement is part of the entertainment. And – this is important – you don't sit down at a table. Tapas are best on foot, standing at the bar or balancing wineglass and tapa on a little shelf.

The variety of tapas is quite stunning. Most tapa bars serve ten to twenty different dishes, but some specialise in just one. So, for instance, a particular bar may serve only ham and sausages, another only *bacalao* dishes, others exclusively shellfish or snails. Tapas range from very traditional home cooking to innovative and trendy.

Tapas divide into roughly four categories: ready to eat, salads and cold dishes, fried foods, and *tapas de cocina,* hot cooked dishes. It's perfectly acceptable to mix and match them in any order.

Ready to eat includes olives, toasted almonds, aged cheese and the special Spanish ham, *jamón serrano.* In many tapa bars these hams hang from the beams alongside sausage links and garlands of garlic. The ham is very thinly sliced and served raw. One type of serrano ham, made from the breed of Iberico pig, is especially esteemed and justifiably expensive. Some bars serve a *surtido de ibérico,* an assortment of Iberico ham, cured loin and sausages. Others feature *pinchos* – tidbits such as pickles, anchovies, and eggs speared on toothpicks.

Salads and cold dishes run the gamut from stuffed eggs, potato salad and bean salad to seafood cocktail, marinated mussels and fish roe. *Tortilla de patatas,* a thick potato omelette cut into squares and served cold, is a classic. Fried foods are among the glories of tapa bars – batter-fried prawns, golden croquettes, crisp aubergine.

Tapas de cocina may be served in *cazuelitas,* earthenware ramekins. They include meatballs, notably in an almond-saffron sauce; tripe stew; chicken sautéed with garlic; kidneys in Sherry sauce. Almost any dish – beef stew to braised partridge – can be and is served in tapa-sized portions. Some are cooked to order on a *plancha,* griddle.

Tapas are not necessarily finger food, as some stews and sauced foods may require a spoon or fork. Bread accompanies tapas, a must for mopping up delicious sauces. A tapa is a small individual portion; a *ración* is a larger portion suitable for sharing.

Tapas have their pace, which is leisurely. Spaniards can put away quite a lot of food while just standing at the bar, sipping wine and having an animated conversation with friends.

La Mancha and its wines are deeply embedded in Madrid's tapa culture. By the nineteenth century, Valdepeñas had become the wine of choice for the taverns of Madrid, supplied by muleteers who hauled it to the capital in wineskins. With the coming of the railroad in 1861, a daily 'wine train' delivered carriage-loads of wine to the capital. To this day, Madrid *tascas* feature wines and foods of La Mancha.

MANCHEGO CHEESE *and* POTATO CROQUETTES

Croquetas de Queso

Pass a tray of these cheesy croquettes at your next wine party. They are sure to be a hit. The recipe is adapted from a book about Manchego cheese, *La Mancha y el Queso Manchego,* published by the department of agriculture of Castilla–La Mancha. For authenticity's sake and flavour too, use true Manchego. However, a mature Cheddar could be substituted.

Cooking the potatoes unpeeled prevents them from absorbing a lot of cooking water. They will be almost as flaky as a baked potato.

MAKES FIFTY 4CM/1¼IN CROQUETTES

700g baking potatoes (3 medium)

1 tablespoon olive oil, plus about 1 litre/1½ pints for deep-frying

170g Manchego, grated

1 tablespoon finely chopped spring onion

4 tablespoons finely chopped fresh flat-leaf parsley

½ teaspoon salt

Pinch of dried thyme

Pinch of hot pimentón or cayenne

4 eggs (2 separated)

1 teaspoon wine vinegar

80g fine dry breadcrumbs

Cook the unpeeled potatoes in boiling water until tender, about 30 minutes. Drain thoroughly. Split them in half and scoop the flesh into a bowl, discarding the skins. Add 1 tablespoon oil and mash the potatoes with a fork or potato masher until fairly smooth.

Stir the cheese into the potatoes. Add the spring onion, parsley, salt, thyme and hot pimentón.

Separate 2 eggs. Place the whites in a clean bowl. Stir the yolks into the potato mixture.

At high speed, beat the whites until stiff. Beat in the vinegar.

Fold half of the egg whites into the potato mixture until thoroughly combined. Fold in the remaining whites.

Beat the remaining 2 eggs in a shallow bowl. Spread the breadcrumbs on a tray.

Use a teaspoon to scoop up a mound of potato-cheese. Drop it into the beaten egg and roll it to coat all sides. Lift it out with the spoon and a fork, allowing excess egg to drain off. Place the croquette in the crumbs. Continue shaping croquettes until the tray is filled. Spoon some of the crumbs over the croquettes and, using a fork, roll them to coat all sides.

Lift the croquettes out of the crumbs, patting very gently to shape each into a ball. Place them on another tray as they are shaped.

Place enough oil in a deep frying pan to reach a depth of 2cm/¾in. Heat the oil until it is shimmering but not smoking (180°C/350°F). Fry the croquettes in 4 or 5 batches, turning them once, until they are golden brown, 1½ to 2 minutes. Skim out and drain briefly on kitchen
paper. Serve hot.

NOTE: *Croquettes can be fried up to 4 hours in advance and kept at room temperature. Place them on a baking sheet and reheat them in a preheated 200°C/180°C/GM6 oven until hot (about 10 minutes). Fried croquettes can be frozen for up to 1 month. Remove them from the freezer 15 minutes before heating. Place on a baking sheet and bake in a preheated 190°C/170°C/GM5 oven for 15 minutes.*

'DOUBLE' EGGS

Huevos Dobles

'Double' eggs, because there are eggs on the inside and eggs on the outside. Looking very much like Scotch eggs, these are fun, though time-consuming, to prepare. The coating is thicker and crisper if the eggs are dipped twice in flour, egg and crumbs.

Serve each person one egg. Tomato sauce makes a good accompaniment.

The recipe makes more stuffing mixture than needed for the 6 egg whites. Any leftovers make a fine sandwich spread.

SERVES 6 AS A STARTER

6 hard-boiled eggs

1 tablespoon olive oil, plus about 450ml/¾ pint for deep-frying

4 tablespoons finely chopped onion

4 tablespoons finely chopped serrano or cooked ham

¾ teaspoon salt

Pinch of caraway seeds

½ teaspoon Dijon mustard

Pinch of hot pimentón or cayenne

1 tablespoon plus 350ml/12 fl oz milk

2 tablespoons butter

5 tablespoons flour, plus 70g for dredging

1 to 2 eggs

70g fine dry breadcrumbs

Tomato Sauce, home-made (page 26) or ready-made passata, for serving (optional)

Peel the eggs and pat them dry. Cut each in half lengthways. Transfer the yolks to a small bowl.

Heat 1 tablespoon oil in a small frying pan. Sauté the onion and ham over medium heat until the onion is softened, 5 minutes. Scrape the mixture into the bowl with the yolks. Add ¼ teaspoon of the salt, and all of the caraway seeds, mustard, pimentón, plus 1 tablespoon of the milk. Mash the yolks until smooth. Press the yolk mixture into the hollows of the egg whites.

Cover a tray with a layer of clingfilm. Place the egg halves, stuffed side down, 5cm/2in apart in a single layer. Refrigerate.

Melt the butter in a saucepan. Stir in 5 tablespoons flour and stir until smooth over low heat.

Remove the pan from the heat and stir in the remaining 350ml/12 fl oz milk very gradually, until the mixture is smooth. Return to medium heat. Cook, stirring, until the sauce is thick and smooth, 5 minutes.

Spoon the hot sauce over the egg halves, coating them smoothly with the sauce. Refrigerate the eggs until the coating is chilled and solidified, at least 3 and up to 24 hours.

Roll one egg half over, stuffing side up. Pick up another egg and place it on top, so the stuffing is enclosed, but don't press down yet. Repeat with the remaining eggs. Return the tray to the refrigerator.

Place flour for dredging in a shallow pan. Beat 1 or 2 eggs in a shallow dish. Place half the breadcrumbs in another shallow pan.

Dredge each egg in flour. Pat off the excess and now you can gently press the 2 halves together. Roll the eggs in beaten egg. Place them in the tray of breadcrumbs. Sprinkle the remaining half of the crumbs over the eggs. Roll or pat the eggs so they are completely covered with crumbs. Allow to dry on a tray for 15 minutes.

If desired, repeat the breading, dredging the eggs first in flour, then eggs, then in crumbs.

Heat oil to a depth of 2cm/¾in in a deep frying pan until shimmering but not smoking (180°C/360°F). Fry the eggs, turning to brown all sides, 4 to 5 minutes. Remove with a slotted spoon and drain on kitchen paper. Serve hot or warm, accompanied by tomato sauce if desired.

NOTE: *The eggs can be stuffed and fried up to 24 hours in advance and refrigerated. Bring them to room temperature while you preheat the oven to 200°C/180°C fan/GM6. Place in a roasting tin and heat in the oven for 8 to 10 minutes.*

TOMATO SAUCE *Salsa de Tomate Frito*

This is a basic smooth tomato sauce that can be served as an accompaniment to cooked foods, such as the 'Double' Eggs in the previous recipe, or as a cooking medium for foods such as Piquant Cocktail Meatballs (page 31). You can vary the flavour of the sauce by adding other herbs or by using smoked pimentón.

Makes 350ml/12 fl oz

500g drained tinned plum tomatoes

2 tablespoons olive oil

130g chopped onion

2 garlic cloves, chopped

4 tablespoons chopped fresh flat-leaf parsley

1 teaspoon sweet pimentón

Pinch of ground cumin

1 bay leaf

Salt and freshly ground black pepper

Cut out the stem end of the tomatoes and break the tomatoes up slightly.

Heat oil in a saucepan and sauté the onion and garlic over medium heat until the onion begins to turn golden, 5 minutes. Add the parsley and pimentón and stir for 30 seconds. Add the tomatoes, cumin, bay leaf, and salt and pepper to taste.

Bring to the boil, cover and simmer until the tomatoes are thickened, 25 minutes.

Purée the sauce in a blender. If desired, strain sauce to remove any remaining seeds.

Serve the sauce hot or at room temperature.

SALT COD *and* ROASTED PEPPER TOASTS

Tiznao

Tiznao means 'blackened', for the cod and vegetables are charred over hot coals or under the grill. Roasting gives the peppers a bittersweet edge that contrasts nicely with the salty cod. In this recipe, the salt cod is soaked after grilling, not before. If salt cod does not appeal to you, try this recipe using water-packed tinned tuna, well drained, in its place. In La Mancha, *tiznao* is usually served as a starter in small *cazuelitas,* individual earthenware ramekins, with plenty of bread on the side. It makes a fine appetiser, heaped on toasted slices of baguette.

MAKES **18** TOASTS, ENOUGH TO SERVE **6** AS A STARTER

350g salt cod, to make about ½ pint of flaked cod, or else use drained water-packed tinned tuna

2 medium onions

2 red peppers

3 large tomatoes

1 head of garlic

3 tablespoons extra virgin olive oil

2 teaspoons sweet pimentón

Dried chilli flakes

Freshly ground black pepper

¼ teaspoon ground cumin

Salt

18 baguette slices, toasted, for serving

25g black olives, pitted

Preheat the grill to high.

Place the cod on a sheet of heavy-duty foil. Roll up the edges to make a rim. Place on a grill rack and grill about 10cm/4in from the heat until the surface is lightly toasted, 10 minutes. Turn the piece of cod (drain off and discard any liquid that accumulates in the foil packet) and grill until toasted, about 10 minutes. Remove the cod from the oven, discarding the foil, and place it in a bowl. Add water to cover and soak for at least 1 and up to 4 hours, changing the water twice.

Place the onions, peppers, tomatoes and garlic on the grill rack and toast them under the grill, about 10cm/4in from the heat, turning occasionally, until the tomato skins are split, the peppers and onions charred. The tomatoes will take 8 to 10 minutes, the onions, garlic and peppers 20 to 25 minutes.

As they are roasted, transfer the vegetables to a pan and cover with a lid. When cool enough to handle, peel the tomatoes, discarding seeds. Chop coarsely.

Peel the peppers, discarding the seeds and stem. Cut the peppers into thin strips.

Peel the onions, cut them into quarters, and then sliver them.

Slit open the garlic cloves and unwrap the softened garlic cloves. Cut them lengthways into quarters.

Drain the soaked cod. With your fingers, separate it into flakes or crumbs, discarding all skin and bones.

Heat the oil in a frying pan or cazuela. Add the tomatoes and cook over high heat for 5 minutes, until they have sweated out most of their liquid. Add the peppers and cook for 2 minutes. Then add the onions and garlic and season with pimentón, chilli flakes and black pepper to taste, and cumin. Reduce the heat to low and cook, covered, for 15 minutes. Stir in the cod flakes. Remove from the heat and let stand, covered, for at least 30 minutes or up to 2 hours. Add salt to taste.

Serve the *tiznao* heaped on toasted baguette slices or on individual plates, accompanied by toast. Scatter olives on top.

GARLICKY SALT COD DIP

Atascaburras

Atascaburras means 'to choke a donkey'. This cod and potato purée should be that thick. Serve it as an appetiser dip or in individual ramekins as a starter, accompanied by toast or breadsticks. Start this at least a day before serving, to allow the salt cod to soak for 24 hours.

SERVES 4 TO 6

250g salt cod

570g baking potatoes, peeled and quartered (about 3)

4 garlic cloves, peeled

5 tablespoons virgin olive oil

25g walnut halves

1 hard-boiled egg, sliced

Toast Crisps (page 30) or breadsticks for serving

Rinse the pieces of cod to remove excess salt. Cover with water and soak for 24 hours, changing the water 3 times. Drain and rinse the cod.

Put the potatoes in a pan with water to cover. Bring to the boil, then reduce the heat to simmer. Add the cod and cook, covered, very gently until the potatoes are tender, about 20 minutes. Drain, saving about 250ml/½ pint of the cooking liquid.

Crush the garlic in a large mortar or bowl. Gradually add the cooked potatoes, mashing them to a smooth paste. Beat in 4 tablespoons oil and enough of the reserved liquid to make a stiff purée, about 120ml/¼ pint.

With your fingers, flake the cod, discarding all skin and bones. Stir the flaked cod into the potato purée.

Spread the purée in a shallow bowl or in individual ramekins, smoothing the top. Drizzle the remaining tablespoon of oil over the purée. Garnish with walnuts and sliced egg. Serve with Toast Crisps or breadsticks.

TOAST CRISPS *Tostaditas Crujientes*

Slice the bread very thinly, so it crisps in the oven. The crisps keep for several days in an airtight container. They are also good served with soup or pâté.

Makes 24 small toasts

Twenty-four 5mm/¼in baguette slices
½ garlic clove
1 tablespoon extra virgin olive oil

Preheat the oven to 190°C/170°C fan/GM5.

Trim off the bread crusts if desired, then place the slices on a baking sheet.

Cut a crosshatch on the cut side of the garlic clove. Scrub the cut garlic on one side of each bread slice. Brush the slices with oil.

Bake until the bread is golden and crisp, about 8 minutes.

PIQUANT COCKTAIL MEATBALLS

Pinchos de Albondiguillas

You can make these versatile meatballs with minced pork, veal, turkey, chicken, lamb or beef. Quickly fried (a light flouring prevents them from splattering while frying), they can be served piping hot or at room temperature. These are nicely spiced and accented with piquillo peppers, so they require no dipping sauce. Piquillo peppers are tiny sweet red peppers with just a hint of piquancy. They are grown in northern Spain, roasted and tinned, providing a handy flavour boost. If you can't find piquillos (see the back of the book for sources), use any roasted pimiento. The meatballs also may be simmered in Tomato Sauce (page 26) and served with pasta or rice as a main dish.

MAKES **60** BITE-SIZED MEATBALLS, ENOUGH TO SERVE **20** AS A TAPA

900g minced pork shoulder blade

2½ teaspoons finely chopped garlic

60g finely chopped onion

30g chopped fresh flat-leaf parsley

2 teaspoons salt

¼ teaspoon cayenne

1 teaspoon sweet smoked pimentón

1 teaspoon sweet pimentón

½ teaspoon ground cumin

¼ teaspoon dried thyme

½ teaspoon dried oregano

¼ teaspoon freshly ground black pepper

Grating of fresh nutmeg

1 tablespoon wine vinegar

About 4 tablespoons plain flour for dredging

About 120ml / 8 tablespoons olive oil for frying

10 piquillo peppers, from a 215g jar, drained and patted dry

Place the pork in a bowl. Add the garlic, onion and parsley.

In a small bowl, combine the salt, cayenne, smoked pimentón, sweet pimentón, cumin, thyme, oregano, pepper and nutmeg. Add the vinegar and stir to make a smooth paste. Sprinkle the spice mixture into the meat. Knead the meat with your hands to distribute the seasonings evenly.

Allow the meat to stand at room temperature for 1 hour or cover and refrigerate it for up to 24 hours.

Form the mixture into 2.5cm/1in balls. Dredge the meatballs in flour, patting off the excess.

Heat enough oil to cover the bottom of a large heavy frying pan. Fry the meatballs over medium heat in 2 batches, turning to brown them on all sides, until browned and cooked through, about 5 minutes. Transfer the meatballs to kitchen paper to drain.

Cut each piquillo pepper into 6 strips. Fold a strip into thirds, spear it with a cocktail stick and skewer a meatball. Place on a serving platter and serve hot or at room temperature.

NOTE: *The meatballs can be prepared up to 4 hours in advance and reheated on a baking sheet in a 190°C/170°C fan/GM5 oven for 8 minutes.*

PARTRIDGE *and* CHICKEN PÂTÉ

Paté de Perdiz y Pollo

The partridge pâté served in La Mancha restaurants is a smooth, creamy version. No partridge? No problem. Make this pâté with all chicken or substitute quail, veal or pork. Use both white and dark chicken in the mix. And if truffles aren't available or within your budget, simply eliminate them from the recipe. Fresh pork belly, which is uncured bacon, keeps the pâté juicy.

Serve slices of the pâté at room temperature on salad leaves accompanied by Scarlet-Pickled Onions (page 282) and toasts. A fine reserva red Tempranillo wine from La Mancha is the appropriate accompaniment.

SERVES 16 TO 20

450g boned partridge

450g boneless, skinless white and dark chicken

230g fresh pork belly

2 eggs, separated

120ml/8 tablespoons milk

4 tablespoons brandy

4 tablespoons dry or medium Sherry (fino or amontillado)

1 tablespoon salt

230g chicken livers

1 teaspoon freshly ground black pepper

½ teaspoon dried thyme

4 tablespoons finely chopped fresh flat-leaf parsley

60g grated onion

15g black truffles, chopped (optional)

8 rashers bacon

Cut the partridge, chicken and pork belly into cubes. Purée the meat in 2 batches in a processor or blender, adding 1 egg yolk and 4 tablespoons milk to each batch.

Combine the paste with the brandy, Sherry and salt in a bowl. Chop the chicken livers in the processor or blender and mix thoroughly into the paste. Season with pepper, thyme, parsley and onion. Refrigerate the mixture, covered, for at least 1 and up to 8 hours.

Preheat the oven to 180°C/160°C/GM4.

Beat the egg whites until stiff. Stir a third of the whites into the partridge paste. Fold in the remaining whites.

Place half the mixture in a 1.4 litre/2½ pint loaf tin (or in two 700ml/1¼ pint terrine moulds). Scatter the chopped truffle on top, if you're using it. Spread the remaining pâté mixture over. Top with bacon rashers. Place the mould in a pan and add boiling water to come halfway up the sides of the mould to make a bain marie. Cover the top with foil. Bake until the pâté is set (internal temperature of 82°C/180°F), about 1 hour (50 minutes for the smaller terrines).

Allow the pâté to cool, then refrigerate. Unmould the pâté, draining off excess liquid, and slice to serve. The pâté keeps, refrigerated, for up to 2 weeks.

LIVER *and* GAME PÂTÉ, CUENCA STYLE

Morteruelo de Cuenca

This country pâté, somewhat like rillettes, is made with pork liver, partridge, hare and chicken and spiced with an exotic combination of cinnamon and caraway. In the province of Cuenca, outdoorsmen – lumberjacks and shepherds – wrap the potted pâté in straw and bury it in a snowdrift to keep during the winter.

Partridge and hare give the pâté a deep colour and flavour, but the dish is just as delicious made with chicken.

I prefer to cook the pork liver separately, so it doesn't overwhelm the flavours of the chicken and game. Don't like liver? Leave it out and increase the amount of chicken.

The pâté is tastiest when piping hot. It can be served in individual ramekins as a starter, with toasted bread crusts as dippers; as a sandwich filling; as hash, alongside fried eggs; or as an appetiser, spread on toasts and grilled with a topping of pine nuts or chopped walnuts.

MAKES 24 TOASTS, ENOUGH TO SERVE 24 AS AN APPETISER OR 6 AS A STARTER

350g pork liver

3 teaspoons salt

1 pound boneless chicken legs, hare, partridge or rabbit

250g fresh pork belly

1 small onion

4 cloves

1 stick of celery

1 bay leaf

4 country bread slices, crusts removed, toasted

1 teaspoon sweet pimentón

¼ teaspoon ground cinnamon

1 teaspoon coarsely ground black pepper

½ teaspoon caraway seeds

Pinch of ground cloves

½ teaspoon dried oregano

2 garlic cloves, crushed

4 tablespoons pine nuts or coarsely chopped walnuts

2 teaspoons olive oil

24 baguette slices, toasted

Fresh parsley leaves for garnish

Put the pork liver in a pan and cover with salted water. Soak for 1 hour and drain. Bring the liver to the boil in fresh water to cover and simmer for 10 minutes. Drain. Cover with fresh water and 1 teaspoon of the salt. Bring to the boil and simmer until the liver is very tender, about 30 minutes. Allow the liver to cool in the cooking liquid.

Place the chicken in a pan with the pork belly. Cover with 2 litres/3½ pints water. Add the onion stuck with the cloves, celery, remaining 2 teaspoons salt and bay leaf. Bring the water to the boil and cook the chicken and pork belly until very tender, 2 hours. Drain, saving all the liquid.

When the meat is cool enough to handle, strip off any skin, bone and rind, and discard. Chop or shred the meat and reserve.

Drain the cooked liver and chop it finely. Combine the liver with all the meat in a large bowl (making about 950ml/1½ pints).

Break the toasted country bread into pieces and grind it coarsely in a food processor (making 350ml/just over ½ pint). Stir the breadcrumbs into the chopped meat.

Combine the pimentón, cinnamon, black pepper, caraway, ground cloves, oregano and garlic in a small bowl. Stir in 120ml/¼ pint of the reserved stock. Stir the spice mixture into the meat and breadcrumbs. Add 600ml/1 pint more of the reserved stock to the meat mixture.

Place the mixture in a large non-stick frying pan over medium heat. When the mixture begins to bubble, reduce the heat and cook, stirring frequently, until it is very thick, 30 minutes. The pâté can be cooled and kept, covered and refrigerated, for up to 1 week.

To serve, lightly brown the pine nuts in the olive oil in a small frying pan over medium heat, about 2 minutes.

Preheat the grill to high.

Spread a heaping tablespoon of pâté on each of the baguette toasts. Sprinkle with ½ teaspoon toasted pine nuts, pressing them into the pâté. Place the toasts on a grill tray and grill until hot and lightly browned, 2 to 3 minutes. Garnish each toast with a parsley leaf.

BEAN SALAD *with* CHORIZO

Ensalada de Alubias con Taquillos de Chorizo

La Mancha is a land of pulses. Beans, chickpeas and lentils are grown here and not just for an occasional soup. They are favoured fare in everyday meals, all year round. When there are leftover cooked beans, they go into a tasty salad such as this. In Spain, this salad would be served as a first course, but it makes a good side with summer barbecue.

SERVES 6 TO 8 AS A STARTER OR SIDE DISH

450g dried pinto or red kidney beans, soaked overnight

1 bay leaf

Salt

28g chopped fresh flat-leaf parsley

½ teaspoon dried oregano

⅛ teaspoon cumin seeds

60g chopped onion

4 tablespoons chopped red pepper

120g Spanish hard chorizo or salami in 5mm / ¼in cubes

4 tablespoons olive oil

4 tablespoons white wine vinegar

Freshly ground black pepper

30g Spanish empeltre or other black olives

2 hard-boiled eggs, quartered

Sliced radishes and lettuce leaves for garnish

Drain the beans and put them in a pan with water to cover, along with the bay leaf and 1 teaspoon salt. Bring to the boil, skim, then reduce the heat and simmer, covered, until the beans are tender, 1 to 2 hours. Drain the beans and place in a bowl.

Add the parsley, oregano, cumin seeds, onion, red pepper, chorizo, oil and vinegar. Add salt and pepper to taste and combine well. Cover and refrigerate for at least 2 and up to 24 hours.

Remove the beans from the refrigerator and let stand at room temperature for 30 minutes. Transfer the beans to a platter and garnish with olives, quartered eggs, radishes and the lettuce leaves tucked around the beans.

BEEF and HAM SALAD

Salpicón de Carne

Salpicón – essentially leftovers from the midday *olla*, the great stewpot – is what Don Quixote ate for supper most nights. *Salpicón* (*sal* = salt, *picar* = to chop) is a cold hash made by chopping together the leftover meat and vegetables from the pan and dressing them with salt, olive oil and vinegar. In this rendition, I've stuck close to sixteenth-century foodways – no tomatoes, peppers or potatoes. However, in present-day Madrid tapa bars, a dish also called *salpicón* is made with chopped tomatoes, green peppers and shellfish.

You may use boiled beef from the *olla*, leftover pot roast, or roast beef from the deli for this recipe. It can be heaped on salad leaves on individual salad plates, or, if you like a moulded effect, fill a 7.5cm/3in cylinder (such as a pastry cutter) with a quarter of the salad mixture, press it down firmly, then press it out of the mould onto a plate. Repeat with the remaining three servings. You can also serve the mixture hot – stir the beef and ham into the sautéed onions, heat thoroughly – and call it hash.

SERVES 4

230g chopped or shredded cooked beef

120g diced cooked ham

140g diced cooked carrot

28g chopped fresh flat-leaf parsley

3 tablespoons olive oil

130g chopped onion

45g chopped celery

1 garlic clove, chopped

1 teaspoon salt

½ teaspoon freshly ground black pepper

½ teaspoon dried oregano

4 tablespoons white wine vinegar

4 tablespoons mayonnaise

1 teaspoon Dijon mustard

1 tablespoon extra virgin olive oil

1 tablespoon drained capers

1 hard-boiled egg, chopped

Lettuce or other leaves for serving

Combine the beef, ham, carrot and parsley in a bowl.

Heat the olive oil in a skillet over medium heat and sauté the onion, celery and garlic until softened, about 5 minutes. Add to the beef along with the salt, pepper, oregano and 3 tablespoons of the vinegar. Cover and marinate at room temperature for 1 hour or in the refrigerator for up to 4 hours.

While the beef mixture marinates, prepare the sauce. Whisk the mayonnaise until smooth. Stir in the mustard, extra virgin olive oil and remaining tablespoon of vinegar.

Right before serving, fold the capers and chopped egg into the beef salad. Arrange the salad on lettuce or other leaves. Serve with the sauce spooned over the salad.

TOMATO-TUNA SALAD

Pipirrana

I visited the town of Alcázar de San Juan (province of Ciudad Real), famous for wine and cheese, in early September when it was celebrating a local fiesta. At midday groups of friends gathered in the huge central plaza, in the shade of the town hall, where they set up folding tables to prepare this *pipirrana*. Each group had an enormous earthenware bowl in which were combined tomatoes, onions, hard-boiled eggs, tuna, olives and olive oil to make a soupy salad. Invited to partake, I was instructed to scoop it up on chunks of bread. Those with country know-how speared the bread on the tip of a pocketknife and dipped it into the pipirrana.

Pipirrana—also known as *moje,* dunk, because it's soaked up with bread – traditionally was made with fresh or home-bottled tomatoes. Now people use tinned tomatoes from the supermarket, which are surprisingly good with the addition of tuna and fine olive oil. Choose a quality brand of tomatoes.

SERVES 6

1kg drained tinned tomatoes (save the juice for another use)	1½ teaspoons salt
130g finely chopped onion	Up to 5 tablespoons extra virgin olive oil
4 hard-boiled eggs, chopped	Lettuce leaves for serving (optional)
150g drained tinned tuna in olive oil in chunks	Chopped fresh basil or dried oregano for garnish (optional)
160g sliced stoned green and / or black olives	Bread for serving

Core the tomatoes and cut them into pieces. Place them in a large bowl and add the onion, eggs, tuna, olives and salt. Combine the oil drained from the tuna with additional extra virgin olive oil to make 5 tablespoons of oil. Add to the salad and combine gently. Let the salad stand at room temperature for 30 minutes before serving.

Line shallow bowls or ramekins with lettuce if desired. Spoon the salad mixture into the bowls. Garnish with chopped basil or a pinch of oregano, if desired. Serve with bread for dipping into the juicy salad.

LEMON SALAD *with* PRAWNS

Ensalada de Limones con Gambas

In Alcázar de San Juan, a town right in the middle of La Mancha, this is served as a lunchtime dish on fiesta days. In Alcázar and elsewhere in La Mancha, where it is also called *moje,* it's served in a big bowl with lots of bread for dipping into the tangy juices – as is the preceding recipe. The traditional lemon salad does not contain prawns – that was my idea. It makes a surprisingly good prawn 'cocktail'. Some chopped avocado is a good addition, too.

SERVES 4

3 medium lemons

40g chopped spring onion

45g stoned black olives, halved lengthways

¼ teaspoon salt

3 hard-boiled eggs, chopped

2 tablespoons extra virgin olive oil

120g peeled small prawns

Lettuce or other salad leaves for serving

Chopped fresh coriander for garnish

Slice off both ends of the lemons. Set a lemon on end on a chopping board. With a sharp knife, slice down, removing both peel and pith in one cut. Turn the lemon and continue peeling it in this manner. Slice the lemon crossways and discard any seeds. Chop the lemon. Repeat with the remaining 2 lemons. Put the chopped lemon in a bowl.

Add the spring onion, olives, salt and eggs to the lemon. Stir in the oil. Let the salad stand for 1 hour.

Cook the prawns in boiling salted water for 2 minutes. Drain and rinse in cold water.

Line salad plates with lettuce leaves or other greens. Spoon the lemon mixture on top. Scatter the prawns over the lemon. Garnish with coriander and serve.

SHEEPSHEARERS' RICE SALAD with HAM and CHEESE

Ensalada de Esquileo

This recipe is adapted from *Guisos, Viandas y Otras Pócimas* by Joaquín Racionero Page. Although he doesn't say why the salad is the sheepshearer special, I suspect it's because the rice and its accoutrements could be prepared in advance and packed in a pouch to be carried to the country where the shearers worked. According to Pedro Condés, administrator for the Manchego Cheese Board, the sheep still have to be sheared every year, although the wool is worth nothing.

SERVES 6 AS A STARTER OR 4 AS A MAIN COURSE

220g cooked Spanish round-grain rice

60g diced cooked ham

60g cooked peas

35g diced cooked carrot

50g diced Manchego cheese

40g diced flame-roasted red pepper, preferably piquillo

40g chopped spring onion

100g diced peeled fresh tomato

40g sliced green olives

¼ teaspoon whole-grain mustard

¼ teaspoon dried oregano

2 tablespoons white wine vinegar

Salt and freshly ground black pepper

3 tablespoons extra virgin olive oil

Salad leaves for serving

Combine the rice in a mixing bowl with the ham, peas, carrot, cheese, red pepper, spring onion, tomato and olives.

Mix the mustard, oregano, vinegar, ½ teaspoon salt, and pepper to taste together in a small bowl. Whisk in the oil until the dressing is emulsified. Stir into the rice salad and mix well. Let stand at room temperature for at least 15 minutes or up to 2 hours.

Serve the rice salad heaped on salad leaves.

SALAH OF PICKLED PARTRIDGE *or* CHICKEN

Ensalada con Escabeche

Partridge in spiced escabeche is one of La Mancha's emblematic dishes. If you find pickled partridge at gourmet shops, serve it in this delectable salad. The salad is almost as good made with Chicken Wings in Escabeche. Strip the meat from the bones, discarding most of the skin too. You'll need the meat from about 8 wings (16 wing pieces) to serve 4. Use some of the carrots from the marinade in the salad too. The salad can be garnished with pickled mushrooms and onions. Or omit the pickles and scatter pomegranate seeds over the salad.

SERVES 4

150g mixed salad leaves

450g boned pickled partridge or Chicken Wings in Escabeche (page 170) plus pickling liquid

8 hard-boiled quail eggs, halved, or 4 hard-boiled hen eggs, quartered

Cherry tomatoes or sliced plum tomatoes

¼ teaspoon dried oregano

2 tablespoons chopped spring onion

Pickled Mushrooms (page 281; optional)

Scarlet-Pickled Onions (page 282; optional)

Olives or capers

4 teaspoons extra virgin olive oil

Chopped fresh flat-leaf parsley

Divide the salad leaves among 4 salad plates. Top with the boned partridge or chicken. If there are carrot pieces in the escabeche, scatter them around the partridge or chicken.

Garnish the partridge with hard-boiled eggs, tomatoes, oregano, spring onion, pickled mushrooms and onions, if you're using them, plus the olives or capers.

If the escabeche liquid is jellied, heat it briefly in a microwave or a saucepan to liquefy. Drizzle 2 teaspoons of the pickling liquid over each salad. Drizzle 1 teaspoon oil over each. Garnish with chopped parsley.

TOMATOES STUFFED *with* POTATO-CAPER SALAD

Tomates Rellenos con Ensaladilla Rusa

Ensaladilla rusa – 'Russian' salad – is a classic in Madrid tapa bars. Besides potatoes and carrots, it usually contains peas. In this version, tangy capers replace the peas and boost the flavour. This recipe makes only enough potato-caper salad to stuff the tomatoes. You can quadruple the quantities to make a fine luncheon salad.

Chilling the potato for several hours makes it easy to dice.

SERVES 4

1 medium baking potato (250g), skin on

1 carrot, peeled

Salt

1 tablespoon white wine vinegar

4 medium tomatoes (700g)

4 tablespoons diced red or green pepper

1 tablespoon chopped spring onion

1 tablespoon chopped fresh parsley

1 heaping tablespoon drained capers

4 tablespoons mayonnaise

2 tablespoons extra virgin olive oil

Pinch of hot smoked pimentón (optional)

Lettuce leaves for serving

Cook the potato and carrot in boiling water until they are fork-tender, about 15 minutes for the carrot, 25 minutes for the potato. Drain and chill them for 4 hours.

Peel the potato. Cut the potato and carrot into 1cm/⅜in cubes. Place in a bowl and sprinkle with ½ teaspoon salt and the vinegar.

Cut the tops off the tomatoes and scoop out and discard the seeds and pulp, leaving tomato shells. Salt the shells and leave upside down to drain.

Add the pepper, spring onion, parsley and capers to the potato and carrot. In a small bowl, whisk the mayonnaise until smooth. Then whisk in the olive oil, little by little, until the mayonnaise is smooth and glossy. Stir the mayonnaise into the potato salad.

Fill the tomato shells with the salad. Sprinkle with pimentón if desired. Serve the tomatoes on lettuce leaves.

MANCHEGAN SALAD *with* CHEESE

Ensalada a la Manchega

Fresh salads are extremely popular in Castilla–La Mancha. Simple ones may serve as a side dish with a meat main course, in place of cooked vegetables. This salad is usually presented as a starter, placed in the centre of the table. Someone does the honours of liberally anointing the salad with good olive oil and wine vinegar, a sprinkle of salt, and it's ready to enjoy. At a family meal, everyone helps himself directly from the platter.

SERVES 4

1 garlic clove, crushed

½ teaspoon salt

1 teaspoon Dijon mustard

25g chopped spring onion

3 tablespoons white wine vinegar

5 tablespoons extra virgin olive oil

2 tablespoons chopped fresh parsley

170g torn leaf lettuce, broad or curly-leaved endive, or mixed salad leaves

1 large tomato, cut into wedges

160g peeled and diced cucumber

120g Manchego cheese, cut into 1cm/½in cubes

1 hard-boiled egg, quartered

80g drained tinned tuna

12 black or green olives

4 tinned white asparagus spears (optional)

Combine the garlic, salt, mustard, spring onion and vinegar in a small bowl and whisk to combine. Whisk in the oil until the dressing is emulsified. Stir in the parsley.

Spread the lettuce on a large platter. Place tomato wedges around the edges. Scatter the cucumber and cheese over the top. Put the egg wedges on top. Scatter the tuna and olives over. Arrange the asparagus on the salad if you're using it.

Whisk the dressing again and drizzle it evenly over the salad. Serve immediately, without tossing the salad.

GREEN BEAN SALAD *with* GRAPES *and* ANISE

Ensalada de Judías Verdes con Uvas

Fermented grape juice makes wine. Distilled wine makes *aguardiente*, a clear, strong alcoholic drink usually flavoured with aniseeds. In La Mancha it is customary to preserve fruits such as grapes and cherries in aguardiente, which becomes subtly infused with the fruit. In bars and restaurants you will see beautiful decanters and flasks of the liqueur with fruit. It is served in tiny glasses as a digestive. The fruit can be drained and served separately.

This salad, incorporating grapes in aguardiente, was inspired by a recipe in a little book, *La Cocina Tradicional en la Provincia de Toledo*, prepared by a chef at the national parador of Oropesa (Toledo). Paradors are a national network of hotels, often situated in monumental castles, monasteries and ancestral palaces. The original recipe calls for serving the salad with sautéed escalopes of venison. It's equally good with chicken breast or lamb.

Add the dressing to the beans immediately before serving so the vinegar doesn't leach the bright green from the beans.

SERVES 4

75g seedless red grapes, halved	1 garlic clove, crushed
2 tablespoons *aguardiente de anís* or anisette	½ teaspoon Dijon mustard
450g green beans	1 tablespoon white wine vinegar
30g thinly sliced celery	2 tablespoons extra virgin olive oil
20g thinly sliced spring onion	½ teaspoon salt
1 hard-boiled egg	Red leaf lettuce for serving

Place the halved grapes in a small bowl and add the aguardiente or anisette. Allow to macerate for 2 hours. Drain the grapes and discard the aguardiente.

Cut off the tops and tails of the beans and either sliver them lengthways or cut crossways into 5cm/2in pieces. Cook the beans in boiling salted water until crisp-tender, 7 to 8 minutes. Drain and refresh in cold water. Drain.

Place the beans in a bowl and add the celery, spring onion and grapes.

Cut the egg in half. Transfer the yolk to a small bowl. Dice the white into the bowl containing the beans.

To make the dressing, mash the yolk with the garlic, mustard, vinegar, oil and salt. Stir the dressing well. Immediately before serving, toss the dressing with the beans. Garnish a serving bowl with the lettuce and fill it with the dressed beans, or divide the bean salad among 4 individual serving dishes, garnishing each with a few lettuce leaves.

Tortillas,
Egg *and* Cheese Dishes,
Savoury Pastries
and Sandwiches

The story of Don Quixote's adventures is essentially the world's first road-trip novel. On the road with Rocinante. Zen and the art of windmill tilting. Travels with Sancho Panza.

After one of their early adventures together, Sancho (*panza* means 'belly') proffers his humble repast of onion, cheese and bread, slyly suggesting that it wouldn't suit the likes of a valiant knight like Don Quixote. Don Quixote, quite hungry by this point, declares that, though it's a point of honour with knights errant not to eat but once in a month, when they do eat, he declares, they take what's nearest to hand, except for the occasional sumptuous banquet, of course. So the two share the humble meal companionably.

Another time they sup with shepherds – Don Quixote seated on an upturned watering trough – on braised goat meat, cheese and edible acorns.

When I was on the road in La Mancha, I frequently stopped at roadside ventas for a morning breakfast or mid-afternoon snack. To go with coffee I ordered tortilla, a thick potato omelette or a plate of cheese accompanied by bread and olive oil. Simple pleasures, filling food.

The recipes in this chapter are especially suitable for light meals – brunch, lunch, supper and snack. In Spain, egg dishes – and they range from the beloved tortilla, an omelette with potatoes, to vegetable-egg combos, baked dishes and timbales – are rarely served for breakfast. They are favoured for tapas and snacks, light suppers, sometimes starters.

Manchego is Spain's best-known cheese – so famous that its name is illegally 'borrowed' by cheeses made elsewhere. Cheese is principally enjoyed on its own, as a tapa with red wine or sandwiched in a crusty roll as a snack. However, in combination with eggs, cheese makes some delicious luncheon dishes, such as Baked Eggs with Cheese, Cheese Flans with Ham, and Chard and Cheese Pie.

Savoury pastries, some of which overlap with egg and cheese dishes, also make appetising lunch or supper dishes. Add a salad and the meal is complete.

You'll find here a basic recipe for Spanish bread, so delicious when freshly baked with good flour. Enjoy it fresh with meals and for sandwiches. Because it contains no fat and no preservatives, it doesn't stay fresh long. However, stale bread is a primary ingredient in Spanish cookery – toasted and drizzled with fine olive oil for a *tostada* (page 85), crumbled and fried with bacon bits as in *migas* (page 275) or soaked in stock to thicken garlic soup.

SPANISH POTATO TORTILLA

Tortilla de Patatas

Here is the classic all-time favourite Spanish egg dish, *tortilla de patatas*. A Spanish tortilla is in no way even remotely related to the Mexican flat corn or flour wrapper – except that both are round. In Spain, a tortilla is a round cake of eggs and other ingredients, a sort of omelette. But neither is a tortilla the same thing as a frittata. And, to make a tortilla properly, you need a lot of olive oil to slowly, slowly poach the potatoes.

You will find tortilla served in chunks at just about every Madrid tapa bar, the perfect accompaniment to a glass of wine, but it's also good for breakfast, lunch, supper or a picnic.

Use a well-seasoned omelette pan or lightweight non-stick frying pan for the tortilla. A cast-iron pan will be too heavy for turning the tortilla.

Cook the potatoes in lots of olive oil and drain it off. Return only a spoonful of oil to the frying pan to cook the tortilla, and save the remainder for another use.

SERVES 4 FOR LUNCH, 20 AS A TAPA

120ml/scant ¼ pint olive oil

900g baking potatoes (about 4 medium), peeled and chopped into 2.5cm/1in pieces

1 teaspoon salt

2 tablespoons chopped onion

6 eggs

Heat the oil in a 25cm/10in frying pan over medium heat. Add the potatoes and turn them in the oil to coat them thoroughly. Reduce the heat to medium-low and cook the potatoes very slowly, stirring frequently, without browning, for 10 minutes. Sprinkle them with ½ teaspoon of the salt.

Add the onion and continue cooking, stirring frequently, until the potatoes are fork-tender, 20 minutes more.

Beat the eggs in a large bowl with the remaining ½ teaspoon salt.

When the potatoes are tender, place plate or a lid over the frying pan and tip the pan to drain excess oil into a small heatproof bowl.

Stir the potatoes into the bowl of beaten eggs.

Return a little of the reserved oil to the frying pan and pour in the potato-egg mixture. Cook over medium heat until the omelette is set, about 5 minutes, adjusting the heat so the tortilla does not brown. Shake the frying pan to keep the tortilla from sticking.

Place a flat lid or plate on top of the frying pan. Hold it tightly and tip to drain out any excess oil into the heatproof bowl. Then invert the tortilla onto the plate.

Add a little reserved oil to the pan and slide the tortilla back in to cook on the other side, about 3 minutes more. Slide it out onto a serving dish and serve hot or at room temperature. For tapa servings, cut the tortilla into 5cm/2in squares, making 20 pieces. For lunch servings, cut it into wedges, serving 4.

TORTILLA *with* ARTICHOKES *and* HAM

Tortilla con Alcachofas

You would need to cut up dozens of fresh artichokes to have enough for this recipe. Frozen artichoke hearts make prepping easy. They acquire a great flavour from slow cooking in olive oil with ham.

SERVES 4 TO 6

5 tablespoons olive oil

130g chopped onion

2 garlic cloves, chopped

Three 250g packets frozen artichoke hearts or bottoms, thawed, or three 400g tins (720g drained)

100g serrano or cooked ham, chopped

1 teaspoon salt

Freshly ground black pepper

6 eggs

1 tablespoon chopped fresh parsley

Heat 4 tablespoons of the oil in a well-seasoned 25cm/10in omelette pan or non-stick frying pan over medium heat. Sauté the onion and garlic until softened, 5 minutes.

If the artichoke hearts are whole, cut them into quarters or eighths or into roughly 5cm/2in pieces. Add them to the skillet and sauté for 10 minutes. Add the ham, ½ teaspoon of the salt, and pepper to taste. Cook, covered, for 8 to 10 minutes more, until the artichokes are very tender.

Beat the eggs in a large bowl with the remaining ½ teaspoon salt and the parsley. Add the cooked artichoke mixture to the eggs and stir well to combine.

Heat the remaining tablespoon of oil in the frying pan and pour in the egg-artichoke mixture. Smooth the top, but do not stir. Cook over medium heat until the eggs are almost set, without allowing the bottom of the tortilla to brown too fast, about 8 minutes. Use a spatula to firm the sides of the tortilla as it cooks, sliding it between the tortilla and the sides of the pan.

Remove the pan from the heat. Place a flat lid or plate on top of the tortilla. Holding it tightly, turn the frying pan upside down and turn the tortilla out on the plate or lid. Slip the edge of the spatula under it and edge it back into the pan, uncooked side down. Don't worry if a few pieces of artichoke escape. Cook until the bottom is set, 3 to 4 minutes longer.

Slide the tortilla out onto a clean serving plate. Serve hot or at room temperature, cut into 4 to 6 wedges.

CAPUCHIN TORTILLA *with* ASPARAGUS

Tortilla Capuchina

This tortilla is so much more delicious than the simple ingredients might suggest. Something crisp and green on the side is all you need for a fine lunch.

SERVES 4 TO 6

450g fresh asparagus cut into 2.5cm/1in pieces

6 tablespoons olive oil

350g peeled, diced potatoes (about 2 medium)

1½ teaspoons salt

½ medium onion, chopped

4 tablespoons chopped raw bacon (optional)

Coarse fresh breadcrumbs made from 3 to 4 slices of bread

6 eggs

1 tablespoon chopped fresh parsley

Cook the asparagus in boiling water until just tender, about 4 minutes. Drain, refresh in cold water, and drain well. Set aside.

Heat 5 tablespoons of the oil in a non-stick 25cm/10in frying pan. Add the potatoes and sprinkle with ½ teaspoon salt. Cook the potatoes over medium heat, turning them frequently, until almost cooked, 5 to 10 minutes, adjusting the heat so the potatoes do not brown.

Stir in the onion and bacon, if you're using it, and continue to sauté over medium heat for 5 minutes. Add the asparagus and breadcrumbs and sauté for 3 minutes. Remove from the heat.

In a mixing bowl, beat the eggs, parsley and remaining teaspoon of salt.

Stir the contents of the frying pan into the bowl of beaten eggs. Wipe out the frying pan so no bits are stuck to the surface. Add the remaining tablespoon of oil and heat. Pour the egg mixture into the frying pan. Use a spatula to spread it evenly, but do not stir. Cook over medium heat until the tortilla is nearly set, about 3 minutes. Shake the frying pan slightly to keep the tortilla from sticking on the bottom.

Working over a bowl to catch any possible drips, place a flat plate or pan lid on top of the tortilla. Hold it tightly and turn the frying pan upside down, turn the tortilla out onto the plate or lid. Slide the tortilla back into the frying pan, uncooked side down. Cook until set on the bottom, 2 minutes.

With a spatula, lift the edge of the tortilla while tipping the frying pan and slide the tortilla out onto a serving dish. Serve hot or at room temperature, cut into 4 to 6 wedges.

CRACKLY FRIED EGGS

Huevos Estrellados

Spanish fried eggs are a very special category. The egg should emerge from immersion in hot olive oil with the white a little crackly around the edges – *estrellada* – and the yolk still unset. The procedure is more like poaching, only the medium is oil, not water. The eggs must be very fresh and at room temperature. Fry them one at a time. Fried eggs accompany *migas,* fried breadcrumbs (page 275), and *pisto,* vegetable medley (page 245).

SERVES 4

5 to 8 tablespoons olive oil

4 eggs

2 garlic cloves, coarsely chopped

Salt and freshly ground black pepper

Pour enough oil in a 20cm/8in frying pan to measure 1cm/⅜in deep. Heat the oil over medium-high heat until it is shimmering, almost smoking.

Break one egg into a saucer or small cup. Slip it into the hot oil. Add a quarter of the chopped garlic. The egg white will bubble up around the yolk. Use a heatproof spoon or skimmer to spoon hot oil over the top of the egg. The edges of the egg white will turn brown and crackly. The egg will cook in less than 1 minute.

Skim the fried egg out of the oil. Continue frying the remaining eggs in the same oil, adding garlic to each egg. Sprinkle with salt and pepper.

EGG, POTATO and GARLIC SCRAMBLE

Revuelto de Huevos y Patatas con Ajo

I first tasted this at an olive oil mill, where it was served as part of *desayuno molinero,* a typical olive miller's breakfast. It was called *huevos mal educados* – badly behaved eggs – because the eggs, instead of being perfectly fried discs, are broken up into the potatoes and fried with garlic.

In this recipe, whole unpeeled cloves of garlic cook with the potatoes and flavour the oil. You can choose whether or not to squeeze out and eat that nugget of flavour once they're cooked.

SERVES 4

900g baking potatoes (about 4)	Pinch of chilli flakes or cayenne pepper
6 garlic cloves	1 teaspoon salt
5 tablespoons olive oil	¼ teaspoon ground cumin
5 tablespoons chopped spring onion (about 25g)	4 eggs
40g chopped green pepper	2 tablespoons chopped fresh parsley

Peel the potatoes. Cut them lengthways into quarters, then slice them 5mm/¼in thick. Crush the garlic with the flat side of a knife. Slice off the root end, but do not peel them.

Heat the oil in a large non-stick frying pan. Add the potatoes and garlic and sauté over medium-high heat for 5 minutes. Don't let the potatoes brown. Add the spring onion, green pepper, chilli flakes, salt and cumin. Sauté over high heat for 1 minute. Cover and lower the heat. Cook, stirring occasionally, until the potatoes are tender, about 10 minutes.

Push the potatoes to one side and break an egg into the pan. Move the potatoes again and add another egg. Likewise, add the remaining 2 eggs. Let the eggs cook over medium heat for 2 minutes, until the whites are set. Sprinkle with parsley.

With a wooden spatula, scoop up and turn the potatoes, breaking up the eggs. Make 4 or 5 turns. Remove the pan from the heat. Cover and allow the eggs to finish cooking in the heat from the potatoes, 2 minutes. Serve hot.

EGGS with BROAD BEANS

Revuelto con Habas

This egg and bean scramble is frequently made with tinned broad beans, available at any time of year, but it's best with fresh broad beans in the spring.

Choose young, freshly picked broad beans. Cook them in boiling water, then drain and plunge into cold water. This keeps the outer skins tender. You will need about 2.5kg/6lbs of broad beans in their pods to get the correct amount of shelled beans.

SERVES 4

500g shelled broad beans	8 tablespoons bread in very small cubes
2 tablespoons olive oil	90g grated tomato pulp (page 62)
45g diced bacon	½ teaspoon salt
½ medium onion, chopped	Freshly ground black pepper
1 garlic clove, chopped	5 eggs

Cook the beans in boiling water to cover until tender, 15 minutes. Drain and cover them with cold water.

Heat the oil in a frying pan over medium heat. Sauté the bacon, onion and garlic for 3 minutes. Add the diced bread and sauté for 2 minutes. Stir in the tomato pulp.

Drain the beans and add them to the frying pan with the salt, pepper to taste, and 120ml/scant ¹1₄ pint water. Cook, covered, for 10 minutes. Uncover the frying pan and cook for 5 minutes more, leaving a little liquid with the beans.

Break the eggs into the frying pan. Cook for 2 minutes, until the whites begin to set. Stir just the whites to mix with the beans and cook for 2 minutes. One by one, stir the yolks into the beans. Cook just until they are softly scrambled, 2 minutes.

Serve hot.

SATURDAY EGGS and BACON

Duelos y Quebrantos

This tasty dish of eggs scrambled with bacon is what Don Quixote ate on Saturdays. Roughly translated, *duelos* means 'toils and travails' or 'grief' (a duelo is also a wake preceding a funeral), and *quebrantos* means 'afflictions' or 'cracked'. The dish may have originated in the old custom in some parts of La Mancha for shepherds to deliver to their masters any animals that died or were injured during the week. The meat was salted and dried to make sheep or goat jerky (*tasajo*), and the bones were cracked and cooked in the *olla* to make a Saturday stew thickened with eggs. Presumably, it was the master who had lost his stock who suffered the duelos – and ate them.

But some Cervantes scholars declare the addition of bacon or salt pork contrary to the custom of Cervantes' time, for Saturdays were days of semi-abstinence, when fatty meat and salt pork were not allowed, but animal 'parts' were permitted. A soup of offal – chicken feet, gizzards, lamb's brains, tripe – would be thickened with beaten eggs. From that is derived another interpretation of the dish as eggs with lamb's brains, often with the addition of bacon – a modest venial sin in exchange for a great deal of pleasure.

SERVES 4

3 tablespoons olive oil

35g/4 tablespoons chopped onion

65g diced bacon, pancetta or fatty ham

70g diced Spanish soft chorizo (1 link)

6 eggs

1 tablespoon chopped fresh parsley

Freshly ground black pepper

Triangles of bread fried in olive oil for serving (optional)

Heat the oil in a large frying pan over medium heat. Add the chopped onion, bacon and chorizo and fry for 4 minutes.

Beat the eggs with the parsley. Pour the eggs into the frying pan and stir until softly set. Serve immediately with a little black pepper. Accompany the eggs with fried bread if desired.

GARLICKY ASPARAGUS *and* EGGS

Ajo de Espárragos

In Spain this vegetable dish with eggs probably would be presented as a first course or as the main dish for a light supper. It's also an ideal brunch dish. Serve it with toast 'buttered' with extra virgin olive oil.

SERVES 4

800g chopped thin asparagus

3 tablespoons olive oil

1 medium onion, chopped

3 garlic cloves, chopped

1 bay leaf

90g chopped serrano ham

2 teaspoons sweet pimentón

2 tablespoons plain flour

1 teaspoon salt

Freshly ground black pepper

4 eggs

Pinch of hot smoked pimentón or cayenne

Cook the asparagus in boiling salted water until crisp-tender, about 3 minutes. Drain, saving the liquid.

Heat the oil in a frying pan or cazuela over medium heat and sauté the onion, garlic and bay leaf until the onion is softened, 3 minutes. Add the ham and asparagus and sauté for 3 minutes. Remove and discard the bay leaf.

Remove the pan from the heat and stir in the sweet pimentón and flour. Return the pan to medium heat and stir in 300ml/½ pint of the reserved cooking liquid. Season with salt and pepper. Stir the asparagus and cook until the sauce thickens slightly, about 3 minutes.

Lower the heat so the sauce just simmers. Break the eggs on top of the asparagus. Sprinkle them with hot pimentón. Cover the frying pan and poach the eggs until the whites are set but the yolks still runny, 4 to 5 minutes. Remove the pan from the heat and let stand, covered, until the eggs are set, 1 minute more. Serve in shallow soup plates.

Instant Tomato Purée

Over the years I've learned many tricks from Spanish cooks, such as this one for quickly preparing puréed tomatoes. Cut the tomatoes in half and grate them on the coarsest side of a box grater. Collect all the pulp and juices. Discard the flattened skin – which also serves as a shield for your knuckles! You will need about 700g/1½lb of tomatoes to make 600ml/1 pint of grated tomato pulp.

EGGS POACHED in TOMATO PURÉE with CHEESE

Huevos Escalfados en Puré de Tomate con Queso

Not all cheese in La Mancha is Manchego with DO. Several excellent cheeses are made of a combination of milks – cow, sheep and goat. Some are marketed fresh and uncured, so they are fairly soft and creamy. Such a soft cheese would be perfect for this dish of eggs poached over a bed of tomato purée. Fresh mozzarella would be a good substitute. Serve the eggs with plenty of fresh bread for dunking.

SERVES 4

3 tablespoons olive oil

Grated tomato pulp from 680g tomatoes (page 62)

1 teaspoon salt

Freshly ground black pepper

8 thin slices cheese (120g)

60g serrano ham, thinly sliced (optional)

8 eggs

⅛ teaspoon hot smoked pimentón or a pinch of cayenne

Heat the oil in a 30cm/12in frying pan over high heat. Add the tomatoes and season with ½ teaspoon of the salt, and pepper to taste. Cook for 1 minute, lower the heat to medium, and cook the tomatoes for 10 to 12 minutes. Quite a lot of liquid will remain.

Remove the pan from the heat. Lay the slices of cheese on top of the tomato purée. Divide the ham, if you're using it, into 8 pieces. Place them on top of or between the slices of cheese. Break the eggs, one by one, into a small cup and slide them into the pan on top. Sprinkle with the remaining ½ teaspoon salt and the pimentón.

Cover the frying pan and place over high heat for 1 minute. Reduce the heat to medium and cook gently until the whites are just set but the yolks are still runny, 6 to 7 minutes. Let stand for 1 minute before serving.

Use a large spoon to lift eggs, cheese and tomato sauce out of the frying pan. Serve in shallow soup plates.

EGGS BAKED in SPINACH NESTS

Huevos en Nidos de Espinacas

When this egg dish is part of a larger menu, one egg per person is fine. But if it's to be the whole meal, use 2 eggs for each. The eggs can be baked in metal or ceramic ramekins or in individual earthenware cazuelas. Cazuelas are slow to heat, but they retain heat after being removed from the oven. Remove the cazuelas when the whites are barely set and the eggs will finish cooking from residual heat.

Use Manchego or a smoky cheese such as San Simón from Galicia in north-west Spain or Idiazábal from the Basque Country.

SERVES 4

350g shredded spinach	170g diced tomato
3 tablespoons olive oil	1 teaspoon salt
35g/4 tablespoons chopped onion	Freshly ground black pepper
1 garlic clove, chopped	4 to 8 eggs
35g/ 4 tablespoons diced bacon (optional)	25g/4 tablespoons grated cheese

Preheat the oven to 200°C/180°C fan/GM6.

Cook the spinach in boiling water until wilted, 2 to 3 minutes. Drain and press out excess liquid.

Heat the oil in a medium frying pan over medium heat and sauté the onion, garlic and bacon, if you're using it, for 2 minutes. Turn the heat to high and add the tomato, salt and pepper to taste. Reduce the heat to medium and cook until the tomatoes are thick, about 10 minutes. Add the spinach to the tomatoes and cook for 3 minutes.

Divide the spinach mixture among 4 lightly oiled ramekins or individual cazuelas. Use a spoon to make 1 or 2 indentations in the spinach. Break 1 or 2 eggs into each ramekin. Sprinkle cheese over the eggs.

Bake until the whites are set but the yolks are still runny, about 10 minutes. Serve immediately.

BAKED EGGS *with* CHEESE

Costrada Manchega

This makes an admirable luncheon or supper dish, serving four with two eggs each or up to eight with one egg per person. Manchego is preferred, but the recipe works with any flavourful cheese, such as Gruyère or Cheddar.

❧ SERVES 4 TO 8

8 slices sandwich bread

3 tablespoons olive oil

280g cheese, grated, preferably Manchego

120ml / 4 fl oz dry white wine

⅛ teaspoon cumin seeds

⅛ teaspoon finely chopped fresh rosemary

8 eggs

Salt and freshly ground black pepper

1 garlic clove, sliced crossways

Chopped fresh parsley

Preheat the oven to 190°C/170°C fan/GM5.

Remove the crusts from the bread and lightly toast the slices. Arrange them in a single layer in an oiled baking pan. Brush them with 1 tablespoon of the oil.

Combine the cheese, wine and cumin seeds. Spread the cheese mixture over the bread. Scatter the rosemary on top. Break an egg on top of each slice of bread. Sprinkle with salt and pepper to taste.

Heat the remaining 2 tablespoons oil in a small frying pan and sauté the garlic until golden. Spoon the oil and garlic over the eggs and cheese.

Bake until the whites are set but the yolks are still runny, about 10 minutes. Sprinkle with chopped parsley to serve.

'FRIDAY PIE' with FISH

Pastel de Viernes

On Fridays during Lent, housewives prepare meatless meals – thus the name of this tasty dish, Friday pie. It is traditionally made with *bacalao,* dry salt cod, first soaked, then flaked. I have substituted tinned tuna, making this 'pie' easy to prepare and a delicious lunch any day of the week. Accompany it with Tomato Sauce (page 26) and a fresh salad.

You probably will not need additional salt – taste the mixture after adding the tuna and before incorporating the eggs.

SERVES 4 TO 6

2 tablespoons olive oil

½ medium onion, chopped

1 tablespoon plain flour

250ml/scant ½ pint semi-skimmed or full-fat milk

Freshly grated nutmeg

Freshly ground black pepper

350g drained tinned tuna

45g/4 tablespoons sliced black, green or pimiento-stuffed olives

4 eggs, beaten

1 tablespoon fine dry breadcrumbs

Preheat the oven to 180°C/160°C fan/GM4.

Heat the oil in a saucepan over medium heat and sauté the onion until softened, 3 minutes. Stir in the flour and cook for 1 minute. Whisk in the milk and cook, stirring constantly, until the mixture thickens, 4 minutes.

Remove from the heat and add nutmeg and pepper to taste, then the tuna, olives and eggs.

Coat a 23cm/9in pie pan with cooking spray. Sprinkle with the breadcrumbs. Pour the tuna mixture into the pan and spread evenly.

Bake until the pie is set and a skewer inserted comes out clean, about 45 minutes. Serve hot or at room temperature.

AUBERGINE TIMBALE

Cuajado de Berenjenas

Spanish cooking has a number of variations on *cuajado*, a sort of timbale with vegetables, eggs and cheese. Precursors of the ever-so-popular *tortilla*, made of eggs with potatoes or other vegetables, and somewhat like the Italian frittata, the cuajados come from Spain's medieaval Sephardic Jewish culture, where an all-dairy meal (no flesh) was served on some holidays. In fact, modern-day Sephardim call these meatless meals by the Spanish word *desayuno*, or 'break-fast' – meaning a substantial brunch or lunch.

This aubergine timbale indeed makes a delightful brunch dish or an elegant starter. It looks quite special, with its shiny black skin. I like to serve it sliced, on salad leaves with a sharp, tangy dressing (such as yogurt with Dijon mustard and Sherry vinegar) to highlight the richness of the cheese and aubergine.

✼ SERVES 6 TO 8 AS A STARTER

4 medium aubergine (about 1kg)

1 tablespoon grated onion

3 eggs

100g fresh breadcrumbs

190g grated cheese, such as Manchego

1 teaspoon salt

½ teaspoon freshly ground black pepper

1 tablespoon wine vinegar

Olive oil for the pan

Preheat the grill to high.

Pierce the bottoms of the aubergine twice with a skewer (to prevent steam from accumulating as they heat). Roast them under the grill (or over charcoal, or in the oven, or in a microwave), turning once, until they are soft when tested with a skewer, about 10 minutes per side. Do not let the skin char. Remove and cool slightly.

Preheat oven to 190°C/170°C fan/GM5.

Remove and discard the aubergine stems. Cut the aubergine open lengthways and scoop out the flesh, reserving the skins. Purée the flesh in a blender or food processor with the onion and eggs.

Place the puréed aubergine in a bowl and fold in the breadcrumbs, cheese, salt, pepper, and vinegar.

Oil the bottom and sides of a 2 litre/3½ pint ovenproof casserole or a 20cm/8in cake pan. Place the aubergine skins, shiny side down, on the bottom of the pan, overlapping them slightly and allowing them to extend partway up the sides. Spoon the aubergine and cheese mixture into the pan, smoothing the top. Cover with a lid or foil. Place the pan in a larger, ovenproof container and add boiling water to reach halfway up the outsides of the pan to make a bain marie. Carefully place the bain marie in the preheated oven.

Reduce the oven heat to 180°C/160°C fan/GM4. Bake the timbale until set and a skewer inserted in the centre comes out clean, about 55 minutes. Remove and let cool for 15 minutes.

Loosen the sides of the timbale. Place a serving plate on top and carefully invert the timbale onto the plate. Serve warm or cold.

NOTE: *The timbale can also be baked in a loaf tin without the aubergine skins.*

CHEESE FLANS *with* HAM

Flan de Queso con Jamón

Egg whites folded into the custard mixture give these flans a delicate mousselike texture. Serve them with steamed broccoli or grilled asparagus as a luncheon main course or with prawns or crab and salad leaves as a starter. Prepared with milk plus cream, these flans are very rich. For a lighter version, use all milk. Manchego works best, but any well-flavoured cheese can be used instead.

SERVES **8**

2 tablespoons olive oil

3½ tablespoons plain flour

470ml / ¾ pint milk

250ml / scant ½ pint double cream

120ml / scant ¼ pint Tomato Sauce, home-made (page 26) or tinned (not concentrate)

4 eggs (2 separated)

230g cheese, grated

90g chopped serrano or cooked ham

Pinch of cayenne

Pinch of dried oregano

1 teaspoon salt

Freshly ground black pepper

Preheat the oven to 180°C/160°C fan/GM4. Oil eight large (240ml) custard cups or individual flan moulds and set them in a baking tin, for your bain marie.

Heat the oil in a saucepan over medium heat and stir in the flour. Cook, stirring, for 1 minute. Whisk in the milk and cream and cook until the custard begins to thicken, 5 minutes. Whisk in the tomato sauce and cook, stirring, for 2 minutes.

Separate 2 of the eggs, putting the whites in one bowl and beating the yolks and the 2 whole eggs in another. Whisk the beaten eggs and yolks into the sauce. Remove from heat and stir in the cheese, ham, cayenne, oregano, salt, and pepper to taste.

Using a clean whisk, beat the egg whites until they hold stiff peaks. Beat a third of the whites into the custard mixture. Fold the remaining whites thoroughly into the custard.

Ladle the custard mixture into the custard cups, filling them only three-quarters full. To create your bain marie, pour enough hot water into the baking bain marie to come halfway up the outside of the custard cups. Carefully transfer the pan to the oven. Bake until the custards are set (a skewer inserted in the centre will come out clean), 40 to 45 minutes.

Remove the flans from the bain marie and let them cool for at least 15 minutes. Loosen the sides with a knife and unmould the flans onto individual plates. Serve warm or at room temperature.

AN ARTISANAL CHEESEMAKER
IN LA MANCHA

Sheltered in a barn from the fierce sun of a La Mancha summer, two hundred sheep of the Manchega breed are baaing politely, waiting for lunch. The sheep were milked at 5 A.M. and taken out to graze the golden, stubbled wheat fields on the farm. José Araque Carrascosa, former shepherd, now a master cheesemaker, is proud of his stock.

José's father before him was a shepherd in the small town of La Solana. And his granddad, his great-granddad, and his great-great-grandfather too were shepherds. They tended flocks of sheep in the upland plains of central Spain.

'They say La Solana breeds shepherds,' says José. La Solana means 'a place in the sun'. A few centuries ago this was a favoured wintering destination for great flocks of sheep that moved in a seasonal migration from the northern provinces to the south. From mediaeval times the sheep were a source of fantastic wealth for their wool. Now the wool is virtually worthless, but the cheese – once a by-product, made by shepherds to conserve the milk – is like gold.

Cheesemaking was a cottage industry – literally made in the family home – and the cheeses were sold locally. In 1990 José decided to register the family business with the Consejo Regulador de la Denominación de Origen Queso Manchego, the regulating board that authenticates all cheese with the Queso Manchego label.

With his wife, Paqui, who learned cheesemaking from her mother-in-law, José continued making artisanal cheese from the milk from his own ewes. When his cheeses started taking prizes at important gastronomy and livestock fairs, José and Paqui decided to expand their cheesemaking capacity and moved the operation to a shiny new facility with the latest equipment.

His cheese, labelled artisanal Manchego, is made from raw, unpasteurised milk. The milk comes from several family herds, all within a fifteen-mile radius – close enough so that he can monitor the milk's quality and sanitation.

José and Paqui make cheese every other day, so the milk is held for up to two days in refrigerated tanks. Then it is piped to a big temperature-controlled vat where it is warmed to 30°C/86°F. Paqui monitors the process. When the temperature is right, she weighs out the *cuajo,* rennet, a curdling agent.

When the milk begins to thicken into curds, Paqui sets in motion the *lira* (lyre), a mechanical arm with steel threads that rotate, cutting the curds into smaller and smaller bits. In former times the curds had to be cut by hand, a slow process requiring patience. With mechanisation, she can process as much as fifteen hundred gallons of milk in one go, almost single-handedly.

The whey is drawn off from the vat of clabbered milk. It is piped to holding tanks, then to tankers, and sold to the baking industry. A small part of the whey Paqui heats gently to make *requesón,* cottage cheese, for local consumption (delicious drizzled with honey and sprinkled with a few walnuts). She also separates the *nata,* the rich, sweet cream that rises to the top of the whey. Ewes' milk is highly valued for cheesemaking because it is much richer in fat, protein and milk solids than cows' milk. It takes 5 litres of sheep's milk to make 1 kilogram of cheese.

José scoops out some fresh curds from the new batch of cheese to taste. They are sweet, almost sunny.

The next step requires all hands – two of the couple's sons and a niece. The curds sluice through various funnels on their way to becoming cheese. The moulds used are high-tech plastic with tiny holes that facilitate the release of whey. They are imprinted with a crosshatch pattern that mimics the woven *esparto* grass strips with which Manchego cheese traditionally was moulded.

Curds are heaped into the moulds. As the moulds emerge on the miniature conveyor belt, Paqui slaps each one with the disc that identifies it officially as Manchego. The curds in their moulds go to a press that squeezes out the remaining whey.

During this alchemy, as fresh milk becomes solid, the two sons, Antonio and José Manuel, take charge of removing the fresh cheeses made two days before from the saltwater bath where they have been submerged. A cheese lift raises them from the brine and sends them to the end of the line, where they are stacked in crates.

José moves the cheeses to the *secadero,* drying room, where they are stacked and turned for thirty days. From the secadero the cheeses move to a cold curing room, *maduración.* Here they stay for a minimum of sixty days. The aroma begins to mellow, smells of cheese. The cheese develops a light coating of mould, which favours the maturing process. Later they will be brushed to clean off the mould. Then they move to a keeping chamber. Or, in the case of José's aged cheeses, some of them are submerged in olive oil, which keeps them even longer.

After the minimum sixty-day ageing, and after sample cheeses are tested in the laboratory of the Manchego regulating board, the board issues the official label. This is authentic Queso Manchego.

The Manchego found in American and British delicatessens and supermarkets is primarily industrial. All of the requirements are the same – the milk must come from certified ewes of the Manchega breed and be produced within the designated areas of La Mancha (parts of the provinces of Ciudad Real, Toledo, Cuenca and Albacete). Only coagulant and salt can be added to the cheese. The cheese must be matured for a minimum of sixty days. The only difference is that industrial Manchego cheese is produced from pasteurised milk with the addition of natural ferments. The cheese is subjected to the same lab analysis and meets all the size and flavour specifications of the regulating board. Only cheese authenticated as Denominación de Origen Queso Manchego can carry the official logo with the silhouette of Don Quixote.

CHARD and CHEESE PIE

Torta de Acelgas con Queso

Fresh white cheese, *queso fresco*, often made from goat's milk, makes a solid filling between the two layers of chard. It has a mild flavour of fresh milk, quite unlike cured cheeses. If unavailable, use crumbled ricotta in its place. Bacon adds a subtle smokiness, but if you prefer a vegetarian pie, omit it.

SERVES 6 TO 8

1 recipe Flaky Pastry (page 79)

Flour for rolling the pastry

900g chard, stems chopped and leaves shredded

2 tablespoons olive oil

30g pine nuts

30g chopped bacon (optional)

1 medium onion, chopped

2 garlic cloves, chopped

1 egg

½ teaspoon freshly ground black pepper

⅛ teaspoon freshly grated nutmeg

⅛ teaspoon ground ginger

Pinch of ground cinnamon

1 teaspoon salt

2 tablespoons raisins (optional)

350g fresh white cheese, such as *queso fresco*, sliced 5mm / ¼in thick

Roll out the pastry on a lightly floured surface. Fit it into a 30cm / 12in loose-bottomed flan tin. Trim off any excess dough and reserve it. Chill the pastry case.

Cook the chard in boiling salted water until tender, 15 minutes. Drain and refresh in cold water. Drain very well, pressing to eliminate all liquid.

Preheat the oven to 180°C / 160°C fan / GM4.

Heat 1 teaspoon of the oil in a frying pan over medium-high heat and sauté the pine nuts until they are lightly toasted, about 30 seconds. Skim them out and reserve.

Add the remaining oil to the frying pan. When hot, sauté the bacon, onion, and garlic until the onion is softened, 5 minutes. Add the chard and sauté for a few minutes more.

Beat the egg in a bowl with the pepper, nutmeg, ginger, cinnamon and salt. Add the chard mixture along with the raisins, if you're using them. Combine well.

Pour half of the chard mixture into the pastry case. Arrange the sliced cheese on top. Cover with the remaining chard. Scatter the toasted pine nuts over the top and press them gently into the chard.

Roll any remaining pastry into cords to crisscross the top of the pie. Pinch them to the edges of the pastry case.

Bake the pie until the pastry is light golden, 35 to 40 minutes. Cool on a rack for 10 minutes. Release the pastry from the sides of the flan tin. Remove the outer ring and cut into wedges. Serve warm or cold.

EMPANADAS FILLED *with* SPICY CHICKEN

Empanadas Rellenas con Pollo

Pack these tasty empanadas for a picnic lunch.

MAKES 5 EMPANADAS

2 tablespoons olive oil

½ medium onion, finely chopped

1 garlic clove, chopped

½ boneless, skinless chicken breast, diced
(about 250g)

1 roasted and peeled red pepper, tinned or fresh,
chopped

2 tablespoons Tomato Sauce, home-made (page
26) or ready-made passata

2 tablespoons dry white wine or water

½ teaspoon salt

¼ teaspoon dried oregano

Cayenne

¼ teaspoon ground cumin

1 hard-boiled egg, chopped

Flaky Pastry (page 79)

Flour for rolling the pastry

1 egg yolk

Heat the oil in a frying pan over medium heat and sauté the onion and garlic until softened, 5 minutes. Add the diced chicken and sauté until the chicken loses its pink colour, 2 minutes. Stir in the roasted pepper, tomato sauce, wine, salt, oregano, cayenne to taste and cumin. Cook, covered, for 8 minutes. Uncover and cook to reduce the liquid, but leave the mixture juicy, not dry. Stir in chopped egg.

Preheat the oven to 200°C/180°C fan/GM6.

Roll out the pastry on a floured surface. Cut four 15cm/6in circles. Gather up the pastry scraps, roll out, and cut one more circle.

Place about 4 tablespoons of the chicken filling on one half of each circle. Brush the edge of the circle lightly with water and fold the pastry over the filling. Crimp or roll the edges to seal the empanadas. Place them on a baking sheet. Combine the egg yolk with 2 teaspoons water and brush the tops of the empanadas with it. Bake until golden, about 30 minutes. Serve hot or at room temperature.

ASPARAGUS TART

Torta de Espárragos

The classic version of this tart is made with silky tinned white asparagus. I much prefer the stand-up flavour of fresh green asparagus. Cook it laid flat in a frying pan of boiling salted water until tender. Any flavourful cheese, such as Gruyère or Cheddar, can be used in place of Manchego for the gratin topping.

❧ SERVES 6 TO 8

Flaky Pastry (page 79)

2 tablespoons plain flour, plus flour for rolling the pastry

60g butter

½ medium onion, finely chopped

½ teaspoon smoked pimentón

470ml/¾ pint full-fat milk

1 teaspoon salt

Pinch of dried thyme

Freshly ground black pepper

2 egg yolks

1.8kg asparagus (2 to 4 dozen spears, depending on thickness), trimmed to 15cm/6in and cooked

1 large mushroom, thinly sliced

50g coarsely grated Manchego

Preheat the oven to 180°C/160°C fan/GM4.

Roll out the pastry on a lightly floured surface to a 36cm/14in circle and fit it into a 30cm/12in loose-bottomed flan tin. Line the pastry with foil and weigh down with dried beans or rice. Place on a baking sheet and bake until the edges are lightly coloured, 15 minutes. Remove the foil and beans. Return the pastry case to the oven and bake for 8 to 10 minutes longer, or until the crust is pale gold and just begins to pull away from the sides of the pan. Allow to cool.

Heat the butter in a saucepan over medium heat. Add the onion and sauté until softened, 5 minutes. Stir in the 2 tablespoons flour and cook for 1 minute. Stir in the pimentón. Whisk in 400ml/14 fl oz of the milk and cook, stirring constantly, until the mixture begins to bubble and thicken. Add the salt, thyme, and pepper to taste. Reduce the heat to very low and cook this savoury white sauce, stirring frequently, for 5 minutes.

In a heatproof bowl, combine the egg yolks with the remaining milk. Whisk in some of the hot white sauce, then stir the yolk mixture into the pan of white sauce. Cook, stirring constantly, until the mixture thickens and begins to simmer. Lower the heat and cook for 5 minutes, stirring frequently.

Preheat the grill to high.

Spread half of the custard in the baked pastry case. Arrange the spears of asparagus, tips out, on top, in spokes. Cover with the remaining custard mixture. Press the mushroom slices lightly into the custard. Sprinkle with grated cheese.

Place the pie on a baking sheet about 10cm/4in from the heat and grill until the top is bubbly and lightly browned, about 5 minutes. Serve hot or at room temperature.

FLAKY PASTRY

Pasta Quebrada

Use this pastry for empanadas and both sweet and savoury pies. Be sure to let it rest at room temperature for at least 1 hour. The pastry works well whether the crust is filled with raw ingredients and baked, or baked 'blind' and then filled with a cooked filling. The raw pastry freezes well. Thaw completely before rolling out on a floured board.

MAKES ENOUGH PASTRY FOR A 28CM/11IN PIE OR FIVE 15CM/6IN EMPANADAS

250g plain flour, plus flour for rolling the pastry

1 teaspoon baking powder

½ teaspoon salt

60g unsalted butter, cut into small pieces

2 egg yolks

4 tablespoons olive oil

Sift the flour, baking powder and salt into a mixing bowl. Rub the butter into the flour until the mixture is crumbly.

Combine the egg yolks and oil. Make a well in the flour and pour in the yolks. Use a fork to blend the flour into the yolks. Add 3 tablespoons cold water to make a soft pastry that can be patted into a ball.

Turn the pastry out onto a board and knead it very briefly. Cover and leave at room temperature for 1 hour before rolling out on a floured board.

NOTE: *To double the recipe for the pastry, making 10 empanadas, use the following proportions:*

470g flour, plus flour for rolling the pastry

1½ teaspoons baking powder

1 teaspoon salt

120g unsalted butter

3 egg yolks

120ml/4 fl oz olive oil

7 tablespoons water

BASIC BREAD DOUGH

Masa para Pan

One 7g sachet easy-blend dried yeast

1 teaspoon sugar

1 teaspoon salt

600g strong flour

350ml/12 fl oz warm (48°C/120°F) water

Olive oil for the bowl

Combine the yeast, sugar, salt and 550g of the flour in a large mixing bowl. Make a well in the centre and add the warm water. Mix with a wooden spoon. Turn the dough out onto a board and knead the remaining 50g flour into it. Knead the dough until smooth and elastic, about 8 minutes. Pat into a ball.

Oil a clean bowl. Place the ball of dough in it and turn the dough to coat all sides with oil. Cover the bowl with a dampened cloth and place in a warm, draught-free place to rise until doubled in bulk, about 1 hour.

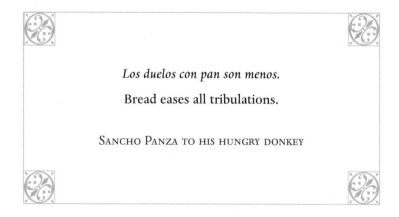

Los duelos con pan son menos.

Bread eases all tribulations.

SANCHO PANZA TO HIS HUNGRY DONKEY

The dough is now ready for use in any recipe that requires bread dough. If the dough is to be baked as bread, shape the loaves, place them on a floured baking sheet, and cover with a dry cloth. Allow to rise until not quite doubled in bulk, about 1 hour.

Preheat the oven to 220°C/200°C fan/GM7. If you're using a baking stone, place it in the lower third of the oven and preheat it.

When the loaves have risen, use a baker's peel or a thin baking sheet to slide under the risen loaves and ease them onto the preheated stone. Otherwise, bake them directly on the baking sheets.

Bake for 15 minutes, lower the oven temperature to 180°C/160°C fan/GM4, and bake until the loaves are golden brown and have a hollow sound when tapped on the bottom, 15 to 20 minutes longer, depending on the shape.

PICNIC ROLLS *with* PORK, SAUSAGE *and* EGG

Hornazos de Romería

A *romería* is a pilgrimage to a saint's shrine in the countryside. It's an occasion to pack a picnic basket full of goodies and head for the hills. This bread roll, with sliced meat and egg baked right into it, is favourite fare for romerías in La Mancha. It's also typical for Carnaval, the Spanish version of Mardi Gras. A variation typical for Easter follows.

MAKES 6 ROLLS

1 recipe Basic Bread Dough (page 80), risen once

130g plain flour

½ teaspoon bicarbonate of soda

120ml/4 fl oz plus 3 tablespoons olive oil

6 thin slices boneless pork loin (about 250g)

Salt and freshly ground black pepper

½ teaspoon dried oregano

½ teaspoon wine vinegar

1 small garlic clove, finely chopped

6 thin slices serrano ham (85g)

2 links Spanish hard chorizo (140g), cut into 1cm/½in slices

Cornmeal (polenta) for the baking sheet

3 hard-boiled eggs, halved lengthways

After the bread dough has risen once, knock it back and place it in a large mixing bowl. Combine the flour and bicarbonate of soda. Add 120ml/4 fl oz of the olive oil to the dough in 3 parts, alternating with the flour. Use your knuckles to work the oil into the dough.

When the dough has absorbed the oil, turn it out on a board and knead until very smooth. As the dough is somewhat slippery, additional flour will not be needed on the work surface.

Place the dough in a bowl, cover with a damp cloth, and allow to rise in a warm place until doubled in bulk, about 1 hour.

Place the sliced pork loin on a plate and sprinkle with salt and pepper to taste, oregano, vinegar and garlic. Allow to stand for 30 minutes.

Heat the remaining 3 tablespoons oil in a frying pan and fry the sliced loin very quickly, about 45 seconds per side. Remove. Quickly fry the ham in the same oil. Do not allow it to crisp.

Remove from the pan. Fry the sliced chorizo, turning to brown both sides. Remove the frying pan from the heat, but leave the chorizo in the oil.

Knock back the dough and divide it into 7 equal pieces (tennis ball sized, about 150g). Pat and roll a ball of dough out to a 150ml/6in circle. Place it on a baking sheet that has been sprinkled lightly with cornmeal. Continue with 5 more dough circles.

Cut the sliced pork loin in half lengthways. Place half an egg, cut side down, in the centre of each circle of dough (except the spare one). Place a strip of loin on either side. Press ham and sliced chorizo around the egg. Drizzle the oil remaining in the frying pan over the 6 rolls.

Use the remaining ball of dough to roll thin cords. Cut them into approximate 15cm/6in lengths and crisscross 2 cords over each roll, pinching to attach them to the edges of the round. Allow the rolls to rise while the oven is heating.

Preheat the oven to 200°C/180°C fan/GM6.

Bake the rolls for 12 minutes. Lower the oven temperature to 180°C/160°C fan/GM4 and bake until the crust is golden, 8 to 10 minutes longer. The rolls should sound hollow when tapped on the bottom. Cool them on a rack.

VARIATION: Hornazos para Pascua. *This sugared variation of hornazos has a coloured hard-boiled egg baked in the centre for Easter. With or without the egg, it makes an excellent breakfast roll.*

Prepare the dough for hornazos as directed. While the dough is rising, prepare the following topping.

1 tablespoon olive oil	½ teaspoon grated orange zest
110g coarsely chopped almonds	1 egg
50g plus 1 tablespoon sugar	1 tablespoon milk
1 teaspoon ground cinnamon	Cornmeal (polenta) for the baking sheet

Heat the oil in a small frying pan over medium heat and sauté the almonds until toasted, about 40 seconds. Add 50g of the sugar and cook for 1 minute, until the sugar begins to melt. Remove from the heat and add the cinnamon and orange zest.

Divide the dough into 8 balls. Pat them into 11cm/4½in circles and place on a baking sheet that's been sprinkled with cornmeal. Spread the almond topping on the circles. Beat the egg and milk together. Drizzle a little over the almonds. Sprinkle with the remaining sugar.

Bake the rolls as directed above.

TOAST *with* OLIVE OIL

Una Tostada

This is my favourite breakfast. In its simplest version, it consists of thickly sliced country bread, grilled or toasted, drizzled with extra virgin olive oil, and sprinkled with a little salt. Some people rub the toast with a cut garlic clove. Vary the toppings – tinned sardines or leftover fried fish, anchovies, aged Manchego or fresh goat's cheese, raw onion, thinly sliced serrano ham, roasted sweet peppers, grated tomatoes (in La Mancha this is known as *tomatón,* but elsewhere in Spain it's 'Catalan toast'). As the savoury toppings suggest, you can serve the *tostada* as an appetiser as well as breakfast.

Slice bread about 4cm/1½ in thick. Toast it under the grill or in a preheated hot oven, turning once, until lightly toasted on both sides. Place the toasts on a platter. If desired, rub the toasts with garlic. Drizzle with extra virgin olive oil, allowing 1 to 2 teaspoons oil per slice of bread. Serve with the toppings of your choice.

CRISP HAM *and* CHEESE SANDWICHES

Bocaditos de Jamón y Queso

These crispy shallow-fried sandwiches go nicely with smooth tomato soup (page 97) or a sliced tomato salad.

SERVES 4

8 slices bread from a small sandwich loaf

85g cheese, preferably Manchego, grated

2 tablespoons finely chopped spring onion

1 teaspoon Dijon mustard

Pinch of dried thyme

Freshly ground black pepper

6 tablespoons olive oil

2 eggs

60g serrano or cooked ham, thinly sliced

2 tablespoons milk

5 tablespoons (about 25g) fine dry breadcrumbs

Remove the crusts from the bread and cut the slices in half diagonally.

In a bowl, combine the cheese, spring onion, mustard, thyme, pepper to taste and 2 tablespoons of the oil. Beat one of the eggs and add to the cheese mixture. Spread the cheese mixture on half of the bread slices. Top with sliced ham and cover with the remaining bread.

Beat the remaining egg with the milk in a shallow bowl. Place the breadcrumbs on a plate. Dip the sandwiches into the egg, letting excess drip off. Cover them in breadcrumbs. Place on another plate.

Heat 2 tablespoons of the remaining oil in a frying pan over medium heat. Fry half of the sandwiches until nicely browned, 2 to 3 minutes per side. If possible, balance the sandwiches upright to brown the cut edges too. Add the remaining oil to the frying pan as needed and fry the remaining sandwiches. Serve them hot.

Soups,
Potages
and One-Pot Meals

The *olla* is the great soup pot, source of everything delicious – comfort food from Mother's kitchen, lusty stews with pulses and sausage, delicate broths, and sumptuous meals-in-a-pot. The olla represents both sustenance and jubilation. Every day and fiesta.

In this chapter are some light soups, such as Consommé of Quail and Wild Mushrooms, to be served as a first course; vegetable soups, such as Manchegan Soup with Asparagus, which might be a starter or, in larger portions, a luncheon main course; two versions of Castilian garlic soup; and a fish soup. The olla includes *potajes,* potages, which are hearty stews with pulses, and *cocidos* – meals in which the broth is served as a soup course followed by all the meat and vegetables that cooked in the pot.

In Spanish home cooking, soups are rarely based on stocks. For example, rustic garlic soup is really no more complicated than olive oil, garlic, bread and water. Nevertheless, I have suggested a simple stock (page 94) to use for most of these soups. Fresh chicken stock from the supermarket can be used instead. Some soups, such as Chickpea Purée with Crisp Croûtons, are concocted especially to use up leftover *caldo,* stock, from the midday boiled dinner. This is a full-flavoured stock from slow cooking with chicken, beef and ham bone. You can approximate it by adding a piece of unsmoked ham and a beef bone to the recipe for simple stock. Or simply use water.

CONSOMMÉ OF QUAIL *and* WILD MUSHROOMS

Caldillo de Codorniz y Setas

I have served this deeply flavourful consommé as a welcoming libation for a holiday buffet party on a blustery winter day. In lieu of canapés, I passed the soup in demitasse cups with the sautéed breast meat and mushrooms speared on cocktail sticks.

Begin preparations for the consommé one to three days before serving. Any wild or cultivated mushroom can be used – chanterelles are divine; oyster mushrooms are fine.

Boning the quail breasts is fast and easy. Use a small sharp knife to slit down along the ridge of the breastbone. Cut through the skin at the neck and release the half-breast where the wing is attached. Cut away the other half-breast in the same manner. Leave the skin attached to the breasts.

Brandy de Jerez (brandy aged in Sherry casks in Jerez de la Frontera) lends a deep, mellow flavour to the soup. Dry fino or amontillado Sherry could be used instead. Sherry is the perfect accompaniment to the consommé.

꩜ SERVES **12 TO 16** AS AN APERITIF OR **6 TO 8** AS A SOUP COURSE

6 to 8 quail (about 1kg), breasts removed

2 teaspoons olive oil

½ onion

350g wild or cultivated mushrooms

3 litres chicken stock, home-made (page 94)

1 leek, sliced

2 carrots, sliced

1 stick of celery

85g chopped tomato

Salt and freshly ground black pepper

½ teaspoon dried thyme

2 bay leaves

Fresh parsley sprigs or stems

2 egg whites and crushed eggshells to clarify the stock

120ml/4 fl oz Brandy de Jerez or other brandy

1½ tablespoons extra virgin olive oil

40g shredded baby spinach leaves

Preheat the oven to 200°C/180°C fan/GM6.

Wrap the quail breasts in clingfilm and refrigerate them until shortly before serving. Spread the remaining quail carcasses in a roasting tin and drizzle with the 2 teaspoons oil. Place the unpeeled onion in the tin with the quail and roast it, turning the quail occasionally, until well browned, about 45 minutes.

Transfer the quail and onion to a large saucepan. Add 4 tablespoons water to the roasting tin and scrape up all the drippings. Add them to the saucepan.

Set aside 60g of the mushroom caps or slices to finish the soup. Chop the remainder and add them to the saucepan along with the stock. Bring to the boil and skim off any foam that rises to the top. Add the leek, carrots, celery, tomato, 1 teaspoon salt, pepper to taste, thyme, bay leaves and parsley. Cover and simmer the stock for 1½ hours. Remove from the heat and cool slightly.

Strain the stock in a colander, pressing on the solids to extract all the liquid. Discard the solids. Cool the stock, then refrigerate, covered, for at least 12 hours and up to 2 days.

Skim off and discard the fat from the top of the stock. Place the stock in a clean large saucepan over medium heat and add the egg whites and crushed eggshells. Heat, stirring occasionally, until the stock begins to simmer. Lower the heat so it barely simmers for 15 minutes, without stirring, rotating the pot a quarter of a turn at intervals. Keep a close watch so the stock never boils. As the egg white cooks and floats to the top, it will carry along solids that cloud the stock. Remove from the heat and allow to stand 10 minutes.

Place a fine sieve over a clean pan. Gently push the egg-white froth to one side and carefully ladle the stock into the sieve. Discard the foam.

Shortly before serving, place the pan of clarified stock over medium heat and add the brandy. Bring to a simmer.

Sprinkle the quail breasts with salt and pepper to taste. Heat the extra virgin olive oil in a frying pan over medium heat and sauté the breasts, skin side down, until browned, about 1 minute. Turn and sauté for 1 minute on the other side. The breasts will be pink in the centre. Remove and keep them warm.

Sauté the reserved mushroom caps or slices in the same oil, about 1 minute on each side.

When the stock begins to boil, lower the heat so that it simmers and add the shredded spinach. Cook for 2 minutes, until the spinach is wilted.

Serve the consommé in 150ml/¼ pint cups with the breast and mushroom cap speared on a cocktail stick or in shallow soup bowls with the breast and mushroom placed in the bowls. If desired, slice the breast crossways and fan it out in the bowls.

MANCHEGAN SOUP *with* ASPARAGUS

Sopa Manchega con Espárragos

The rounds of toasted baguette soak up the golden broth and turn into pillowy dumplings. This soup finishes in the oven, so use a 2 or 3 litre / 3½ or 5 pint cazuela or ovenproof casserole that can go from oven to table.

SERVES 8 AS A FAIRLY DELICATE FIRST COURSE OR 4 AS A MORE SUBSTANTIAL MEAL

¼ teaspoon saffron threads

450g green asparagus, preferably thin spears

4 tablespoons, plus 1 tablespoons olive oil

1 onion, finely chopped

40g finely chopped ham (optional)

2 garlic cloves, crushed

1½ litres / 2½ pints chicken stock, home-made (page 94)

Salt and freshly ground black pepper

Eight 2.5cm / 1in thick slices day-old baguette

¼ teaspoon caraway seeds, lightly toasted and coarsely crushed

1 egg

Crush the saffron threads in a mortar. Place the powdered saffron in a small bowl and add 4 tablespoons warm water. Let it infuse for at least 10 minutes.

Break off and discard the ends of the asparagus. Cut off the tips and set aside. Chop the stalks into 1cm / ½in pieces and reserve. Blanch the tips in boiling salted water for 1 minute. Refresh under cold water, drain and reserve.

Heat 4 tablespoons of the oil in a soup pot over medium heat. Sauté the onion and ham, if you're using it, until the onion begins to brown, about 8 minutes. Add the crushed garlic and chopped asparagus. Sauté for another 5 minutes.

Add the chicken stock and saffron water. Season with salt and pepper to taste. Bring to the boil, then simmer the soup, covered, for 20 minutes.

Preheat the grill to high.

Place the baguette slices on a rack and brush with the remaining tablespoon of oil. Place under the grill until they are browned on one side. Remove.

Place the baguette slices, toasted side up, in one layer in a cazuela or an ovenproof casserole.

Preheat the oven to 230°C/210°C fan/GM8.

When the soup is cooked, stir the crushed caraway seeds into it. Ladle the soup over the baguette slices. Beat the egg with 1 tablespoon water. Dribble it over the tops of the toast. Scatter the blanched asparagus tips on top. Place in the oven until the top is slightly browned, about 20 minutes. Turn off the oven and let the soup stop bubbling, then carefully remove the cazuela. Ladle the soup directly from the cazuela into soup bowls.

SIMPLE CHICKEN STOCK *Caldo Sencillo*

This simple stock can be used for making other soups in this chapter. I find it useful to make the stock in quantity and freeze it in two or three containers, so I always have it handy for soup making.

Makes 2 litres/3½ pints

1–1.4kg chicken carcasses, backs and wings

1 leek, halved

1 carrot, halved

2 celery stalks, halved

Handful of fresh parsley stems

2 tablespoons wine vinegar

1 tablespoon salt

Freshly ground black pepper

Pinch of dried thyme

2 bay leaves

Place the chicken pieces in a large soup pot. Add 3 litres/5 pints water and bring to the boil. Skim off the froth and scum that rises to the top. Add the remaining ingredients and bring back to the boil. Cover and simmer for 2 hours.

Strain the stock into a clean pot, discarding all the solids. Cool the stock, then refrigerate. When chilled, lift off and discard any fat that has congealed on top of the stock.

The stock can be kept, covered and refrigerated, for up to 4 days or frozen for up to 2 months.

CAULIFLOWER-POTATO SOUP *with* CHEESE FLAN

Sopa de Vigilia con Coliflor y Flan de Queso

Vigilia signifies a meatless meal. Some families observe vigilia on Christmas Eve, before attending midnight mass and taking communion. Whether made with water or a richly flavoured chicken stock, this soup makes a delightful addition to a special dinner.

SERVES 6 TO 8

FOR THE CHEESE FLAN

3 eggs, beaten

350ml/12 fl oz milk

Pinch of cayenne

¼ teaspoon dried thyme

1 teaspoon salt

100g grated Manchego

Preheat the oven to 180°C/160°C fan/GM4.

Combine the flan ingredients and pour into an oiled 1½ litre/2½ pint loaf tin. Cover the pan with foil. Place it in a larger pan for the bain marie and partially fill the bain marie with boiling water. Bake until a skewer inserted in the centre comes out clean, about 20 minutes. Remove the foil and bake for 10 minutes more.

Keep the flan warm in the bain marie while you prepare the soup.

FOR THE SOUP

3 tablespoons olive oil

1 medium onion, chopped

1 tablespoon sweet pimentón

Pinch of cayenne

Pinch of ground cumin

450g baking potatoes (about 2 medium), peeled and finely chopped

450g cauliflower florets

2 litres/3½ pints water or stock

1 tablespoon salt

Freshly ground black pepper

1 bay leaf

1 tablespoon wine vinegar

Chopped spring onion for serving

Chopped fresh parsley for serving

Heat the oil in a large saucepan over medium heat and sauté the onion for 5 minutes. Remove the pot from the heat and stir in the pimentón, cayenne and cumin. Add the potatoes and cauliflower along with the water. Season with the salt, pepper to taste, bay leaf and vinegar.

Bring the soup to the boil and simmer, covered, until the potatoes are tender, about 35 minutes. Let it cool slightly. Remove the bay leaf and purée the soup in a blender or with a hand blender. Reheat the purée gently.

Cut the cheese flan into slices and lift them out of the loaf tin with a spatula, discarding any accumulated liquid. Place a slice in each soup bowl and ladle the soup over. Garnish with spring onion and parsley.

NOTE: *If you don't want to turn on the oven to make the flan, you can make it in the microwave, using a microwave-safe ring mould. Microwave on full power for 2 minutes; microwave on ¾ power for 3 minutes. Test with a skewer. If the flan is still not set, microwave for 30 seconds and test again.*

TOMATO SOUP *with* BACON

Sopa de Tomate con Bacón

Bacon and smoky pimentón de la Vera give this simple tomato soup a heady aroma. Use any well-flavoured stock – chicken, beef or lamb. Purée the tomatoes in a blender, then pass the soup through a conical sieve. You will be surprised by how many tomato pips get strained out. Serve the soup garnished with moulded cubes of cheese flan (page 95) or with croûtons of fried bread. Change the flavour completely with the addition of peeled prawns.

SERVES 6

2 tablespoons olive oil

3 rashers bacon, chopped

1½ medium onions, chopped

2 garlic cloves, chopped

4 tablespoons fine fresh breadcrumbs

1 teaspoon sweet smoked pimentón

Pinch of hot smoked pimentón or cayenne

900g finely chopped peeled fresh plum tomatoes or tinned tomatoes, drained, liquid reserved

1½ litres / 2½ pints chicken stock, home-made (page 94), or any meat stock

Salt and freshly ground black pepper

Pinch of dried thyme

1 tablespoon fresh parsley leaves

Fresh herbs (parsley, basil, coriander or mint) for garnish

Moulded cheese flan for garnish (optional; page 95)

Heat the oil in a soup pot and fry the bacon until lightly crisped. Skim out the bacon and reserve. Add the onion and garlic to the fat and sauté over medium heat until the onion is golden, about 5 minutes. Stir in the breadcrumbs and fry for 1 minute longer.

Remove the pot from the heat and blend in the sweet and hot pimentón. Add the tomatoes, return the pot to the heat, and cook over high heat for 5 minutes, stirring frequently, until the tomatoes begin to sweat out their liquid.

Add the stock, salt to taste (depending on the saltiness of the stock), pepper to taste, the thyme and the parsley. If you're using tinned tomatoes, add the reserved tomato juice. Bring to the boil, reduce the heat to a simmer, and cook, covered, for 45 minutes. Let stand for about 20 minutes to cool slightly.

Purée the soup using a hand blender, or in batches in a regular blender. Pass the soup through a conical sieve, pressing on the solids. Discard the solids.

Reheat the soup before serving. Serve garnished with bacon bits, chopped fresh herbs and, if desired, cubes of moulded cheese flan.

CREAM OF PUMPKIN SOUP

Crema de Calabaza

This recipe is adapted from one given to me by Carlos Falcó, Marqués de Griñón, who makes superlative wines on his estate, Dominio de Valdepusa, in Toledo province.

Use deep orange pumpkin or calabaza for this soup.

Served chilled, pumpkin soup is a refreshing summer luncheon main course. Hot, it makes a fine starter for a festive harvest dinner.

SERVES 6

3 tablespoons olive oil

1 medium onion, chopped

70g finely chopped carrot

110g chopped red pepper

2 garlic cloves, chopped

570g pumpkin, peeled, seeded and cut into 2½cm / 1in cubes

230g peeled finely chopped baking potato

1.2 litres / 2 pints chicken stock, homemade (page 94)

1 tablespoon white wine vinegar

1 strip orange zest

Pinch of dried thyme

1 bay leaf

Dash of ground cloves

½ teaspoon salt

250ml / scant ½ pint full-fat milk or single cream

Chopped fresh mint or finely chopped apple for serving

Heat the oil in a soup pot over medium heat and sauté the onion, carrot and pepper for 5 minutes. Add the garlic and pumpkin and sauté for 5 minutes more.

Add the potato, stock, vinegar, orange zest, thyme, bay leaf, cloves and salt. Bring the soup to the boil, cover, and simmer until the pumpkin is very tender, 25 minutes.

Remove the orange zest and bay leaf. Purée the soup in a blender or with a hand blender. Strain it, discarding any remaining solids. Stir in the milk.

To serve hot, reheat the soup without allowing it to boil. Garnish with chopped apple. To serve cold, allow the soup to cool, then refrigerate, covered, until chilled and garnish with chopped mint.

GREEN PEA SOUP

Sopa Verde

Make this soup in the spring, when fresh peas arrive in the market. Cooking the pea pods produces a 'stock' that intensifies the soup's flavour.

SERVES 6 AS A FIRST COURSE

450g chicken carcasses, backs and wings

1 ham bone or 250g unsmoked ham

1 leek, sliced

½ onion, peeled

1 bay leaf

1 teaspoon dried thyme

1 stick of celery

sprigs of flat-leaf parsley

Salt and freshly ground pepper

900g fresh peas in pods

3 tablespoons olive oil

3 slices bread, cut into 1cm / ½in cubes

Chopped fresh herbs (parsley, fennel fronds or mint) for garnish

Chopped spring onion for garnish

Put the chicken, ham, leek, onion, bay leaf, thyme, celery and a sprig of parsley in a large pan with 2½ litres/4 pints of water. Add 1 teaspoon each salt and pepper. Bring to the boil, then lower the heat and simmer for 1 hour. Strain and reserve the stock. Discard the chicken and vegetables. If desired, reserve the ham to add to the finished soup.

Shell the peas, reserving the pods. Put the pods in a pot and cover with 700ml/1¼ pints of water. Bring to the boil and cook for 15 minutes. Strain and reserve the liquid. Discard the pods.

Return the pea water to the pan and bring to the boil. Add ½ teaspoon salt, another sprig of parsley and the peas. Cook until the peas are very tender, 10 to 20 minutes, depending on their size. Reserve 4 tablespoons cooked peas. Purée the remainder in a blender until smooth.

Combine 1½ litres/2½ pints of the strained chicken stock and the puréed peas in a soup pot. Bring to the boil and simmer for 15 minutes. Taste for salt. Heat the oil in a small frying pan and fry the bread cubes until they are golden and crisp, about 6 minutes. Serve the soup garnished with the chopped herbs, spring onion, fried bread cubes, reserved peas, and, if desired, shredded ham.

FIFTEEN-MINUTE FISH SOUP

Sopa al Cuarto de Hora

I tested this classic Madrid recipe against the clock, and it really does work – if you've got the chopping done and the water boiling before you start the timer. Use any firm-fleshed fish, such as monkfish or snapper, in this soup. The clams are opened in the soup, which means you eat them out of the shells. If you prefer, first steam them open, discard the shells, and add them to the soup in the last minute of cooking. The classic version of this soup is made with peas, but I like this variation with chard.

SERVES 6

4 tablespoons olive oil

½ medium onion, chopped

175g chopped tomato

75g chopped chard or 125g peas

1½ litres / 2½ pints boiling water or fish stock

¼ teaspoon fennel seeds

1½ teaspoons salt

Freshly ground black pepper

4 tablespoons chopped ham, preferably serrano

Pinch of saffron threads, crushed (optional)

170g fish fillets, cut into 2½cm / 1in pieces

230g small clams (if unavailable, use mussels)

110g cooked rice

4 tablespooms dry Sherry

170g peeled small prawns

Heat the oil in a large saucepan over medium-high heat and sauté the onion for 1 minute. Add the tomato, chard and boiling water. Raise the heat to high and cook for 1 minute. Add the fennel seeds, salt, pepper to taste, ham, saffron and fish. Let the soup bubble for 10 minutes.

Add the clams, rice, Sherry and prawns. Cook for 3 minutes more and serve.

GARLIC SOUP

Sopa de Ajo

I cannot imagine a more heartwarming soup for a blustery winter's day. In La Mancha, this soul-satisfying dish is also appreciated as a hangover cure, to be imbibed after a night of
partying.

Chicken stock gives depth of flavour to a soup usually made simply with water. Whole, unpeeled cloves of garlic cook in the stock. Serve them with the soup and let each person squeeze out the softened garlic into the soup.

SERVES 4

Sixteen 1cm/⅜in baguette slices

4 to 8 unpeeled garlic cloves

4 tablespoons extra virgin olive oil

4 tablespoons finely chopped onion

85g finely chopped serrano ham

2 teaspoons sweet pimentón

4 tablespoons grated tomato pulp (page 62)

1½ litres/2½ pints chicken stock, homemade (page 94)

4 eggs

Chopped fresh parsley for garnish

Preheat the oven to 180°C/160°C fan/GM4.

Place the sliced baguette on a baking sheet. Bake for 6 minutes and turn the slices. Bake for 6 minutes more, or until golden.

Cut a slit into each of the unpeeled garlic cloves. Heat the oil in a deep frying pan, cazuela, or soup pot over medium heat. Add the garlic cloves and fry them for 3 minutes, turning to brown. Skim out the garlic and reserve.

Add the onion and ham to the oil and sauté for 1 minute. Stir in the pimentón, then add the tomato pulp. Cook for 1 minute. Return the garlic to the pan. Add the stock and bring to the boil. Reduce to a simmer, cover, and cook for 10 minutes.

Add the toasted bread to the soup. Cover and cook for 5 minutes. Break the eggs into the soup.

Cover and poach until the egg whites are set and the yolks still liquid, 4 minutes.

Serve the soup from the same cazuela, lifting out egg, bread and stock into individual soup bowls. Garnish with parsley.

No comas ajos ni cebollas,
porque no saquen por el olor tu villanería.

Don't eat garlic or onions,
so that they don't take you for a peasant.

DON QUIXOTE'S ADVICE TO SANCHO PANZA WHEN
HE GOES OFF TO BECOME GOVERNOR OF THE ISLAND

DOUBLE GARLIC SOUP

Sopa de Ajo Emparejado

Double the flavour – crushed garlic cloves plus green garlic shoots make a heady brew. This recipe is adapted from one in *Guisos, Viandas y Otras Pócimas,* by Joaquín Racionero Page.

⸙ SERVES 4

2 tablespoons plus 2 teaspoons olive oil

450g potatoes, peeled and cut into 2cm/¾in cubes

4 tablespoons finely chopped red pepper

2 garlic cloves, crushed

2 teaspoons sweet pimentón

Pinch of chilli flakes

100g chopped drained tinned tomato

3 tablespoons plain flour

1.2 litres/2 pints chicken stock, homemade (page 94)

Salt

1 fresh mint sprig

100g chopped green garlic shoots, including green tops

Heat 2 tablespoons of the oil in a soup pot over medium heat. Add the cubed potatoes and fry them, stirring frequently, until they begin to brown, 5 minutes. Add the red pepper and sauté for 1 minute more. Remove the pot from the heat and stir in the crushed garlic, pimentón and chilli flakes. Add the tomatoes and return to medium heat. Cook for 2 minutes, stirring.

Combine the flour and 250ml/scant ½ pint of water in a jar with a tight lid. Shake the mixture until the flour is thoroughly mixed. Pour it into the soup pot, stirring to blend. Add the stock, little by little, stirring well. Season to taste with salt. Add the sprig of mint. Bring to the boil and simmer the soup, covered, until the potatoes are cooked, 10 minutes.

While the soup is cooking, heat the remaining 2 teaspoons oil in a small frying pan. Sauté the chopped green garlic over low heat until softened but not browned, 5 minutes.

Stir the sautéed garlic shoots into the soup. Cook for 5 minutes without stirring, until red-coloured oil begins to rise to the top. Discard the mint sprig. Let the soup rest for 5 minutes before serving.

THE GARLIC CAPITAL OF SPAIN

Sturdy garlic soup, a classic peasant dish of Spain's central Castilian region, is simple stuff: fry chopped garlic in olive oil, stir in some red pimentón; add water, salt and chunks of bread; embellish with poached eggs and serve piping hot. But in the La Mancha town of Las Pedroñeras a singular chef, Manuel de la Osa, has turned garlic soup upside down – and chilled it too.

The garlic soup at Manuel's restaurant, Las Rejas, arrives in a martini cocktail glass. Where the olive would come to rest is a poached egg yolk. A jellied, garlic-infused stock makes the cocktail. On top are a flag of crisp-fried serrano ham, a croûton or two and a drizzle of parsley-infused olive oil. Sancho Panza – who spurned fancy palace food – might have approved with a wink and a grin.

Las Pedroñeras – literally, rockville – is a village southeast of Madrid, smack in the middle of Don Quixote country. The village lays claim to the title of Spain's capital of garlic. A single growers' cooperative in the town, San Isidro del Santo, produced in one year more than fifteen thousand tonnes of the fragrant bulb. Most of it is the esteemed *ajo morado,* purple garlic, a variety of hard-necked garlic that has papery white layers enclosing cloves shrink-wrapped in violet skins. Purple garlic is both sweet and pungent, with a powerful bite. The purple garlic of Las Pedroñeras enjoys its own protected denomination of origin.

When Manuel de la Osa created the cold jellied garlic soup for the town's annual garlic fair, it became an instant classic. Although the menu at Las Rejas changes with the seasons and with the chef's inspiration, the garlic soup remains. Like most of his dishes, even the wildest flights of fancy, it is based in the traditional kitchen.

Manuel is one of Spain's most acclaimed chefs (Las Rejas earned a Michelin star in 1994) in a country that boasts some of the top chefs in the world. Nevertheless he is essentially a small-town guy. He grew up in Las Pedroñeras, where his father ran a bar on the central plaza. His grandmother, mother and aunts did the cooking.

'I am rooted in La Mancha,' says Manuel. 'In my grandmother's kitchen I took in the smells and tastes that still guide me.

'I take traditional dishes and transform them. I might use advanced techniques, from a long tradition of French cuisine. Or combine flavours and textures in new ways. I liberate the imagination.'

Ajo arriero, salt cod in muledriver's style – which is to say with lots of garlic – starts from a simple country dish but, in Manuel's kitchen, becomes more complex in flavour and texture, with the addition of smoked cod, almonds, clams and a garnish of caviar. He pairs partridge with tuna. Matches fatty pancetta and rare squab breast with a sauce of sweet quince jelly. Airy foam of lemon verbena tops gelatinous cod tripe rolled around flaky cod. An intensely flavoured green tomato soup with minted olive oil reflects on Andalusian gazpacho.

Manuel's cooking starts with the finest products of the land – artisanally produced Manchego cheese, extra virgin olive oil from small producers in the highlands of the Montes de Toledo, the finest lamb, garlic from Las Pedroñeras, wild game taken locally. And, of course, superb wines. Las Rejas has an impressive listing of wines with La Mancha denomination of origin. (Vineyards occupy more acreage than garlic fields in Las Pedroñeras.)

He playfully combines the local with the exotic when the result produces something special. So, although neither foie gras nor caviar is a local product, both make an appearance.

'I don't mix just for the sake of mixing,' says Manuel. 'There is an underlying sense of what works.' Which comes through in his *potaje con pulpo,* cabbage and octopus soup. Or a hauntingly earthy combo of puddled cheese (Manchego and Parmesan melted with sheep's milk), truffles, hazelnuts and tomato jam.

About that garlic soup. Manuel says that garlic is abused in his home town.

'I use about one-tenth the quantity of garlic as in a traditional garlic soup. Badly treated, garlic *se repite.* It comes back up on you.'

HEARTY VEGETABLE SOUP *with* BEANS *and* SAUSAGE

Olleta

Adapted from a recipe in Lorenzo Diaz's *La Cocina del Quijote,* this soup, says the author, should be cooked in an earthenware pot over a fire of grapevines or oakwood.

This rendition favours spring vegetables – broad beans, chard and artichokes. But the soup is equally delicious with winter cabbage or summer courgettes. Serve the soup with bread and cheese for a hearty meal.

If you are using fresh artichokes, don't cut them up until the soup is bubbling. Then trim off the outer leaves, slice off the tops, and trim the artichokes to the hearts.

SERVES 6

1 tablespoon olive oil

170g pork sausages or Spanish soft chorizo, sliced or crumbled

1 medium onion, chopped

4 garlic cloves, chopped

1 teaspoon sweet pimentón

200g tinned crushed tomato

2 litres / 3½ pints water or light stock

150g shelled broad beans (450g in shells)

170g green beans in 2½cm / 1in pieces

120g turnip, finely chopped

140g chopped chard (2 to 3 stalks)

120g finely chopped carrot (2 to 3 carrots)

2 artichoke hearts, quartered (from 2 small artichokes; 225g)

1½ teaspoons salt

Freshly ground black pepper

260g cooked or drained tinned cannellini beans (one 420g tin)

100g Spanish round-grain rice

Heat the oil in a soup pot over medium heat. Add the sausage and sauté until it begins to brown, 2 minutes. Add the onion and garlic and sauté for 3 minutes. Remove the pot from the heat and stir in the pimentón. Add the tomatoes and water and bring to the boil.

When the stock is boiling, add the vegetables, salt and pepper to taste. Bring back to the boil, then cover and simmer until the vegetables are just tender, 20 minutes.

Add the cannellini beans to the soup. Uncover and cook for 5 minutes. Add the rice and cook for 12 minutes. Remove from the heat, cover, and allow to stand for 5 minutes before serving.

CHICKPEA PURÉE *with* CRISP CROÛTONS

Puré de Garbanzos con Pan Frito

This purée, with chickpeas, carrots and potatoes, can be made with the leftovers of a grand *cocido* (page 120). If you are starting with uncooked ingredients, you will need about 200g dried chickpeas to make 400g cooked. Soak them in water for 12 hours. Add them to boiling water and simmer until tender, about 2 hours. Straining the soup after it is puréed eliminates the chickpea hulls and makes for a smoother soup. Use a conical sieve, pushing on the solids.

SERVES 6

2 tablespoons plus 1½ tablespoons olive oil

4 tablespoons diced salt pork or bacon

120g sliced carrot

1 medium onion, chopped

1 garlic clove, chopped

1 medium potato (225g), cut into pieces

400g cooked chickpeas

4 tablespoons Tomato Sauce, homemade (page 26) or ready-made passata

2 litres/3½ pints water, stock or chickpea-cooking liquid

Pinch of cayenne

Salt and freshly ground black pepper

Pinch of dried thyme

1 bay leaf

60g bread in 1cm/½in cubes

½ teaspoon coarsely chopped garlic

¼ teaspoon smoked hot pimentón

Heat 2 tablespoons of the oil in a soup pot over medium heat. Fry the salt pork until the fat is rendered and the pork is crisp, 2 minutes. Remove the pot from heat and tip it so the fat drains to one side. Skim out the salt pork and reserve.

Return the pot to the heat and add the carrot, onion and chopped garlic. Sauté over medium heat until softened, 4 minutes. Add the potato and cook for 1 minute. Add the chickpeas, tomato sauce and water. Season with cayenne, salt and pepper to taste, thyme and bay leaf. Bring to the boil, cover, and simmer until the potatoes and carrots are tender, 20 minutes. Discard the bay leaf.

Purée the soup in batches in a blender. If desired, strain the purée.

Shortly before serving, reheat the puréed soup. In a small frying pan, heat the remaining 1½ tablespoons oil over medium-high heat. Toss the diced bread in the oil until lightly toasted, 2 minutes. Add the ½ teaspoon garlic and reserved salt pork. Fry for 1 minute.

Serve the soup in shallow bowls. Scatter the croûtons, garlic and salt pork over the soup. Top each serving with a pinch of pimentón.

LENTILS with SAUSAGE

Lentejas con Chorizo

In Spanish homes, this is served as a first course for the *comida de mediodia,* midday dinner, the principal meal of the day, served at about two in the afternoon. The main course that follows would be a small piece of meat, chicken or fish, perhaps with a side of vegetables, followed by fresh fruit for dessert. Nevertheless, this lusty lentil stew easily makes a full meal. Just add salad and good bread to round out the menu.

The most common variety of lentil in Castilla–La Mancha is the *rubia castellana,* big, flat discs of a pale greenish brown colour, and sold in the UK as 'green lentils'. They cook up ever so softly, without turning to mush. The tiny, dark brown *pardina* lentils (or puy lentils), which always stay al dente, can be substituted. Castilla–La Mancha grows 90 per cent of the lentils produced in Spain, but, as this is insufficient to meet demand, much is imported. At my local shop in southern Spain, the castellana lentils come from Canada!

Be sure to use soft water (use bottled or filtered if your water is naturally hard) for cooking lentils. This helps the legume skins soften.

Pork belly, consisting of ribbons of lean and fat, is pancetta or bacon before it is salted and cured. Any fatty bits of fresh pork or even spareribs could be used. Soft chorizo is a fattier version of the hard chorizo. Morcilla, blood sausage, if available, is especially good with lentils. Any sausage, preferably unsmoked, could be substituted for the chorizo.

SERVES 4

450g dried green castellana lentils (green lentils)

115g pork belly (uncured pancetta)

115g Spanish chorizo

115g morcilla (optional; or use black pudding)

1 teaspoon olive oil

2 whole cloves

1 small onion, peeled

1 head of garlic

2 carrots, sliced

1 whole tomato or 2 sun-dried tomatoes, cut up

1 bay leaf

1 teaspoon salt

Freshly ground black pepper

1 teaspoon pimentón, smoked or unsmoked

Chilli flakes (optional)

225g potato (1 medium), peeled and cut into 2½cm / 1in cubes

Scarlet-Pickled Onions (page 282) and hot peppers, such as peperoncini, for serving

Place the lentils in a cazuela or large saucepan and add 1½ litres/2½ pints of water.

Cut the pork belly into 1cm/½in strips. Slice the chorizo and morcilla, if you're using it, crossways. Heat the oil in a small frying pan over medium heat and fry the pork and chorizo until lightly browned, about 4 minutes. Tip the frying pan to drain the fat to one side, skim the pork and chorizo out, and add them to the lentils. Discard the fat.

Stick the cloves into the onion and tuck it into the lentils. Slice the top off the head of garlic and remove the outer, papery skin. Add the whole head of garlic to the lentils with the carrots, tomato, bay leaf, salt, and pepper to taste. Stir the pimentón into 1 tablespoon water until smooth, then stir it into the lentils. Add the chilli flakes, if you're using them.

Bring to the boil, lower the heat to a simmer and cover the lentils. Cook gently for 15 minutes. Add the potatoes and cook for 30 minutes more.

Remove and discard the onion and bay leaf. Remove the tomato, cut out the core and discard the skin. Use the edge of a spoon to break the tomato into pieces and return them to the lentils. Squeeze the soft-cooked garlic cloves from their skins into the lentils. Let stand, covered, for 15 minutes before serving. Each person adds pickled onions and peppers to taste.

DON QUIXOTE'S FRIDAY LENTILS

Lentejas para Viernes

On Fridays Don Quixote ate lentils. Or so Cervantes tells us in the first paragraph of the novel. Because it was Friday – a day of abstinence from meat in the Catholic Church – they were certainly lentils *viudas*, 'widowed', bereft of meat or sausage. Nevertheless, well flavoured with the olive oil of the region, garlic, onions and spices such as cumin and pepper, they were probably a substantial and tasty meal. Potatoes – a plant from the New World – were not widely known in Don Quixote's day. In their place, *castañas pilongas*, dried chestnuts, were cooked with the lentils. If you choose to use them, soak the chestnuts in water to cover for 12 hours.

Use the tiny dark brown *pardina* lentils (or else puy lentils) for this dish, which is served 'dry', not soupy. With a salad, bread and cheese, lentils make a fine vegetarian meal. They are also a good side dish with duck, ham or pork.

🌿 SERVES 4 AS A MAIN DISH OR 6 TO 8 AS A SIDE DISH

450g dried small brown lentils such as *pandina* lentils or Puy lentils

One 2½cm / 1in piece lemon zest, slivered

2 bay leaves

1 teaspoon salt

¼ teaspoon saffron threads, crushed (optional)

3 tablespoons olive oil

225g carrot, finely chopped

1 medium onion, chopped

30g celery, finely chopped

3 garlic cloves, chopped

¼ teaspoon cumin seeds

Pinch of ground cloves

½ teaspoon freshly ground black pepper

1 hard-boiled egg, chopped (optional)

Lemon wedges for serving

Place the lentils in a large pan or cazuela and add 1½ litres / 2½ pints of water, the slivered zest, bay leaves and salt. Bring to the boil and cook, covered, for 8 minutes. Drain the lentils, saving the liquid. Discard the bay leaves.

If you're using saffron, soak it in 2 tablespoons hot water for 15 minutes.

Heat the oil in a large pan or cazuela over medium heat and sauté the carrot, onion and celery for 5 minutes. Add the garlic and sauté for 3 minutes. Add the cumin seeds and sauté for 1 minute.

Stir in the cooked lentils and 470ml/¾ pint of the reserved liquid. Add the cloves, pepper, saffron and additional salt, if necessary. Bring to the boil, then lower the heat and simmer, covered, for 20 minutes, or until the lentils and carrot are tender. Allow to stand for 10 minutes before serving.

If desired, serve garnished with chopped egg. Serve with lemon wedges to squeeze into the lentils.

BLACK-EYED BEANS *with* TOMATO SOFRITO

Potaje de Carillas con Sofrito

Black-eyed beans are especially delicious cooked with fatty sausage, pancetta or ham hocks. But, if you prefer a vegetarian version, simply omit the pancetta. The *sofrito* of fried onion, peppers and tomatoes provides lots of flavour.

SERVES 4

400g black-eyed beans, soaked for 8 to 12 hours

50g sliced leek

150g sliced carrot

2 bay leaves

2 tablespoons olive oil

85g diced pancetta, bacon or fatty ham

1 medium onion, chopped

1 medium green pepper, chopped

3 garlic cloves, chopped

Chilli flakes

½ teaspoon smoked pimentón

180g peeled, seeded and chopped tomato

1 teaspoon salt

¼ teaspoon ground cumin

¼ teaspoon dried oregano

1 tablespoon chopped fresh parsley

Pinch of ground cloves

Freshly ground black pepper

1 tablespoon white wine vinegar

Drain the soaked black-eyed beans and place them in a large pan with 1½ litres/2½ pints of fresh water. Bring to the boil and skim off the froth. Add the leek, carrot and bay leaves. Cover and simmer the peas for 30 minutes.

Meanwhile, heat the oil in a frying pan over medium heat and sauté the pancetta, onion, green pepper and garlic for 5 minutes. Stir in chilli flakes to taste and the pimentón and immediately add the tomato. Season with salt, cumin, oregano, parsley, cloves and pepper to taste. Cook for 8 minutes.

Add 120ml/scant ¼ pint of cold water to the black-eyed beans. Bring back to the boil and stir in the mixture from the frying pan. Cover and simmer until the peas are very tender, 1 to 1½ hours. Stir in the vinegar and cook for 5 minutes longer.

BEANS *with* GARLIC SAUCE

Bolos con Ajiaceite

This garlic sauce, known elsewhere in Spain as *alioli,* adds a sumptuous touch to ordinary beans. Spoon it over the cooked beans and let each person stir the sauce in. The sauce is also delicious as a dressing with other cooked vegetables.

SERVES 4

450g dried pinto beans, soaked for 12 hours

450g meaty ham bone or pork hock

½ onion, peeled

1 celery stalk, sliced

2 bay leaves

Pinch of dried thyme

2½ teaspoons salt

2 carrots, sliced

2 medium potatoes, peeled and quartered

1 egg

2 garlic cloves, peeled

120ml/4 fl oz olive oil

1 tablespoon wine vinegar

Drain the beans and place them in a large saucepan with 1½ litres/2½ pints of water. Bring the beans to the boil and skim off all the foam that rises to the surface. Add the ham bone, onion, celery, bay leaves and thyme. Bring back to the boil, reduce the heat, cover, and simmer the beans for 1½ hours.

Add 250ml/scant ½ pint of cold water to the beans and bring them back to the boil. Add 2 teaspoons of the salt along with the carrots. Reduce the heat to a simmer and cook the beans until very tender, 1 hour. Add the potatoes to the beans. Cover and cook until the potatoes are tender, 30 minutes. Skim out 2 chunks of potato. Keep the beans warm over low heat.

Place the egg and garlic in a blender and blend until smooth. Add the 2 chunks of potato and blend. Blend in the oil to make a thick sauce. Blend in the remaining ½ teaspoon salt and the vinegar.

Place the beans in a large serving bowl. Separate the meat from the ham bone and add to the beans. Spoon half of the garlic sauce over the beans. Serve the remaining sauce separately.

CHICKPEAS *and* SPINACH *with* COD DUMPLINGS

Potaje de Garbanzos y Espinacas con Rellenos

This potage is typical for *Viernes Santo,* Good Friday, when observant Catholics don't eat meat. The chickpeas are so nicely flavoured that you won't miss the sausage. *Rellenos,* a cross between fritters and dumplings, are first fried, then simmered. They are typical of the province of Cuenca.

Fresh cod can be used in place of the dry salt cod and, if it's not Holy Week, chopped, cooked ham can replace the fish. A sweet version of rellenos – without the cod, of course – is poached in milk and dusted with cinnamon and sugar.

SERVES 6

FOR THE DUMPLINGS

225g salt cod, soaked in several changes of water for 24 hours, or 225g chopped fresh cod

4 tablespoons sliced spring onion

4 tablespoons coarsely chopped fresh parsley

50g fresh breadcrumbs

1 egg

Freshly ground black pepper

Pinch of ground cloves

3 tablespoons olive oil

Squeeze out the soaked salt cod, place it in a pan and cover with fresh water. Bring to a simmer and remove from the heat. Drain, saving 2 tablespoons of the liquid. Cool.

Remove and discard all skin and bones from the cod. Chop or flake the fish coarsely and reserve.

Finely chop the spring onion and parsley in a food processor. Add the breadcrumbs and cod and process until thoroughly chopped. Add the egg, pepper to taste and cloves. Add 1 to 2 tablespoons of the reserved cooking liquid to make a paste that holds together.

Heat the oil in a heavy frying pan over medium heat. With hands or 2 tablespoons, lightly shape the cod mixture into 4cm/1½in patties. Fry them until golden on both sides, 3 to 5 minutes. Set aside until the chickpeas and spinach are cooked.

FOR THE CHICKPEAS AND SPINACH

370g dried chickpeas, soaked for 12 hours

2 bay leaves

2 teaspoons salt

2 tablespoons olive oil

1 medium onion, chopped

1 teaspoon sweet pimentón

½ teaspoon hot smoked pimentón or cayenne

90g peeled and chopped tomato

225g fresh spinach, chopped

450g potatoes (about 2 medium), peeled and cut into 2½cm/1in pieces

1 hard-boiled egg

1 garlic clove, crushed

2 tablespoons toasted pine nuts

Put the chickpeas in an olla or soup pot and cover with water (about 1.7litres/2¾ pints). Bring to the boil and skim off the froth that rises to the surface. Add the bay leaves. Cover and simmer for 30 minutes.

Add the salt to the chickpeas and cook for 30 minutes more.

Heat the oil in a frying pan over medium heat and sauté the onion for 5 minutes. Remove the pan from the heat and stir in the sweet and hot pimentón. Add the tomato and continue sautéing for 3 minutes. Add the onion-tomato mixture to the chickpeas along with the spinach and potatoes. Bring to the boil, cover, lower the heat and simmer until the potatoes are tender, about 20 minutes.

Mash the egg yolk with the garlic. Dilute with some of the liquid from the olla and stir into the chickpeas.

Add the fried cod dumplings to the chickpeas and cook gently for 5 minutes, until they are thoroughly heated.

Serve the chickpeas, spinach and dumplings in deep soup bowls. Chop the egg white finely and scatter over the chickpeas along with a few pine nuts.

OLLA PODRIDA, ROTTEN STEW — AND THE MORE ROTTEN, THE BETTER

In the second part of the tale of Don Quixote, Sancho Panza finally gets his wish to govern an island, which he manages with some craft, aplomb and adroitness. At the dinner table, however, he runs into problems. Don Quixote already has counselled Sancho to lay off onions and garlic, to keep his breath sweet (so no one would know he was a peasant). He also suggests moderation in eating and drinking.

Come poco, y cena más poco; que la salud de todo el cuerpo se fragua en la oficina del estómago. Sé templado en el beber, considerando que el vino demasiado, ni guarda secreto, ni cumple palabra.

'Eat little at dinner and less for supper, for good health is forged in the workshop of the stomach. Be temperate in drinking, for too much wine won't keep a secret nor fulfill a promise.'

But it is a presumptuous doctor who keeps whisking away Sancho's food, supposedly to keep him from doing himself harm by eating the wrong victuals, who really gets him riled up.

When, finally, Sancho is allowed a supper of beef and onion hash and slow-cooked calves' feet, he digs in with as much relish as if it were fine pheasant from Rome, veal from Sorrento, quail from Seville or goose from Lavajos. Sancho declares to the doctor who has been keeping him on restricted rations:

'Look, Doc, from now on, don't even think about feeding me dainties, nor fancy foods, because you'll just upset my stomach.'

He declares he's got a finicky digestion, used to goat meat, fatty salt pork, beef jerky, turnips and onions. Any of that hoity-toity palace food will just turn his stomach.

Lo que el maestresala puede hacer es traerme estas que llaman ollas podridas, que mientras más podridas son, mejor huelen.

'What the head waiter can do is bring me some of what's called *ollas podridas* – rotten stews, which the more rotten they are the better they smell.'

Rotten stew? Oh, yummy.

Olla podrida, considered the 'mother of all stews', once was a dish fit for kings, containing all manner of game and meat – chicken, beef, mutton, salt pork, squab, partridge, thrush, pork loin, sausages, hare, salt beef, beef tongues, pigs' ears and trotters. The poor folks' version contained rancid ham bone, salt pork, chickpeas and turnips. Very slowly cooked until the meat was falling off the bones, the stew acquired the descriptive name 'rotten', just as overripe fruit gets mushy and falls away from the stone.

Another explanation for the name is that the olla usually incorporates salted meats, salt pork fat (*tocino*), and chunks of serrano ham and ham bone. The old ham bone, called *añejo*, meaning 'well-cured, aged', imparts a pronounced rancid aroma to the potage which, tongue-in-cheek, could be called 'rotten'.

Or perhaps Sancho Panza, famous for fractured phrases and twisted refrains, was making a little pun. Perhaps by *podrida* – rotten – he actually meant *poderida,* powerful, meaning a stew pot filled with rich meat, an aristocrat's stew pot, not a rotten one. As the governor of an island, surely he deserved no less!

ONE-POT FEAST

Cocido Relleno para Días de Fiesta

Holiday means feast, a celebration. Whether a saint's day, Christmas Day, a wedding or Sunday dinner with the family, there is no more festive dish than the *cocido*, a meal-in-a-pot cooked in the great *olla,* soup pot. Containing beef, ham, stewing hen, vegetables, sausages and chickpeas, it provides a soup for a first course, then a main course, side dishes and sauces. This version has a meat dumpling as well, *relleno,* that can be served with the soup or as a separate course.

The chickpeas need to soak for eight to twelve hours, so start them a day before you plan to serve. The cocido requires almost three hours of slow cooking. As you are not likely to have stewing hen, which needs long cooking, remove the chicken when it is very tender (about 1½ hours of cooking) so that it doesn't fall apart in the soup.

Both red chorizo and black morcilla sausages go into the cocido, although they are usually cooked in a separate pot so they do not colour the cocido broth. Soft, or cooking, chorizo is fully cured but is softer than chorizo for cold cuts, as it has a higher fat content. If chorizo and morcilla are not available, you could substitute pork sausage, bratwurst, andouille, Polish sausage, or black pudding.

You will need three pots for this preparation. Use your largest (6 litre / 10 pint capacity) to cook the meats and vegetables. While the cocido is simmering in the big pot, prepare the meatball mixture. About an hour before serving time, start a second pot of water to cook the pumpkin, potatoes and sausages. Have ready a third pot and a fine-mesh sieve to strain the broth for the soup.

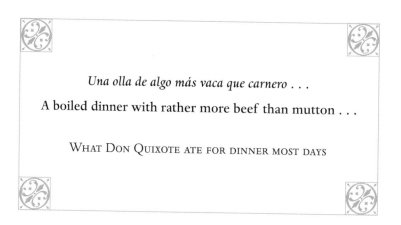

Una olla de algo más vaca que carnero . . .

A boiled dinner with rather more beef than mutton . . .

WHAT DON QUIXOTE ATE FOR DINNER MOST DAYS

Serve the broth with noodles and meatballs as the first course. Cut the meats and sausages into serving-size pieces and present them on a big platter. Put the vegetables and potatoes in another serving dish; the chickpeas in a bowl with some of the pumpkin sauce spooned over them; and the cabbage with its garlic-pimentón sauce in another bowl. Pass the pumpkin sauce separately. Each person spoons it over meat and vegetables to taste. Accompany the platters of food with Scarlet-Pickled Onions (page 282), gherkins or peppers.

Feast!

SERVES 6

FOR THE BIG POT

200g dried chickpeas

900g ham hock or shank, preferably unsmoked

450g boneless shin or stewing beef

½ large chicken (900g)

Giblets and liver from 1 chicken (optional)

6 peppercorns

1 stick of celery

1 small onion, halved

3 fresh parsley sprigs with stems

3 large carrots

1 large turnip, quartered

3 leeks

1½ teaspoons salt

Place the chickpeas in a large bowl and add water to 3 times their depth. Soak the chickpeas overnight or for at least 8 hours. Drain the chickpeas and discard the soaking liquid.

Place the ham hock, beef, chicken and giblets, if you're using them, in a large stew pot. Add 3 litres/about 5 pints of water and bring to the boil. Skim off and discard the foam that rises to the top. Keep skimming the pot for 5 to 10 minutes, until no more foam rises.

Add the drained chickpeas to the boiling liquid. Skim again when the liquid boils. Reduce the heat so the liquid bubbles very gently. Add the peppercorns, celery, onion and parsley. Cover the pot and cook for 1½ hours. The chicken will be fully cooked. Lift it out and place it on a platter. Make a tent with foil over the top to keep it warm. Remove the giblets and liver and cut into small dice. Reserve for the soup.

While the main pot is cooking, prepare first the mixture for the *rellenos,* meatballs, and next the second pot for cooking the sausages and potatoes.

Add the carrots, turnip, leeks and salt to the big pot. Bring back to the boil, then reduce the heat and simmer for 30 minutes.

Add the prepared meatballs (recipe follows) to the pot and poach them for 30 minutes.

Use a skimmer or slotted spoon to transfer the meats to a large serving platter. Separate the chicken into serving pieces. Slice the beef across the grain. Remove the skin and bone from the ham hock and slice the meat. Keep the meats warm.

Place the vegetables on a separate serving dish and keep warm.

Strain the soup through a fine-mesh sieve into a clean pot. Place the chickpeas in a serving bowl. Discard the cooked onion, celery and parsley.

FOR THE RELLENOS
4 country bread slices (115g), crusts removed
180ml milk
1 egg, beaten
1 garlic clove, finely chopped
1 teaspoon grated lemon zest
½ teaspoon salt

¼ teaspoon freshly ground black pepper
2 tablespoons finely chopped fresh parsley
Pinch of ground cinnamon
Pinch of ground cloves
Pinch of freshly grated nutmeg
350g minced pork, veal, chicken or turkey

While the cocido is cooking, prepare the meatballs. Crumble the bread into a bowl. Toss with the milk and allow to stand for 15 minutes, until the bread softens. Break it up with a fork. Add the beaten egg, garlic, lemon zest, salt, pepper, parsley, cinnamon, cloves and nutmeg. Stir to combine well.

Add the minced meat and mix very well. Wet your hands and shape the mixture into 12 golf-ball-sized balls.

Poach the meatballs in the strained soup broth. Serve 2 per person with the broth and noodles as a first course (instructions follow). (The meatballs also can be cooked in the cocido pot. Add them to the soup before serving.)

FOR THE PUMPKIN SAUCE AND SAUSAGES

2½ teaspoons salt

225g peeled pumpkin

1 large tomato

115g Spanish chorizo (2 links)

225g morcilla (if unavailable use black pudding)

570g potatoes (about 3 medium)

1 garlic clove

1 tablespoon white wine vinegar

½ teaspoon ground cumin

About 1 hour before serving, bring 2 litres/3½ pints of water to the boil in a pot with 1½ teaspoons of the salt. Add the pumpkin, whole tomato, chorizo, morcilla and potatoes. Cover and cook until the pumpkin and potatoes are tender, about 30 minutes.

Lift out the pumpkin and tomato and reserve, saving the cooking liquid. Skim out the chorizo and morcilla and add to the platter of meats from the big pot, cutting them into serving-sized pieces. Place the potatoes with the carrots and turnips.

When cool enough to handle, remove the skin from the tomato. Combine the tomato, pumpkin, garlic, vinegar, remaining ½ teaspoon salt and cumin in a blender with 120ml/scant ¼ pint of the broth from the main pot. Blend until smooth. Serve some of this sauce spooned over the chickpeas and the rest in a jug to accompany the vegetables.

FOR THE CABBAGE

450g cabbage, shredded

1 teaspoon olive oil

1 garlic clove, finely chopped

Chilli flakes

1 teaspoon sweet pimentón

Bring the reserved cooking liquid to the boil and add the cabbage. Cook until very tender, 15 minutes. Drain, saving 3 tablespoons of the liquid. Place the cabbage in a serving bowl.

Heat the olive oil in a small frying pan over medium heat. Add the garlic and chilli flakes and sauté until the garlic begins to colour, about 2 minutes. Remove from heat and stir in the pimentón. Stir in the reserved cabbage liquid. Pour over the cabbage.

FOR THE SOUP

2 litres/3½ pints strained cocido broth	Chopped cooked giblets and liver (optional)
12 rellenos (meatballs; recipe page 122)	225g vermicelli noodles
	1 tablespoon finely chopped fresh mint

Bring the strained broth to the boil. Add the meatballs and simmer, covered, for 15 minutes. Add the chopped giblets reserved from the cocido pot if you're using them. Bring the broth to the boil and add the noodles. Cook until done, 6 to 12 minutes, depending on whether they are fine or thick. Serve the soup in shallow bowls. Garnish with chopped mint.

ACCOMPANIMENTS

Scarlet-Pickled Onions (page 282)	Pickled peppers (*guindillas*), such as peperoncini

Serve the broth with noodles and meatballs as a first course. Serve a platter of carrots, turnips, leeks and potatoes. Serve a bowl of chickpeas with accompanying pumpkin sauce. Serve the bowl of cabbage. Serve the platter of cut-up chicken, ham hock, beef, chorizo and morcilla. Accompany with pickled onions and peppers.

Fish and Shellfish

I was having an early-morning coffee at a café in a small La Mancha town. A delivery van pulled up at the door. *Pescados Juanito,* Johnny's Fish. I supposed a crate of frozen fish was being delivered to the freezer in the restaurant's kitchen. The guy got out with a tray heaped with absolutely fresh sardines, still glistening and rigid. This was a place about as far away from the sea as you can get.

La Mancha is full of surprises. One of the biggest was discovering impeccably fresh fish in the markets and at very good prices. Every bit as good as what I can buy at the fish market near where I live in southern Spain, only about two blocks from a fishing port on the Mediterranean.

That's because Madrid, in the geographic centre of the Spanish peninsula and a long way from the ocean, is a distribution hub for seafood. Fresh fish and shellfish arriving at major ports on the Bay of Biscay, Atlantic or Mediterranean are packed on ice and shipped in refrigerated trucks to Madrid. From Madrid, one of the biggest wholesale fish markets in the world, fish is moved out to the provinces.

Of course, it wasn't always that way. Before refrigeration and automotive transport, the only fresh fish came from streams, rivers and lagoons. From far-off oceans came salt fish of various sorts, carried overland by muledrivers. To this day La Mancha has a variety of preparations for *bacalao,* dry salt cod.

Freshwater trout gets top billing in this chapter. Wild trout once was abundant in the rivers and streams of Castilla–La Mancha, but nowadays farmed fish is marketed. Some of these recipes would work equally well with ocean fish such as small bass. From the ocean are hake in a luscious saffron sauce, sea bass with pine nuts, roasted red bream for Christmas and sole in wine sauce.

TROUT STUFFED *with* HAM *and* MUSHROOMS

Truchas Rellenas con Jamón y Setas

Fresh trout doesn't need much sprucing up. But if you have a good source and can enjoy it frequently, it's great to have a few variations on the tried and true. This recipe also works nicely with serving-sized sea bass.

SERVES 4

4 trout, each about 350g, filleted (8 fillets)

Salt

1 tablespoon olive oil, plus olive oil for frying

60g chopped shallot

85g chopped mushrooms

Pinch of dried thyme

250ml / 8 fl oz dry white wine

4 tablespoons fresh breadcrumbs

60g serrano or cooked ham, thinly sliced

Flour for dredging

1 tablespoon fresh lemon juice

1 tablespoon chopped fresh parsley

Sprinkle the fillets with salt and let stand while you prepare the stuffing.

Heat 1 tablespoon oil in a small frying pan over medium heat. Add the shallot and sauté for 2 minutes. Add the mushrooms and sauté for 5 minutes. Add the thyme and 4 tablespoons of the wine and cook until the liquid is evaporated. Stir in the breadcrumbs. Remove from the heat and let cool slightly.

Spread the mushroom mixture on each of 4 trout fillets. Top with sliced ham. Top with another fillet, pressing gently to close. (The fillets will hold together without being tied.)

Dredge the trout in flour, patting off the excess. Heat olive oil to a depth of ½cm / ¼in in a heavy frying pan over medium heat. Fry the trout, in 2 batches, if necessary, until browned, about 4 minutes. Turn them and cook for about 4 minutes more. Transfer to a serving platter and keep warm.

Pour off all but 2 tablespoons of the oil from the frying pan. Add the lemon juice and remaining wine. Boil for 3 minutes, until reduced by half. Add the parsley to the sauce and pour over the fish.

TROUT *and* MUSHROOMS *in* CAZUELA, GUADALAJARA STYLE

Trucha con Setas en Cazuela, al Estilo de Guadalajara

Guadalajara, a province in Spain (not Mexico) east of Madrid, at the top of the Castilla–La Mancha region, is famed for its trout.

Over the years I have become dedicated to cazuela cooking. A cazuela is an earthenware casserole that can go from top of the stove to oven to table. Once you become used to cooking in a cazuela, you can sauté foods and brown them nicely, then add liquid for a slow braise. Earthenware takes a long time to heat up, but then it maintains a steady and even cooking temperature.

SERVES 4

4 trout fillets, 140 to 170g each

Salt and freshly ground black pepper

450g oyster mushrooms or other mushrooms, sliced

60g serrano ham, cut into julienne strips

2 garlic cloves, chopped

4 tablespoons olive oil

80ml dry white wine

Pinch of dried thyme

Chopped fresh parsley for garnish

Sprinkle the trout fillets with salt and pepper to taste and set aside for 20 minutes. Preheat the oven to 200°C/180°C fan/GM6.

Place the sliced mushrooms in a 23cm/9in cazuela. Scatter the ham and garlic on top. Drizzle with half of the oil.

Heat the cazuela over medium heat until the mushrooms begin to sizzle, about 3 minutes.

Place the trout fillets on top, skin side up, overlapping them slightly. Drizzle with the remaining oil, wine and thyme. When the liquid begins to simmer, after about 2 minutes, place the cazuela in the oven. Bake until the trout flakes easily, about 15 minutes.

Transfer the fillets with a slotted spoon to serving plates, skin side down. Spoon the mushrooms and juice over them. Sprinkle with parsley and serve.

TROUT, JEWISH STYLE

Trucha a la Judía

The original version of this delectable dish probably consisted of no more than fish, olive oil and onions, while the modern version is a sweet-sour confit with tomatoes, a nice counterpoint to trout. This dish can also be made with fillets of sea bass or mackerel.

SERVES 4

4 trout fillets, 140 to 170g each

Salt and freshly ground black pepper

2 tablespoons olive oil

170g sliced plum tomato, juice reserved

4 tablespoons fresh lemon juice

1½ teaspoons sugar

28g chopped fresh flat-leaf parsley

Sprinkle the trout with salt and pepper to taste and let stand for 30 minutes.

Heat the oil in a frying pan over high heat and add the tomato. Cook for 2 minutes. Add the lemon juice, sugar and parsley. Reduce heat to medium and cook until thickened, about 10 minutes.

Place the trout fillets on top of the tomato mixture, skin side down. Cook for 4 minutes. Turn skin side up and cook for 4 minutes longer.

Serve the trout with the tomato sauce spooned over the fillets.

A TROUT FISHERMAN IN CUENCA

North of the provincial capital of Cuenca, heading towards the high sierra, is an idyllic region of fast-moving trout streams, mountain retreats, forested valleys, tumbling waterfalls and an 'enchanted city', where wind and rain over several millennia have carved karstic limestone into phantasmal shapes. Hugging the rocky cliffs above the River Júcar is the village of Villalba de la Sierra. Across the bridge and nestled in a wooded area next to the river is El Tablazo, a hotel in a converted flour mill on a small lake. Javi Alegría, fisherman and outdoorsman, runs a trout fishing concession on the lake. Here I caught my first-ever fish.

'Grip the reel here and hold the line down with your finger, then swing the line out beyond those reeds, letting go of the line at the same time.' Javi Alegría gives me some basic instructions and hands me the fishing rod. The hook on the end is baited with three kernels of sweetcorn.

I cast, and the line gets snagged. I do it again. And wait. Willows ring the small lake, dribbling branches in the shimmery water. I can hear the sound of the nearby river bouncing over stones. I pull the line in just a little. The float bobs, I feel a tug. Oh my goodness! I slowly reel in the line until, dangling before me, is a lovely rainbow trout. I am so excited that my shouts disturb the peaceful scene.

Javi laughs. *'Pescador que pesca un pez, pescador es.'* Catch one fish, fisherman is he. Or fisherwoman. I was hooked. I landed two more of the beautiful fish and proudly delivered them to the hotel kitchen. My friends and I dined on our catch that evening.

Javi stocks the lake at El Tablazo with farmed rainbow trout and opens the fishing concession to guests. He weighs the catch on the way out and charges accordingly. Javi says even fly fishermen come to the lake because they can fish year-round. But when I ask to take his picture with a string of trout, he gets embarrassed and refuses. He doesn't really want to be seen with dead trout.

Javi fly-fishes *sin muerte,* catch and release. He showed me his selection of nymphs and dry flies. After the thrill of landing the trout, with no barb on the hook, it is released unscathed. Not dinner. If his mother wants to cook trout for dinner, he pulls them from the stocked lake. He fly-fishes on the Júcar, just a few metres from the lake, and in rivers higher into the sierra.

Javi grew up in Cuenca. His father was a *guardamonte* – forest ranger and game warden. Javi worked in government reforestation projects but got out because he didn't like the politics of land management. He and his brother took over El Tablazo in the 1990s.

'Environment is delicate,' he says. And people have abused it. People of all sorts – hunters, fishermen, farmers, city people. 'I love fishing. The beautiful part is landing a trout. But, in good conscience, I don't want to kill it.'

When I met Javi, in the autumn after early rains, he was off on a mushroom-hunting expedition. In the winter, when the hills are dusted with snow, he hunts partridge and rabbit. In April the season for trout opens.

In bygone days trout was everyday fare in the cooking of Castilla–La Mancha. Every millstream was a source of trout. The River Tajo in Toledo was so abundant that it was pickled in escabeche. Now trout that appears at the market or in restaurants is always farmed rainbow trout. Castilla–La Mancha has more than two hundred miles of trout streams, mainly in Cuenca, Guadalajara and Albacete provinces. With management of fishing and watercourses, stocks of wild trout are slowly recovering.

Here's a recipe for stuffing and baking trout that Javi shared with me. You need a really big trout – about 1.2kg. Clean it and pat dry with a clean cloth. Season it with salt, white pepper and oregano. For the stuffing, chop pine nuts, bacon and smoked salmon. Stuff the trout with this. Fry the trout in very hot oil until browned on both sides. Then place it in an earthenware cazuela with oil, white wine, water, chopped shallot and any of the stuffing mixture left over. Bake in a preheated 180°C/160°C fan/GM4 oven until the trout flakes easily.

FISH in A TANGY MARINADE

Pescado en Escabeche

In addition to trout, other freshwater fish, such as pike, tench, barbel and carp, are found in the streams and lakes of La Mancha. Before the days of refrigeration *escabeche*, a strong vinegar marinade, was used to preserve cooked fish. Made with farmed catfish, this is a delicious cold dish.

SERVES 6

3 catfish or lake perch fillets, 280 to 340g each

4 tablespoons olive oil

1 medium onion, julienned

4 tablespoons julienned red pepper

2 garlic cloves, slivered

1 carrot, sliced

180ml / 6 fl oz white wine vinegar

¼ teaspoon peppercorns

Pinch of ground cloves

⅛ teaspoon celery seeds

¼ teaspoon dried oregano

4 tablespoons chopped fresh parsley, plus parsley for garnish

2 teaspoons salt

1 bay leaf

Chilli flakes

1 large potato (350g)

Salad leaves for serving

1 hard-boiled egg, quartered, for garnish

Extra virgin olive oil for serving

Cut each fillet into 4 pieces of similar size. Heat the oil in a non-stick frying pan or cazuela over medium heat and fry the fish until lightly browned, about 2 minutes per side. Remove the pieces and place them in one layer in a shallow nonreactive bowl or cazuela.

Add the onion, pepper, garlic and carrot to the oil and sauté for 5 minutes, until the onion is softened. Add the vinegar and 650ml/just over 1 pint of water, the peppercorns, cloves, celery seeds, oregano, parsley, salt, bay leaf and chilli flakes to taste. Bring to the boil and cook for 5 minutes.

Ladle the vinegar marinade with the vegetables and spices carefully over the fish. Allow to stand until cool.

Cook the whole potato in boiling water until tender when pierced with a skewer, about 25 minutes. Drain and cool. When completely cool, peel the potato, cut it in half lengthways, then cut it crossways into 1cm/½in slices. Tuck the slices into the marinade with the fish.

Cover and refrigerate for at least 12 and up to 36 hours.

To serve, lift the fish, potatoes and vegetables out of the marinade and arrange them atop leafy salad leaves. Garnish the plate with egg and parsley. Drizzle with a little extra virgin olive oil and serve.

POACHED HAKE with SAFFRON SAUCE

Merluza al Azafrán

Saffron, grown in La Mancha, contributes subtle flavour to this sauce, which would enhance any poached or grilled fish. It goes especially well with delicate hake, a favourite fish in Spain. Fresh cod, halibut or grouper could be used in its place. For best results, use very fresh fish, not frozen fillets. Leaving the skin on helps to keep a delicate fish from falling apart.

SERVES 4

Salt	2 garlic cloves, chopped
4 pieces hake fillet, about 170g each, skin on	170g peeled, seeded and chopped tomato
½ teaspoon saffron threads	350ml / 12 fl oz Simple Fish Stock (page 135)
3 tablespoons extra virgin olive oil	1 bay leaf
½ medium onion, chopped	3 tablespoons chopped fresh flat-leaf parsley

Salt the fish fillets and allow to stand for 30 minutes.

Crush the saffron in a mortar and dissolve in 2 tablespoons warm water. Let it infuse for 15 minutes.

Heat the oil in a large frying pan or flameproof casserole over medium heat. Sauté the onion and garlic until softened, 5 minutes. Add the tomato and cook for 5 minutes. Add the fish stock and simmer for 15 minutes. Add the saffron water.

Purée the sauce in a blender and strain, discarding the solids.

Pour the sauce into a deep frying pan or flameproof casserole. Add the fish fillets, skin side down, and turn them to coat. Add the bay leaf. Bring the sauce to a simmer and cook, covered, until the fish flakes easily, 8 to 10 minutes.

Discard the bay leaf. Serve sprinkled with parsley.

❧ SIMPLE FISH STOCK *Caldo de Pescado*

At markets where you can purchase whole fish, you will be able to buy heads, bones and trimmings to make a basic stock, essential for fish soups and some sauces. Use trimmings from only white fish (such as snapper or halibut), never those from fatty fish such as salmon. Prawn shells and clam or mussel liquid can be added to the stock. Freeze the stock in 450ml/¾ pint or 700ml/1¼ pint quantities for use in sauces and soups.

❧ Makes 2 litres/3½ pints

450g small white fish or fish heads, bones and trimmings

Prawn shells (optional)

2 teaspoons salt

1 leek

1 strip lemon zest

1 stick of celery

1 small carrot

Parsley stems

Pinch of dried thyme

1 bay leaf

120ml/4 fl oz dry white wine

Combine all the ingredients in a large saucepan with 2.3 litres/4 pints water. Bring to the boil. Cover and simmer for 1 hour. Strain the stock and discard the solids.

SEA BASS *with* GARLIC, PINE NUTS *and* CHILLI

Lubina con Ajillo de Piñones

A classic way of preparing fish in Spain is *a la espalda*, fish grilled 'on its back'. Basically, a whole fish (with the head too) is butterflied and grilled. The spine is lifted out after cooking. Drizzled with a 'sauce' of oil garlic, and hot chilli, it is simple but ever so tasty. This variation includes toasty pine nuts and can be prepared with fish fillets instead of a whole fish.

SERVES 4

Four 170g sea bass or striped bass fillets, skin on

Salt

3 tablespoons plus 1 teaspoon olive oil

3 tablespoons pine nuts

120ml/4 fl oz dry white wine

¼ teaspoon chilli flakes

1 tablespoon sliced garlic (2 to 3 cloves)

1 tablespoon fresh lemon juice

1 tablespoon chopped fresh parsley

Pinch of dried thyme

Sprinkle the fish fillets with salt and allow to stand at room temperature for 30 minutes.

Heat 1 teaspoon oil in a small frying pan over medium-high heat and fry the pine nuts until golden, about 30 seconds. Tip the pan so the oil drains to one side and skim out the pine nuts. Reserve the pine nuts and oil.

Preheat the oven to 190°C/170°C fan/GM5.

Use the oil remaining in the small frying pan to brush a griddle pan or heavy frying pan. Heat the pan until very hot. Sear the fillets, skin side down, until lightly crisped, 1½ minutes. Place the fillets in a single layer, skin side down, in a baking pan.

Drizzle the fish with 2 tablespoons of the remaining oil and the wine. Bake, uncovered, until the fish just barely flakes, 6 to 8 minutes.

While the fish is in the oven, add the remaining tablespoon of oil to the small frying pan and fry the chilli flakes and garlic over medium heat until the garlic is golden, 20 seconds. Remove from the pan immediately so the mixture doesn't burn.

When the fish is cooked, lift the fillets out of the baking pan and place them on heated plates. Pour all the cooking liquid from the baking pan into the small frying pan. Bring to the boil and cook for 1 minute. Add the lemon juice. Remove from the heat and add the pine nuts, garlic, chilli flakes, parsley and thyme.

Spoon this sauce over the fish fillets and serve immediately.

ROASTED BREAM *on* A BED OF POTATOES

Besugo al Horno con Patatas

Besugo is red bream, a much-appreciated fish throughout Spain. It's a reddish pink colour, with white firm but delicate flesh. It's said that besugo doesn't acquire its full virtue until it arrives in (inland) Madrid, where it is considered an essential part of the family Christmas Eve dinner. Prices for this fish skyrocket the week before the holiday.

While it's customary to roast a whole fish, including the head, the recipe works fine even if the head has been removed. A 900g fish (without the head) will serve four if this is a main course. As part of a much larger meal, it will serve six. Try this recipe with red snapper or large bass if you can't find bream.

SERVES 4 TO 6

1 whole fish, gutted and scaled (900g to 1 kg)	2 bay leaves
Salt	4 tablespoons chopped fresh parsley
680g potatoes (about 3 medium), peeled and sliced ½ cm / ¼in thick	2 teaspoons chopped garlic
	50g fresh breadcrumbs
½ medium onion, sliced	1 slice lemon
4 tablespoons olive oil	120ml / 4 fl oz dry white wine

Sprinkle the fish inside and out with salt and allow to stand for 30 minutes.

Preheat the oven to 190°C / 170°C fan / GM5.

Place the potatoes and onion in a bowl and drizzle with 1 tablespoon of the oil and ½ teaspoon salt. Toss to coat the potatoes. Spread them in an oven pan large enough to hold the fish. Tuck the bay leaves into the potatoes. Cover with foil and bake for 10 minutes.

Combine the parsley, garlic, breadcrumbs and 1 tablespoon of the remaining oil in a small bowl.

Pat the fish dry. Cut 2 slashes on the top side of the fish. Cut the lemon slice in half and insert a slice in each slash.

Remove the potatoes from the oven and discard the foil. Use a spatula to turn the potatoes. Place the fish on top of the potatoes. Spread the breadcrumb mixture on top of the fish, patting it into place.

Return the pan to the oven and bake for 10 minutes. Combine the wine with the remaining 2 tablespoons oil. Drizzle a little over the fish and the rest around the fish. Return to the oven until the flesh just barely pulls away from the bone, about 20 minutes longer. (If the fish needs more roasting time, it may be necessary to add water to the pan so that the potatoes don't scorch on the bottom.)

Use 2 spatulas to transfer the fish to a heated serving platter. Place the potatoes around it and serve immediately. Or divide the fish into 4 fillets in the kitchen. Arrange them on individual plates, adding some of the breadcrumbs and potatoes to each serving.

FILLETS OF SOLE *with* WHITE WINE SAUCE *and* GRAPES

Filetes de Lenguado con Uvas

On New Year's Eve, friends go out for a gala supper with *cava,* sparkling wine, then, at midnight everybody gathers in the town plaza to await the twelve bells, swallowing one grape at every bell – assuring good luck for the coming year. Then it's dancing till dawn. These fillets of sole with grapes are a perfect addition to an elegant and festive menu. Use good dry white wine or *cava* in the sauce.

Sole fillets are long and fairly thin, so they can be folded in thirds. Fillets of turbot, flounder or John Dory can be substituted.

SERVES 4

Four 170g sole fillets	120ml/scant ¼ pint dry white wine
Salt	250ml/scant ½ pint Simple Fish Stock (page 135)
60g serrano ham, thinly sliced	Pinch of saffron threads, crushed
2 tablespoons olive oil	150g red or white seedless grapes, peeled
40g chopped shallot	or halved
1 tablespoon all-purpose flour	1 tablespoon cold butter, cut into pieces

Spread the fillets out flat. Sprinkle with salt. Top with sliced ham. Fold the fillets over the ham into thirds (like a letter). Cut bands of foil 6cm/2½in wide. Wrap the bands like a belt around the centre of the folded fillets. Pinch the ends of the foil together to prevent the fillets from unrolling. Place them in an oven pan just large enough to hold them in one layer.

Heat the oil in a small frying pan over low heat. Sauté the shallot until softened but not browned, 4 minutes. Stir in the flour. Add the wine and fish stock and stir. Raise the heat to medium and cook, stirring frequently, for 10 minutes.

Place the crushed saffron in a blender. Add the sauce from the frying pan. Blend to make a smooth sauce.

Preheat the oven to 180°C/160°C fan/GM4.

Pour the blended sauce around the fish fillets. Cover the baking pan with foil and bake until the fish just flakes, 12 to 14 minutes.

Transfer the fillets to a warm platter and snip off the foil bands. Keep warm.

Pour all of the sauce and liquid from the baking pan into the frying pan. Bring to the boil and add the grapes. Simmer for 2 minutes. Add the butter, a bit at a time, swirling or stirring to blend it into the sauce. Do not boil.

Serve the sole fillets with the sauce and grapes.

FARMHOUSE RICE with FISH and SALAD LEAVES

Arroz a la Quintería

A *quintería* is a traditional Manchegan farmstead, where this dish would be made with salt cod. However, nowadays frozen fish is a viable alternative. The salad could be wild spring leaves, such as *collejas*. Here I have used spinach.

Use round-grain Spanish rice for this dish. If you can get it, the Bomba variety is best, because it doesn't 'flower' and open up when cooked. Please avoid the temptation to stir the rice! Let it bubble gently until just al dente.

SERVES 4 TO 5

350g fish fillet, such as cod, snapper or monkfish

4 tablespoons olive oil

260g chopped tomato

1 small head of garlic

1 medium potato (225g), cut into 2½cm / 1in pieces

Chilli flakes

225g shredded spinach

⅛ teaspoon saffron threads, crushed, or 1 teaspoon pimentón

2 teaspoons salt

Freshly ground black pepper

380g Spanish round-grain rice

Cut the fish fillet into 8 to 10 slices or chunks. Heat the oil in a cazuela or sauté pan over medium heat and quickly fry the fish, about 1 minute per side. It does not need to brown. Remove the fish and reserve. Add the tomato to the oil and cook over high heat for 2 minutes. Slice the top off the head of garlic and add to the pan with the potato and chilli flakes. Cook for 5 minutes. Add the spinach and cook for 5 minutes more.

Combine the saffron with 2 tablespoons warm water and allow to stand.

Add 1.2 litres/2 pints of water to the pan along with the salt and pepper to taste. Bring to the boil. Cook, uncovered, over medium heat for 10 minutes. Add the saffron water. Bring the liquid to the boil and add the rice. Return the pieces of fish to the pan.

Let the rice cook over high heat for 3 minutes. Lower the heat so that it bubbles gently and cook for 10 minutes longer. This rice dish is not 'dry' like paella but a little juicy. Remove from the heat, cover the pan and allow to stand for 5 minutes before serving.

OLIVE PICKERS' COD and POTATO STEW

Pote Aceitunero

This one-pot dish comes from the Montes de Toledo, an area famous for its olive oil. January, when groups of pickers gather in the olive groves, can be bitter cold. The pickers make a roaring fire to warm the hands and cook the midday meal. The traditional version is made with *bacalao,* dry salt cod that has been soaked for twenty-four hours to desalt it. In this recipe I have used fresh cod, which needs only minutes to cook. If you use salt cod, cook it very gently with the potatoes. I like the addition of something green – in this case asparagus.

SERVES 4

450g cod fillets, cut into 2cm/¾in cubes

Salt

900g potatoes, peeled and cut into 2cm/¾in cubes

4 tablespoons olive oil

1 bay leaf

1 small dried chilli, such as cayenne

2 garlic cloves, 1 peeled

1 medium tomato

1 medium onion, coarsely chopped

¼ teaspoon ground cumin

½ teaspoon sweet pimentón, preferably smoked

½ teaspoon hot pimentón or a pinch of cayenne

120g sliced cooked asparagus (optional)

1 egg

Sprinkle the cod with salt and let stand at room temperature.

Place the potatoes in a large saucepan or deep frying pan with the oil and sauté over high heat for 2 minutes. Tuck the bay leaf and chilli into the potatoes and add 2 teaspoons salt and 450ml/¾ pint of water. Bring to the boil.

Cut a small slit in one unpeeled garlic clove and add it to the potatoes with the whole tomato and chopped onion. Cover and simmer the potatoes until almost tender, 15 to 20 minutes. Remove and discard the bay leaf and chilli. Skim out the garlic clove and tomato.

Remove the skin from the cooked garlic and tomato and place them in a blender with the peeled garlic clove, cumin, sweet pimentón, hot pimentón and 120ml/scant ¼ pint of liquid from the potatoes. Blend until smooth. Add this sauce to the potatoes and cook for 5 minutes.

Add the cod to the pan and cook until it just flakes, about 3 minutes. Stir in the asparagus if you're using it. Raise the heat so the liquid bubbles. Break the egg into the pan. Use a fork to stir it into the cod and potatoes, about 1 minute. Remove from the heat and allow the casserole to rest 5 minutes. Serve in shallow soup bowls.

CODFISH BALLS *with* WALNUTS

Albóndigas de Bacalao

Salt cod (*bacalao*) was once a staple in the Manchegan kitchen, so housewives learned to prepare it in dozens of appetising ways. These codfish balls, nicely flavoured with cinnamon, nutmeg and pepper, can be made with small pieces of cod left over after cutting up a large piece for another recipe. Use this recipe to make fish balls with scraps of any cooked fish. If the fish balls are to be served as a main course, accompany them with rice and a vegetable such as sautéed chard (page 251).

MAKES ABOUT 16 FISH BALLS, SERVING 8 AS A TAPA OR 4 AS A MAIN COURSE

450g salt cod, soaked in several changes of water for 24 hours	Freshly ground black pepper
1 bay leaf	Fresh lemon juice
2 slices bread	2 tablespoons plain flour
4 tablespoons milk	3 tablespoons olive oil
1 egg	4 tablespoons dry Sherry or white wine
1 tablespoon chopped fresh parsley	⅛ teaspoon saffron threads, crushed
⅛ teaspoon ground cinnamon	Pinch of ground cloves
Grating of fresh nutmeg	Salt if necessary
	25g walnuts, chopped

Drain the soaked cod. Put it in a pan with the bay leaf and cover with fresh water. Bring to just under a boil, then lower the heat to a bare simmer and cook for 5 minutes. Drain, reserving the liquid.

Remove all the skin and bone from the cod. Flake the fish and place it in a blender or food processor.

Place 1 slice of the bread in a saucer and pour the milk over it. When softened, break it up and add to the cod with the egg, parsley, cinnamon, nutmeg and pepper. Process briefly to make a stiff paste.

Moisten your hands with lemon juice and roll the paste into 2½cm/1in balls. Roll them in flour. Heat 2 tablespoons of the oil in a frying pan over medium heat and fry the balls until browned on all sides. Remove.

Add the remaining tablespoon of oil to the frying pan and fry the remaining slice of bread. Place it in the blender or food processor with the wine, saffron, cloves and 120ml/scant ¼ pint of the reserved liquid. Blend to make a smooth sauce.

Place the sauce in a cazuela with 120ml/scant ¼ pint more of the reserved liquid. Cook, stirring, for 10 minutes.

Place the codfish balls in the cazuela and cook for 10 minutes more. Taste for salt. Scatter the walnuts over the top.

SALT COD with ROASTED PEPPERS, MANCHEGAN STYLE

Bacalao a la Manchega

See the instructions on page 10 for how to soak the salt cod. If you can purchase *lomo de bacalao,* cod 'loins', or a centre cut, you will have nice meaty chunks of fish. If buying a whole split (half a salt cod), the skinny tail and bony gill sections yield smaller pieces. Scraps and trimmings can be saved for another dish, such as codfish balls (page 145).

A favourite dish for meatless meals during the Lenten season preceding Easter, this would be served with an egg per person poached on top of the cod, peppers and potatoes.

SERVES 4

570g salt cod, soaked in several changes of water for 24 hours, or 450g fresh cod fillets

1 tablespoon anisette or brandy

4 red peppers

3 tablespoons olive oil

1 medium onion, chopped

260g chopped tomato

680g baking potatoes (about 3 medium), peeled and cut into 2.5cm/1in chunks

3 garlic cloves, peeled

4 tablespoons fresh parsley leaves

1 teaspoon sweet pimentón

½ teaspoon ground cumin

Pinch of saffron threads, crushed (optional)

Freshly ground black pepper

½ teaspoon salt

1 egg per person or 1 hard-boiled egg, quartered

Fresh parsley for garnish

Drain the soaked cod and squeeze it out gently. Remove and discard all skin and bone. Cut the cod into 6cm/2½in pieces. Place them in a bowl and drizzle with the anisette. Allow to marinate for 1 hour, turning occasionally.

Roast the peppers over a flame or under a hot grill, turning them until charred on all sides. Remove and cover the peppers with a lid. When cool enough to handle, peel off the blackened skin, removing the stems and seeds. Cut or tear the peppers into short strips.

Heat the oil in a cazuela or deep frying pan over medium heat. Sauté the onion until softened, 5 minutes. Add the peppers and tomato and cook until the tomato has sweated out some of its liquid, 5 minutes. Add the potatoes.

In a blender, combine the garlic, parsley, pimentón, cumin, saffron if you're using it, pepper and salt with 120ml/scant ¼ pint of water. Blend until smooth. Pour over the potatoes along with a further 120ml/scant ¼ pint of water. Bring to the boil, then simmer, covered, for 15 minutes.

Add the pieces of cod to the cazuela. (If you're using fresh cod, add it during the last 10 minutes of cooking.) Simmer over low heat until the potatoes are tender, 15 minutes more. Do not allow the liquid to boil, or it will toughen the cod.

If using poached eggs, break the eggs on top of the potatoes and cod. Cover and simmer until the whites begin to set, 3 to 4 minutes. Remove the cazuela from the heat and allow to stand, covered, for 5 minutes.

Lift the egg, cod, potatoes and some liquid from the cazuela with a skimmer or large spoon. Serve in shallow soup bowls with a sprinkling of chopped parsley. If you haven't poached eggs with the cod, top each serving with a quarter of hard-boiled egg.

CLAMS, MARINER'S STYLE

Almejas a la Marinera

Mariner's style in land-locked La Mancha? Well, yes. This recipe points up a double Manchegan paradox. For one thing, seafood is super-fresh, distributed from coastal waters to inland markets in twenty-four hours. And, second, weird as it may seem, Spain's national naval museum and archives are situated in El Viso del Marqués, a town in the province of Ciudad Real, far from the sea, in the renaissance *palacio* (mansion) of Don Alvaro de Bazán, an admiral in the Spanish navy in the sixteenth century. Go figure.

SERVES 4

4 dozen Manila or littleneck clams (about 900g); if unavailable, use mussels

3 tablespoons olive oil

½ medium onion, chopped

3 garlic cloves, chopped

1 teaspoon sweet pimentón

Pinch of chilli flakes

2 tablespoons fine dry breadcrumbs

80ml / about 5 tablespoons dry white wine

4 tablespoons chopped fresh flat-leaf parsley

Wash the clams and place them in a basin of water for 2 hours before cooking.

Heat the oil in a deep pan or flameproof casserole over medium heat and sauté the onion and garlic until softened, about 4 minutes. Stir in the pimentón, chilli flakes and breadcrumbs. Add the wine and equal quantity of the water. Bring to the boil.

Lift the clams out of the soaking water and add to the frying pan. Cover and cook over high heat until the clam shells open, 3 to 4 minutes. Discard any clams that do not open. Sprinkle with parsley and serve the clams and their cooking liquid in soup bowls.

PRAWNS *in* CAZUELA

Cazuela de Gambas

A *cazuela* is an earthenware casserole that goes from hob to oven to table. It is slow to heat, but then holds its temperature even after being removed from the oven. In tapa bars, prawns are cooked to order in small, individual *cazuelitas*. Incidentally, it is customary to peel the tails too, so the whole prawn is edible. Serve the prawns with bread for sopping up the juices or spoon it over steamed rice.

SERVES 4

2 tablespoons olive oil	2 garlic cloves, crushed
35g cubed bacon or serrano ham	2 tablespoons dry white wine
100g chopped leek	Salt
Pinch of chilli flakes	5 tablespoons chopped fresh flat-leaf parsley
570g peeled medium prawns	¼ teaspoon smoked pimentón

Heat the oil in a 25cm/10in cazuela or heavy frying pan over medium-low heat. Add the bacon and leek and sauté until the leek is soft but not browned, 10 minutes. Add the chilli flakes.

Turn up the heat until the leeks are sizzling. Stir in the prawns and sauté for 3 minutes. Add the garlic and wine and cook until the prawns are pink, about 2 minutes. Add salt to taste.

Remove the cazuela from the heat and stir in the parsley. Sprinkle with the pimentón and serve immediately.

Poultry and Small Game

La Mancha is still a very rural region, where *quinterías,* small farms, dot the landscape. A cluster of whitewashed buildings house granary, barn, stables, chicken and rabbit coops, living quarters, kitchen and pantry, bake house, well house, wine press. While four-wheel-drive vehicles and tractors have replaced the mules and old-fashioned ploughs, the chickens clucking and scratching in the dirt in the farmyard are as timeless as the land. Producing eggs for daily consumption and the occasional fowl for the pot, chickens are a source of culinary wealth.

La Mancha also has chicken farms, sending cheap, battery-raised birds to supermarkets at astonishingly low cost. Nevertheless, there is nothing so delicious as free-range, preferably organically raised, birds.

The *corral,* or farmyard, on a quintería also typically has rabbit hutches and dovecotes. Young rabbits and pigeons make an admirable addition to the casserole pot – as Don Quixote himself enjoyed for Sunday dinner.

Hunting is much a part of the rural life of La Mancha. A small landowner – one man, one gun, one dog – typically hunts both feathered and furred small game on his lands, partridge, quail, wild rabbit and hare being the most abundant. There are also fancy hunts, *cacerías,* on huge estates owned by aristocrats.

Wild partridge or hare may not be available when you want to cook. It is for that reason I have grouped chicken recipes with those for small game because most are interchangeable. So, if you find a partridge recipe that sounds enticing, you can probably prepare it with chicken or turkey. You will find suggestions for substitutes in each recipe.

CHICKEN with PEPPERS and TOMATOES, TOLEDO STYLE

Pisto con Pollo Toledano

Pisto is the emblematic dish of La Mancha. It derives from the Moorish *alboronía,* originally meat braised with onions and aubergine. As other vegetables appeared on the scene, such as peppers, squash and tomatoes from the New World, they were incorporated into the dish. This version with chicken calls only for onions, tomatoes and peppers, which become both sauce and vegetable side dish. Serve it with bread, rice or noodles to soak up the delicious juices.

SERVES **4** TO **5**

1 frying chicken, cut up, or about 1kg/2½ lbs chicken pieces

Salt and freshly ground black pepper

5 large green peppers

1 tablespoon olive oil

1½ medium onions, chopped

2 garlic cloves, chopped

1kg tomatoes (about 6 to 7 medium), peeled, seeded and chopped

½ teaspoon salt

⅛ teaspoon cumin seeds

1 tablespoon wine vinegar

Stoned olives such as arbequinas (optional)

Season the chicken pieces with salt and pepper and set aside.

Roast the peppers over a flame or under the hot grill, turning them until charred on all sides. Transfer them to a bowl and cover them. When cool enough to handle, peel off the charred skin, using your fingers or scraping with a knife. Discard the stems and seeds. Rinse the peppers under running water. Tear or cut into bite-sized pieces.

Heat the oil in a large cazuela or deep sauté pan over medium heat. Brown the chicken pieces, about 15 minutes. Remove them and reserve. Drain off all but 1 tablespoon of the fat.

Add the onion and garlic to the pan and sauté for 5 minutes. Raise the heat, add the peppers and sauté for a few minutes longer. Then add the chopped tomatoes and cook over high heat for 5 minutes. Stir in the salt, cumin seeds and vinegar. Return the chicken pieces to the pan. Cook, uncovered, over medium heat, turning the chicken once, until the vegetables and chicken are very tender, 40 to 60 minutes. Serve garnished with a few stoned olives.

NOTE: *If desired, the chicken pieces can be skinned, in which case let them brown very briefly before adding the onion.*

MANCHEGO CHICKEN *with* ANISETTE

Pollo Manchego con Aguardiente

Aguardiente de anís is a clear anise-flavoured brandy, sweet or dry, much appreciated throughout Spain. It makes a pleasant digestive after a meal, served neat in a snifter or over ice. Hardy peasants might sip it for breakfast, when it's said to *matar el gusanillo,* kill the little worm of 'hunger'. For this recipe, use dry aguardiente. If not available, substitute anisette. This chicken is good served over rice.

SERVES 4 TO 6

1.1 to 1.4kg/2½ to 3lbs chicken pieces

Salt and freshly ground black pepper

3 tablespoons olive oil

2 garlic cloves, chopped

Pinch of dried thyme

½ teaspoon ground cinnamon

Pinch of ground cloves

Grating of fresh nutmeg

2 tablespoons aguardiente de anís or dry anisette

4 tablespoons dry white wine

Sprinkle the chicken pieces with salt and pepper and set aside for 15 minutes. Heat the oil in a large frying pan or sauté pan over medium heat. Add the chicken and brown it, about 5 minutes. Turn the chicken and add the garlic. Sauté until the chicken is lightly browned on the other side, about 5 minutes longer.

Sprinkle the thyme, cinnamon, cloves and nutmeg over the chicken. Add the aguardiente, wine and 4 tablespoons of water. Cover and simmer until the chicken is very tender, 35 to 50 minutes, depending on the size of the pieces.

CRISPY, CHEESY CHICKEN BREAST
with QUINCE SAUCE

Pechuga de Pollo Empanada con Salsa de Membrillo

A classic combination is Manchego cheese and *membrillo,* sweet quince jelly. Quince is a fruit so rich in pectin that, when cooked with sugar, it sets up solid and can be cut into cubes. Paired with cheese, it makes a tantalising appetiser or dessert. You can buy membrillo imported from Spain at speciality food shops (or see the recipe on page 329).

Here the quince points up the cheese in breaded chicken breasts. If membrillo is not available, substitute sweetened apple sauce for the quince jelly, with the vinegar, but without the addition of water.

I like to use small breast halves (140 to 170g), allowing one per person. If you can get only larger pieces, cook two or three and cut them in half to serve. Garlicky spinach (page 252) is a good side with the crispy chicken.

SERVES 4

120g membrillo (about a 5cm/2in cube), cut into pieces

2 teaspoons Sherry vinegar

4 small boneless, skinless chicken breast (570g/1¼ lbs)

Salt

¼ teaspoon dried basil

85g grated Manchego, preferably cured (if unavailable, use a mature Cheddar)

85g fine dry breadcrumbs

2 eggs, beaten with 2 teaspoons water

About 6 tablespoons olive oil for frying

To make the sauce, combine the membrillo, vinegar and 80ml/about 5 tablespoons of hot water in a blender. Blend until smooth. Set the sauce aside.

Place the chicken breasts between layers of clingfilm and pound to equal thickness, about 1cm/½in. Sprinkle with salt and basil.

Combine the grated cheese and breadcrumbs in a shallow pan. Place the beaten eggs in another pan. Dip each chicken breast first into beaten egg, then into the cheese-crumb mixture, again into egg, and again into the crumbs. Set them on a baking sheet and allow to dry for 30 minutes.

Heat the oil in a heavy frying pan over medium heat until hot but not smoking. Fry the chicken breasts (in 2 batches, if necessary) until browned on both sides and cooked through, about 4 minutes per side. Drain briefly on kitchen paper.

Heat the quince sauce in a small saucepan. Serve it alongside the chicken breasts.

CHICKEN BREAST *with* CRUNCHY VEGETABLES *and* RICE

Pechuga de Pollo con Arroz y Verduras Frescas

In the shadow of Toledo's grand cathedral is the eponymous restaurant of Adolfo Muñoz, passionate proponent of everything gustatory. Adolfo has one of the finest wine cellars in the country, situated below street level in an excavated house dating from mediaeval times. He's a television chef and an enthusiastic promoter of La Mancha's great products, such as saffron and olive oil.

This recipe is adapted from a dish I savoured at Restaurante Adolfo, where it was prepared with squab breast cooked very rare and rice that was slightly crunchy. I have substituted chicken breasts, which should be thoroughly cooked but not overcooked. The vegetables should be slightly crunchy and the rice al dente.

SERVES 6

FOR THE STOCK

1 tablespoon olive oil	1 carrot
450g/1lb chicken carcass or wings	1 celery stalk
½ onion, sliced	Pinch of dried thyme
4 tablespoons dry white wine	1 bay leaf
1 tomato, quartered	1 fresh parsley sprig
	1 teaspoon salt

Heat the oil in a deep heavy pan over medium-high heat and brown the chicken carcass or wings with the onion until flecked with dark brown, 8 to 10 minutes.

Add the wine, tomato, carrot, celery, thyme, bay leaf, parsley, salt and 1½ litres/2½ pints water. Bring to the boil, cover and simmer for 1 hour.

Strain the stock, pressing hard on the solids. Discard the solids. Let the stock stand for 20 minutes. Skim off and discard the fat that rises to the top. Set aside 700ml/about 1¼ pints of the stock to cook the rice. Reserve the remainder for another use (it can be frozen).

FOR THE CHICKEN BREASTS, VEGETABLES AND RICE

4 boneless chicken breasts with skin (about 900g/2lbs)

Salt and freshly ground black pepper

2 tablespoons olive oil, plus oil for the grill

285g long-grain rice

40g diced carrot

30g diced leek

30g diced red pepper

25g diced mushrooms

50g diced asparagus

¼ teaspoon saffron threads, crushed

4 tablespoons dry white wine

Pinch of dried thyme

Pinch of dried rosemary

Season the chicken breasts with salt and pepper. Heat a ridged grill pan and brush with oil. Sear the chicken breasts, skin side down, over high heat, about 1½ minutes. Turn them crossways and grill for 1 minute more. Turn them over and repeat the turns. Transfer the breasts to a frying pan big enough to hold them in one layer.

In a dry heavy frying pan over medium heat, cook the rice, stirring constantly, until golden and toasted, about 8 minutes. Reserve.

Heat 2 tablespoons oil in a saucepan. Add the carrot and leek and sauté for 3 minutes. Add the pepper and sauté for 2 minutes. Add the mushrooms and sauté for 2 minutes. Add the asparagus and sauté for 1 minute. The vegetables should be crunchy.

Add 2 tablespoons hot water to the saffron and allow to infuse.

Add the reserved 710ml/1¼ pints of stock to the vegetables. Add salt to taste. Bring to the boil. Add the toasted rice and saffron infusion and boil for 3 minutes. Remove from the heat, cover tightly and let the rice set for 10 minutes. The rice will be al dente.

Add the wine, thyme and rosemary to the chicken breasts. Bring to the boil, cover and simmer, turning once, until they are cooked through, about 12 minutes.

Slice the chicken breasts on the diagonal. Serve alongside the rice and vegetables. Bring the remaining wine in the pan to the boil and spoon it over the chicken, rice and vegetables.

SAFFRON, FROM FIELD TO KITCHEN

The locals say you can never predict the day of the *manto,* when the saffron fields are blanketed in blooms. It could come as early as October 25 or as late as November 5. It depends on the weather, the autumn rains and the temperature. The picking begins from the time the first few saffron flowers (*Crocus sativus*) begin poking up through red dirt and continues daily for a week to ten days.

As it happens, this year the day of the manto falls on November 1, and at dawn a dense fog covers the low-lying saffron fields on the outskirts of the village of Campillo de Altobuey on the eastern edge of Cuenca province.

The pickers are already at work, men and women, young and not so young, ghostly figures in the grey mist. Bending from the waist, they move down the rows, plucking the tiny mauve-coloured crocuses and piling them in esparto baskets.

Beyond the saffron fields, the countryside stretches across the stubble of wheat and lentil fields, bent sunflower stalks and coppery leaves of vineyards. In the distance olive groves spread across the flanks of a low rise, not quite a hill.

'*Hay que madrugar mucho,*' says Antonio, the foreman on the picking operation. You have to get up really early to pick saffron.

The saffron flowers – they are called *rosas,* roses – must be picked early in the morning, when the petals are barely opened and still glossy. Once warmed by the sun, the flowers open and become limp, making the picking difficult because it's easy to break the flower and damage the stigmas. Besides, as the sun burns off the fog, bees start working the saffron fields. Paca, one of the pickers, reaches for a flower and gets stung by a bee. Within minutes, her arm starts swelling and she retires to take an antihistamine.

Done so close to the earth, picking crocuses is backbreaking work.

'It's an easy job to learn,' says María, 'but, I'll tell you, your back always hurts,'

The saffron from these fields belongs to a small family business, Bealar, which wins prizes for the quality of its saffron.

All morning long Antonio hauls crates filled with saffron crocuses to town in his little van. He delivers them to the *roseras,* the 'ladies of the rose', or *mondaderas,* the women who perform *mondeo,* extracting the three threads of the stigma from each crocus. The stigmas must be removed the same day that the flowers are picked or the flowers become pulpy and the precious stigmas are lost.

The stigmas, once dried, become the spice known as *saffron,* which imparts a bittersweet aroma – somewhat reminiscent of fresh hay – and glorious golden colour to foods with which it cooks. It takes the stigmas of approximately seventy thousand crocuses to make just 454 grams of spice.

The women sit in groups of six to eight around a table. Heaped in the centre are saffron flowers. Swiftly, deftly, the women open the petals of the crocus with the fingers of one hand and, with the other, pull out the three stigmas. They discard the purple flowers in a heap on the floor. The wisps of orange-red saffron stigmas slowly accumulate on plates. Each woman will be paid by the weight of saffron she has prepared. Vicenta holds the record, with 215 grams of saffron in a single day.

During the first few hours of the *mondeo,* the ladies chatter, joke, gossip and exchange recipes around the table. They argue about what to include in the *cocido,* the midday casserole. Amparo insists on beef bone, lean pork, pig's foot, salt pork, stewing hen, chorizo and morcilla sausages, chickpeas, plus potato, celery, leek, carrot, turnip, parsnip and cardoon. But Concha snorts that that was a 'garden without flowers'. She uses only beef and ham bone, chickpeas and potatoes. Many of the local women say they add a pinch of saffron to the caldo, the stock from the cocido, but only on very special occasions. Saffron is too highly valued for everyday flavouring.

Campillo is closer to Valencia than to Madrid, so paella is made here in the true Valencia manner, with rabbit, chicken, rosemary, snails, green beans, butter beans and, of course, saffron to colour the rice golden. In the old style, saffron was also added to lentil stew.

All agree that saffron is essential for *gallina en pepitoria,* chicken braised in an almond-saffron sauce. Sometimes embellished with dumplings, the dish is called *guiso de boda,* wedding stew.

After a couple of hours, the ladies fall silent. A transistor radio plays in the background. Their fingers are stained from the flowers and their feet are awash in the discarded blossoms. Antonio sweeps them into a crate to return to the fields for composting.

Once the wisps of saffron are separated from the flowers they must be toasted lightly to reduce their humidity and to fix their colour and aroma. Antonio spreads the saffron on trays to dry over electric heating elements.

Traditionally, saffron production was a small family enterprise, with each family planting no more than what its members could pick and process in a day – the morning in the fields, the afternoon at the mondeo, the night tending the braziers for the drying operation. The proceeds from saffron, called 'poor folks' gold', hidden beneath the linens at the bottom of a drawer (saffron-scented sheets are reputed to have aphrodisiac qualities), were a girl's dowry, a family's payment for a piece of land, a new tractor. In the old days, members of the extended family who helped with the picking and extracting were paid not in money but in quantities of the spice.

Saffron doesn't grow just anywhere. Since the Moors introduced its cultivation in the ninth century, saffron has found compatible terrain in very few places in La Mancha, where well-drained sandy soil or light clay provides ideal growing conditions. Supposedly, saffron bulbs planted twenty miles away do not flourish.

Bulbs are set out in the summer. They will produce flowers the second year. The third and fourth years are best. By the fifth year, production diminishes. Then the bulbs are lifted and the fields are planted in wheat or lentils (Campillo is famed for its lentils). The bulbs can be planted in new fields, but it takes fifteen to twenty years before they will flower again in the same plot.

The gathering and processing is seasonal work, so it has always been a sideline to farming. Unfortunately, nowadays young people are more likely to find steady jobs in a nearby factory manufacturing machine parts, or in computer technology, so are not available for the saffron harvest.

Spain was once the world's largest producer of saffron, but it has been surpassed in recent years by Iran, which is flooding the market with cheap saffron, some of which is falsely labelled as 'mancha quality'. To protect their reputation (and price), growers and packagers of authentic La Mancha saffron have set standards and labelling requirements. La Mancha saffron has the seal of the Denominación de Origen Azafrán de La Mancha. Every label is numbered and has a mauve saffron flower and a Quixote emblem to prove its authenticity.

The saffron of La Mancha is said to be the best in the world – with the most intense (and enduring) golden colour, the headiest aroma and the most complex taste. Some of these attributes can actually be quantified in a laboratory, but it is in the kitchen where the real gold shines.

WEDDING STEW *with* CHICKEN *and* MEATBALLS

Guiso de Bodas de Camacho

The most memorable meal in the story of Don Quixote is certainly that of the *bodas de Camacho*, the wedding feast of a rich man named Camacho (who doesn't, by the way, get the girl). Don Quixote and Sancho Panza encounter some fifty cooks at work preparing the meal. A whole young bull stuffed with a dozen suckling pigs is roasting on a huge spit. Lamb, hare and chickens are stewing in enormous earthenware ollas. Loaves of bread are piled into a mountain, and whole cheeses, stacked like bricks, form a wall. A treasure chest of spices is at hand. Cooks are frying sweet pastries in great cauldrons of oil, then dipping them into boiling honey syrup.

Sancho cannot contain himself. He begs permission to dip a crust of bread into one of the cook pots and is bidden to skim off what he likes – and take the ladle too! Happy, he scores three chickens and a couple of geese for breakfast.

This chicken stew, rich with ground almonds, might well have been stewing in the earthenware pot at that wedding feast. The addition of meatballs (or chicken balls) turns it into rather a grand version of chicken *pepitoria*, a favourite fiesta dish in Spain.

The meatballs can be prepared up to a day in advance, poached, then refrigerated. Reheat them in the stew during the last fifteen minutes of cooking. While chicken breast makes a delightfully light dumpling, veal, pork, or a combination can be used instead.

Steamed white rice makes the perfect accompaniment to this sensuous chicken dish with its 'gravy' perfumed with golden saffron and ground almonds.

SERVES 6, WITH 18 MEATBALLS

FOR THE MEATBALLS

5 tablespoons fresh flat-leaf parsley leaves

2 tablespoons chopped onion

25g fine fresh breadcrumbs

1 boneless, skinless chicken breast (340 to 400g), cut into 2½cm/1in pieces

1 egg, separated

⅛ teaspoon freshly grated nutmeg

⅛ teaspoon freshly ground black pepper

½ teaspoon salt

1½ tablespoons fresh lemon juice

1 litre/1½ pints chicken stock, home-made (page 94) or fresh stock from the supermarket or water

Use a food processor to finely chop the parsley. Add the onion, breadcrumbs, chicken breast and egg yolk. Process until the chicken is evenly chopped. Add the nutmeg, pepper, salt and 1 tablespoon of the lemon juice.

Beat the egg white on high speed in a small bowl until it holds stiff peaks. Beat in the remaining lemon juice. Fold the egg white thoroughly into the chopped chicken.

Dip your hands in water and lightly roll the mixture into walnut-sized balls.

Bring the stock to the boil. (The stock can be used in the chicken stew.) Reduce the heat to simmer and poach the meatballs for 4 minutes. They may not be completely cooked through but will finish cooking in the stew. Remove and reserve.

FOR THE CHICKEN STEW

1.2 to 1.4kg/2¾ to 3lbs chicken legs and thighs (about 8 pieces)

Salt and freshly ground black pepper

Flour for dredging

4 tablespoons olive oil

4 garlic cloves, peeled

1 cup blanched almonds

½ teaspoon saffron threads

250ml/scant ½ pint dry white wine

⅟₁₆ teaspoon ground cloves

1 tablespoon chopped fresh flat-leaf parsley, plus chopped parsley for garnish

300ml/½ pint chicken stock, homemade (page 94) or fresh stock from the supermarket

2 hard-boiled egg yolks

A few toasted almonds for garnish

Sprinkle the chicken pieces with salt and pepper and let them stand for 20 minutes. Then dredge them in flour, patting off the excess. Place on a tray.

Heat the oil in a large frying pan over medium heat. Add 2 of the garlic cloves and the almonds. Fry until golden, about 1 minute. Remove with a slotted spoon and reserve.

In the same oil, fry the chicken pieces over medium heat until nicely browned on all sides, 5 to 10 minutes. Transfer the pieces as they are browned to a large cazuela or deep sauté pan.

Crush the saffron in a mortar. Add 2 tablespoons hot water and let it steep for 15 minutes.

Place the fried garlic plus the remaining 2 cloves and the fried almonds in a blender with the wine. Blend until the almonds are smoothly puréed. Add the saffron infusion, cloves, ¼ teaspoon black pepper, parsley and 1 teaspoon salt. Add all but 4 tablespoons of the chicken stock.

Pour the sauce over the chicken pieces. Raise the heat until the sauce begins to bubble. Cover the casserole and cook very gently for 30 minutes.

Turn the chicken pieces and stir the sauce. Cover and cook until the chicken is very tender, about 30 minutes more.

When the chicken is tender, mash the hard-boiled egg yolks until smooth. Blend the remaining 4 tablespoons of the stock into the yolks. Stir into the stew. Add the cooked meatballs to the stew and cook for 15 minutes more.

Serve the stew in the cazuela, sprinkled with chopped parsley and a few toasted almonds.

CHICKEN BRAISED *in* SPICED VERJUICE

Pollo al Agraz

Where there are vineyards, there will be food cooked in the juice of the grape. Juice from unripe grapes, known as *verjuice*, adds tartness to this chicken dish, which is adapted from a renaissance recipe in *Carlos V a la mesa*, by L. Jacinto García, describing culinary trends in the 1500s.

If you have access to grapevines, try pressing your own verjuice from underripe grapes. The grapes should be juicy but very tart – two to four weeks before harvest. Use a food mill to crush grapes that have seeds (or a blender for seedless grapes). Strain the pulp, saving the juice and discarding pips and skins. Four parts of grapes will make approximately 1½ parts of verjuice.

Bottled verjuice can be purchased at speciality shops.

SERVES 6

1.8kg/4 lbs chicken pieces or 1 large chicken, cut up

Salt and freshly ground black pepper

1 tablespoon olive oil

85g diced pork belly (uncured pancetta)

100g chopped leek

¼ teaspoon saffron threads, crushed

1½ teaspoons ground ginger

1 teaspoon freshly grated nutmeg

¼ teaspoon ground cinnamon

¼ teaspoon ground coriander

Pinch of ground cloves

240ml verjuice

2 tablespoons fresh lemon juice

4 tablespoons chicken stock, home-made (page 94) or fresh stock from the supermarket or water

2 egg yolks

Sprinkle the chicken pieces with salt and pepper to taste and allow to stand for 30 minutes.

Heat the oil in a large frying pan or sauté pan over medium heat and fry the diced pork belly until the fat is rendered and the meat is browned. Skim out the pieces of pork and reserve.

Brown the chicken pieces in the fat over medium-high heat, about 5 minutes per side. Remove the chicken and reserve.

Pour off all but 1 tablespoon of the fat from the frying pan. Add the leek and sauté until softened, 3 minutes.

Combine the crushed saffron with 4 tablespoons of warm water and allow to steep for 15 minutes. In a small bowl, combine the ginger, nutmeg, cinnamon, coriander, cloves, ¼ teaspoon black pepper and ½ teaspoon salt.

Return the chicken and pork bits to the pan with the leek. Add 180ml/just over ¼ pint of the verjuice, lemon juice, the stock, saffron water and spices. Bring to the boil, then cover and simmer the chicken for 20 minutes. Turn the chicken pieces and cook until very tender, 20 to 30 minutes longer.

Beat the egg yolks in a bowl with the remaining verjuice. Stir into the chicken and cook without boiling, uncovered, until the sauce is slightly thickened, 10 minutes.

CHICKEN *with* WILD MUSHROOMS *and* POSSIBLY TRUFFLES

Pollo con Setas y Trufas cuando hayan

Pepe Expósito in Albacete makes gorgeous artisanal knives. The day I visited him in his workshop, he was packing a favourite, a bowie knife (he explained that this was originally a European knife that the English brought to the United States) of heavy steel with a horn handle. He told me he was going hunting – truffle hunting. From January to February he finds black truffles. In the spring, March to April, he hunts white ones. Pepe told me he brings back truffles ranging in size from a small nut to a fist. He finds them in 'determined places', near watercourses. One site is only minutes away from an industrial estate. Pepe says his wife does the cooking at his house, but when he brings home wild mushrooms or truffles, he prepares them. He cooks truffles very simply, *revueltos*, scrambled with eggs. Or, surprisingly, for forty seconds in the microwave with olive oil and salt.

This chicken recipe works beautifully with any wild mushroom and the addition of truffles, should you happen to find some.

SERVES 6

1 chicken, cut into serving pieces (1.6 to 1.8kg / 3½-4 lbs)	Freshly grated nutmeg
Salt and freshly ground black pepper	120ml / scant ¼ pint dry white wine
1 tablespoon olive oil	350ml / 12 fl oz chicken stock, homemade (page 94) or fresh stock from the supermarket or water
1 medium onion, chopped	450g mushrooms, such as portobello, shiitake, oyster
2 garlic cloves, chopped	Truffles as desired
4 tablespoons chopped fresh parsley, plus extra for garnish	3 tablespoons plain flour

Sprinkle the chicken pieces with salt and pepper to taste and let them stand for 30 minutes.

Heat the oil in a large sauté pan over medium heat and brown the chicken pieces on all sides, 5 to 10 minutes. Pour off most of the accumulated fat. Add the onion and garlic to the pan and sauté until lightly browned, 5 minutes.

Season the chicken with 4 tablespoons of chopped parsley, the nutmeg, wine, and ⅓ of the stock. Cover and cook until the chicken is fork-tender, 40 to 60 minutes.

Clean the mushrooms and truffles with a dampened cloth and trim. Slice big ones into quarters. Place them in a saucepan with the remaining stock. Bring to the boil and simmer, covered, for 10 minutes.

Toast the flour in a small dry frying pan over medium heat until nutty brown, about 2 minutes. Place the flour in a bowl and whisk in about 250ml/a scant ½ pint of the liquid from the chicken. Stir to blend thoroughly.

Add the flour mixture to the chicken with the mushrooms. Bring to the boil, stirring. Cook, uncovered, for 10 minutes.

Serve the chicken and mushrooms garnished with chopped parsley.

CHICKEN WINGS in ESCABECHE

Escabeche de Alitas de Pollo

Escabeche is an ancient way of preserving foods in a spiced vinegar marinade. During the hunting season, partridge, quail and wild rabbit would be roasted or boiled, packed in crocks, and pickled in escabeche to be kept during cold months. Partridge in escabeche is a tinned gourmet product. Escabeche gives a new lease of life to leftover roast turkey and turns ordinary chicken wings into something a little different. These are not a true conserve, so keep them refrigerated and use within two or three days.

Serve the chicken wings at room temperature or reheated. Place on a bed of salad leaves and garnish with cherry tomatoes and sliced eggs. To serve as finger food, reheat the wings to liquefy the sauce and skim them out of the liquid. If desired, wrap the ends in foil and serve with paper napkins, as wings are a bit messy. They can also be used in the recipe for Salad of Pickled Partridge or Chicken (page 43).

Dusting the wings with flour before frying keeps them from splattering in the hot oil and allows them to brown nicely. If you're using leftover roast turkey, simply add it to the marinade and bring to the boil. It does not need to cook further.

MAKES 24 PIECES, SERVING 12 AS A TAPA, 6 AS A SALAD, OR 4 AS A MAIN COURSE

12 chicken wings, tips discarded and wings separated at the joint (2 to 2.2kg/4½-5 lbs)

Flour for dredging

120ml/scant ¼ pint olive oil

1 medium onion, halved and sliced

1 carrot, halved lengthways and sliced

1 leek, white part only, sliced crossways

2 garlic cloves, quartered lengthways

1 small dried red chilli or chilli flakes to taste

2 bay leaves

2 teaspoons dried oregano

2 teaspoons sweet pimentón

1 tablespoon salt

3 cloves

¼ teaspoon black peppercorns

3 slices orange

240ml/scant ½ pint dry white wine

240ml/scant ½ pint white wine vinegar

Dredge the wing pieces in flour and pat off the excess. Heat the oil in a deep frying pan over medium heat. Fry the wings in 2 batches until browned on all sides, about 4 minutes. Remove.

Skim off 1 tablespoon of the oil and place in a clean pan. Add the sliced onion, carrot, leek, garlic, chilli, bay leaves, oregano, pimentón, salt, cloves, peppercorns and orange slices. Place the wings on top. Pour on the wine, vinegar and 600ml/1 pint of water. Bring to the boil, then reduce the heat and simmer, covered, until the wings are tender but not falling off the bone, about 30 minutes.

Remove the pan from the heat and allow the wings to cool in the cooking liquid. Place the wings and liquid in a nonreactive bowl or jar, cover tightly and refrigerate for at least 24 and up to 48 hours.

Serve at room temperature or warmed.

CHICKEN with PINTO BEANS and PASTA RAGS

Pollo con Andrajos

In the villages of the rugged sierra in the south of Albacete province, this dish is prepared with wild hare. I've substituted chicken thighs. The 'rags' are made from a simple flour and water paste, rolled out thinly and cut or torn into irregular pieces. Won ton wrappers, cut into strips, could be used instead of the pasta.

SERVES 4

200g plain flour, plus flour for rolling out the dough

Salt

6 tablespoons hot-to-the-touch water (about 43°C)

700g / 1½ lbs boneless, skinless chicken thighs

Freshly ground black pepper

3 tablespoons olive oil

1 medium onion, chopped

40g chopped green pepper

2 garlic cloves, chopped

1 tablespoon sweet pimentón

280g peeled, seeded and chopped tomato

Chilli flakes

Dash of ground cloves

1 bay leaf

470ml / ¾ pint chicken stock, homemade (page 94) or fresh stock from the supermarket or water

420g drained cooked pinto beans (one tin)

Chopped fresh mint for garnish

Combine the flour and salt in a mixing bowl. Make a well in the centre and pour in the hot water. Stir the flour into the water to make a soft dough. Turn out on a board and knead until smooth and satiny, 5 minutes. Add only enough flour to prevent the dough from sticking to the board. Gather the dough into a ball, cover with a clean towel and leave to rest at room temperature for 30 minutes.

If the chicken thighs are large, cut them in half. Sprinkle with salt and pepper.

Heat the oil in a deep sauté pan or cazuela over medium-high heat. Sauté the chicken pieces until lightly coloured, about 1 minute per side. Remove them from the pan. Add the onion and green pepper and sauté over fairly high heat for 3 minutes. Add the garlic and sauté until the onion begins to brown, 2 minutes more.

Remove the pan from the heat and stir in the pimentón. Add the tomato, return to fairly high heat and cook for 5 minutes more. Add the chilli flakes, cloves, bay leaf and stock. Add salt if needed. Return the chicken to the pan with any accumulated juices. Simmer, covered, until the chicken is tender, 30 to 45 minutes.

While the chicken is cooking, roll out the pasta dough very thinly (1½ mm/⅟₁₆in). Use a knife to cut it into strips about 2cm/¾in wide. Cut the strips into 7cm/3in lengths. Line a baking sheet with nonstick baking parchment. Lift the strips of pasta dough off the board and place them in a single layer on the parchment.

When the chicken is cooked, uncover the pan and raise the heat so the liquid bubbles. Add the pasta gradually, stirring it into the liquid. Cook for 5 minutes.

Add the beans and cook for 5 minutes more. Allow to stand for 10 minutes before serving. Serve in deep bowls garnished with chopped mint.

ROAST CHICKEN STUFFED *with* LIVER *and* SPRING HERBS

Pollo Asado Relleno con Hierbas

The stuffing is like a herby, chicken-liver terrine that cooks inside the chicken. Use your favourite herbs in this poultry stuffing. I like thyme, mint, celery leaves and a little fennel. But rosemary, oregano, basil and tarragon also make a good combination. If possible, choose a free-range or organic chicken for this dish.

SERVES 6, INCLUDING 700ML/ABOUT ¼ PINT STUFFING

FOR THE STUFFING

1 tablespoon olive oil

225g/½ lb chicken livers, chopped

4 tablespoons chopped onion

50g fresh breadcrumbs

1 tablespoon raisins

60g chopped fresh flat-leaf parsley

2 to 4 tablespoons chopped fresh herbs or 1 to 2 tablespoons dried

1 teaspoon salt

¼ teaspoon grated lemon zest

Freshly ground black pepper

4 tablespoons chicken stock home-made (page 94) or fresh stock from the supermarket or dry white wine

Heat the oil in a frying pan over medium-high heat and sauté the chopped chicken livers and onion until the livers lose their pink colour, about 3 minutes.

Combine the breadcrumbs, raisins, parsley, herbs, salt, lemon zest, pepper to taste, chicken stock and sautéed livers and onion.

FOR THE CHICKEN

1 roasting chicken, 1.6 to 2 kg/ 3½ to 4½ lbs

Salt and freshly ground black pepper

3 slices salt pork or bacon

50g chopped leek

½ medium onion, chopped

2 bay leaves

1 fresh rosemary sprig

120ml/scant ¼ pint dry white wine

350ml/12 fl oz chicken stock, home-made (page 94) or fresh stock from the supermarket

Preheat the oven to 190°C/170°C fan/GM5.

Rub the chicken inside and out with salt and pepper. Let stand at room temperature for 1 hour. Stuff the chicken with the herb and liver stuffing. Use poultry skewers and kitchen twine to close the cavity. Cover the chicken breast with salt pork or bacon.

Place the leek and onion in a roasting pan with the bay leaves and rosemary. Place the chicken on top.

Roast the stuffed chicken for 20 minutes.

Reduce the oven temperature to 160°C/140°C fan/GM3. Pour the wine and chicken stock over the chicken. Continue roasting the chicken, basting frequently. The chicken is done when an instant-read thermometer inserted in the thigh registers 74°C, 60 to 90 minutes. Transfer to a serving platter and allow to stand for 15 minutes before carving.

Skim the fat from the drippings in the roasting pan. Strain the drippings, pressing on the solids. Discard the solids. Serve the sauce with the chicken and stuffing.

COUNTRY CHICKEN CASSEROLE *with* RICE

Cazuela de Pollo con Arroz a la Campesina

Serve this for an informal supper. Everything cooks in one pan, so it's an easy dish for entertaining. Not everyone has a cazuela large enough to hold all the ingredients, so I suggest making it in a casserole pot or extra-large sauté pan.

I use a large chicken, cut into joints (legs, thighs, wings and breasts split into 4 pieces), for this tasty chicken and rice dish. I separate the bony backs and use them to make a light stock that adds flavour to the rice. But you could use legs and thighs or legs and breasts and substitute shop-bought stock.

Use Spanish round-grain paella rice for this recipe. If you can get it, the Bomba variety is best, because it does not 'flower' when cooked with lots of liquid. If Spanish rice is not available, use Arborio rice.

SERVES **8**

1.4kg/3 lbs chicken pieces

Salt and freshly ground black pepper

3 tablespoons olive oil

3 garlic cloves

1 bay leaf

75g chopped green pepper

1 medium onion, chopped

175g peeled and chopped tomato

125g fresh or frozen peas

140g fresh or frozen shelled broad beans

140g fresh or frozen green beans, preferably romano or runner beans, cut into short lengths

1.2 litres/2 pints chicken stock, home-made (page 94) or fresh stock from the supermarket

¼ teaspoon saffron threads

10 peppercorns

2 cloves

⅛ teaspoon cumin seeds

1 teaspoon sweet pimentón

Pinch of cayenne

140g peeled diced potato

380g Spanish round-grain rice

Sprinkle the chicken pieces with salt and pepper and allow to stand for 30 minutes.

Heat the oil in a very large cazuela or casserole over medium-high heat. Fry 2 of the garlic cloves and the bay leaf until the garlic is golden and the bay leaf crisped, about 50 seconds. Skim them out and reserve.

Brown the chicken pieces in the same oil, turning to brown all sides, 8 to 10 minutes. (Use high heat for an earthenware cazuela, medium heat for a casserole pot or sauté pan.) Remove the chicken as it is browned.

Sauté the green pepper and onion for 3 minutes. Add the tomato and sauté over high heat for 2 minutes. If you're using fresh peas, broad beans and green beans, add them now. Add 250ml/scant ½ pint of the stock and 1 teaspoon salt. Return the chicken pieces to the pan. Bring to the boil, then reduce the heat so the liquid bubbles gently. Cover the pan and cook for 8 minutes.

In a mortar, crush the saffron to a powder. Put the peppercorns, cloves and cumin seeds in the mortar and grind them coarsely. Add the fried garlic, remaining garlic clove and reserved bay leaf and mash to a paste. Add the pimentón and cayenne. Mix with 4 tablespoons water.

Stir the spice mixture into the chicken. Add the potato. Cover and cook for 5 minutes more. Add the remaining 1 litre/1½ pints of stock. Bring to the boil and stir in the rice. (If you're using frozen peas, broad beans and green beans, add them now.) Taste for salt and add more if necessary. Reduce the heat so the liquid bubbles gently. Cover the pan and cook for 15 minutes, stirring only once during this time.

Remove the pan from the heat and let stand for 10 minutes before serving.

DUCK BRAISED in RED WINE

Pato al Vino Tinto

La Mancha is a region of surprises. You expect the flatness – and much of it is flat – and the arid landscape. Yet areas of steep hills, rocky mountains and canyons astonish the traveller. Even more surprising, perhaps, are vast wetlands, where marshes shelter waterfowl of many sorts.

Such is Tablas de Daimiel, a national park in the province of Ciudad Real, where two rivers, the Cigüela and Guadiana, encountering terrain so flat they have nowhere to flow, spread out into marshlands. Today it is protected, with paths and hides for birdwatching. But in former times the wetlands were a rich source of food for those who lived in the region. Crayfish, carp, wild dove and wild duck (mallard) were free for the taking.

Wild duck is not appreciated for its flavour. Feeding on fish and crustaceans, it acquires a 'fishy' flavour. From that derives the custom of cooking it with assertive flavours, such as sour oranges, tangy olives or strong wine and brandy. This recipe, adapted for farm-raised duck, such as Pekin, derives from a traditional one.

I start out with whole ducks and cut them up, using the legs for a slow braise, the breasts for a fast sauté to be served rare, and the rest of the carcass to make a deep-flavoured stock to add substance to the sauce. (You will not need all of the stock for the sauce. Use it to embellish duck and rice paella.) If you don't want to bother with the duck stock, substitute Simple Chicken Stock (page 94).

However, if you prefer, use whole ducks, simply quartered, or cut-up legs and breasts.

Duck is fatty, so, happily, it doesn't dry out in reheating. If you make this dish a day in advance, you can skim off all the fat that rises to the surface before finishing the sauce, which is thickened with the puréed carrots, onions and leeks. Red wine makes a sauce that's not quite brown, so leave some of the chopped vegetables unpuréed to give the sauce a little colour.

I choose one of the 'new style' La Mancha wines, made with a *coupage* (blend) of traditional Tempranillo grape, plus Cabernet Sauvignon and Syrah, for both cooking and serving with this duck dish.

Spanish polenta (page 279) makes a good side dish. Quince jelly, *membrillo*, is a classic accompaniment.

FOR THE DUCK STOCK

3 farm-raised ducks, each about 2kg/4½ lbs

2 sticks of celery

1 orange, quartered

1 onion, quartered

1 teaspoon salt

2 cloves

8 peppercorns

1 bay leaf

1 fresh rosemary sprig

6 parsley stems

Remove the legs (thigh and drumstick in one piece) of the ducks. Use a sharp boning knife to remove each breast half, keeping the skin intact. Split the remaining carcasses in half. Set aside the duck pieces and put the carcasses in a large, deep sucepan. Add the celery, orange, onion, salt, cloves, peppercorns, bay leaf, rosemary, parsley and 2.3 litres/4 pints of water. Bring to the boil, cover and simmer for 2 hours.

Strain the stock, discarding all the solids. You should have about 2 litres/3½ pints of stock. Cool, then refrigerate for at least 6 hours. When chilled, skim off and discard the fat that congeals on top. Set aside 470ml/¾ pint for this recipe and refrigerate or freeze the rest. It will last for 2 to 3 days in the refrigerator, 8 weeks in the freezer.

FOR THE BRAISED DUCK

1 tablespoon olive oil

375g chopped onion

3 carrots, halved lengthwise and sliced

145g chopped leek

¼ teaspoon dried thyme

Pinch of ground cloves

1 stick of celery

2 strips orange zest

4 tablespoons brandy

470ml/¾ pint full-bodied red wine

1 tablespoon honey

Prick the skin of the duck legs all over with a skewer or sharp-tined fork. Use a small sharp knife to score the skin of the breasts.

Heat the oil in a heavy frying pan over medium heat. Brown the legs on both sides, a few at a time, and remove. Put the pieces of breast in the pan, skin side down, and cook over medium heat until the fat is rendered and the skin crisped, 8 minutes. Turn and brown the flesh side, 2 minutes. Remove and reserve.

Pour off and discard all but 1 tablespoon of the fat from the frying pan. Add the onion, carrots and leek and sauté over medium heat until the onion begins to brown, 8 minutes.

Place the duck legs in a large saucepan or flameproof casserole. Add the contents of the frying pan to the duck. Add the thyme, cloves, celery and orange zest. Pour on the brandy, wine and 470ml/¾ pint of the duck stock. Bring to the boil, then cover and simmer for 40 minutes. Turn the duck legs and simmer until tender, 30 minutes longer.

Add the reserved breasts to the casserole and cook for 10 minutes longer.

Remove all the pieces of duck from the casserole and set aside (or refrigerate). Discard the celery and orange zest. Allow the liquid to stand for at least 1 hour, then skim off all the fat that rises to the top. (Or refrigerate for at least 6 hours and remove the fat once it has congealed.)

Purée all but 300ml/½ pint of the liquid in a blender. Return the purée to the casserole with the half-pint of unpuréed stock and vegetables. Stir in the honey. Heat the sauce. Return all of the duck to the casserole and heat it in the sauce.

PARTRIDGE, START TO FINISH

In early February winter spreads across the highlands of the Montes de Toledo, in western Castilla–La Mancha. It is the last day of the open season for hunting partridge. At a hunting lodge on a large country estate not too distant from the little town of Los Yébenes, a centre for hunting of both large and small game, a group of hunters gathers over steaming coffee to draw lots for the *puestos,* hides, that they will occupy on the hunt. Some of the hunters come from abroad and are staying at the manor house, whose twin spires are visible through the branches of bare trees. Others, like Teodoro, a well-to-do businessman, have driven down from Toledo, bringing dogs and guns.

The hunters (a few women among them) move out in 4WDs, bumping along rutted dirt tracks and fording a small stream. Leaving the vehicles, they hike cross-country to the first shooting site. Sun breaks through the cloud cover, glinting on flat outcroppings of shiny granite. The rough terrain is dotted with thickets of chaparral and carved by ravines. Waking boots release the powerful scents of wild thyme, marjoram and red lavender.

Teodoro, dressed in cropped trousers with gaiters and loden green jacket, is flanked by a loader, who will keep his guns ready to fire, and a *secretario*, who spots the downed birds and later recovers them. Some friends of Teodoro and an observer also occupy his hide. They must stay crouched on a tarpaulin on the ground because, as the hunter swings around to shoot, raised heads are in danger. Teodoro tethers his one-year-old Labrador-cross retriever, Popi, to a stake.

The hunters with their entourages spread along the ridge, taking up ten hides. The *ojeadores,* beaters, announce the start of the hunt with a blast on a conch shell. They move along the ravine's embankment, thrashing the bushes, banging, and yelling *'Vamos, vamos'* (Let's move, come on, let's go).

The first shots ring out, but it is too distant to see the birds fall. The beaters continue towards Teodoro's position, flushing birds before them. Suddenly, with a rush of wings, a covey of partridge lofts skyward. They seem to scatter in the air, some soaring high, others dipping towards the next ridge. Teodoro shoots in rapid succession. One bird falls very near the hide, causing Popi to snap to attention.

When the beaters reach the end of the drive, they signal the end of the shoot with a horn, and everyone scrambles to find the downed birds. Popi excitedly works the hillside, retrieving partridge one after another to Teodoro. The *secretario* strings them on leather thongs and hitches them to his belt. The whole hunting party treks overland to another drive. A light snow is falling.

At the end of the second shoot (typically there are four or five drives in a day of hunting) the *secretarios* spread all the birds taken in a clearing on the ground, arranging them in braces. There are 126 partridge. Teodoro, the best shot, claims 28. Some he will take home with him. He says his mother prepares them *en conserva,* packed in jars in a mild *escabeche.*

Behind the hunters comes the *pollero,* poultryman. He buys the birds from the organiser of the hunt and takes them to a processing plant, where they are cleaned and plucked, ready for sale to restaurants and speciality meat shops.

A day later, in the restaurant kitchen at Casa Apelio in Los Yébenes, three women are processing six hundred partridge from several different shoots. The birds are singed, one by one, over a gas flame, then chilled and packed for freezing. According to Apelio García, the third generation to run Casa Apelio, his restaurant is one of the few in Spain that serves wild native red partridge. (Most buy farm-raised birds.) His aunt Valentina prepares them in a salad, stewed with beans and braised in an onion-wine sauce.

In the restaurant a roaring fire in the hearth warms the dining room, which is hung with deer heads and racks of antlers (Los Yébenes has four working taxidermists). Caged partridges (they are used for hunting *al reclamo*, with decoys) cackle and call from a shelf on one side of the dining room.

To start, there is partridge pâté with toast. The creamy pâté, produced in Los Yébenes by Taller Gastronómico, comes from a tin. The partridge salad features tender boned partridge in a mild escabeche heaped on top of sliced tomatoes, sprinkled with oregano and generously dribbled with the local extra virgin olive oil with denomination Montes de Toledo. The beans, nicely flavoured with garlic and pimentón, stretch one partridge into two or more servings. Partridge braised in a winey onion sauce, a Toledo classic, calls for a smooth *reserva* La Mancha red wine.

Partridge, start to finish.

BRAISED PARTRIDGE, TOLEDO STYLE

Perdiz Estofada a la Toledana

Autumn brings the opening of the season for game birds. This manner of preparing partridge, braised with lots of onions, is traditional in the Montes de Toledo, the mountainous region in the south part of Toledo province. If partridge is not available, try the dish with plump little poussin. Tucking sprigs of thyme and rosemary in the bird's cavity adds a 'wild' taste. The partridge go nicely with pan-sautéed cabbage (page 253) and, of course, a red *reserva,* aged wine, from one of the many wineries in Toledo province.

SERVES 4

4 partridge, small chickens, or poussin (350 to 500g / 12 to 18 oz each)

Salt and freshly ground black pepper

4 fresh rosemary sprigs (optional)

4 tablespoons olive oil

2 onions, halved and sliced

1 carrot, diced

40g diced serrano ham (optional)

6 garlic cloves, chopped

2 tablespoons chopped fresh parsley

½ teaspoon dried thyme

2 bay leaves

1 tablespoon brandy (optional)

350ml / 12 fl oz dry white wine

Sprinkle the birds inside and out with salt and pepper. If desired, tuck a small sprig of rosemary in the cavity of each. Tie the birds with kitchen twine to keep legs and wings close to the bodies. Allow them to stand for 30 minutes at room temperature.

Heat the oil in a deep sauté pan or cazuela over medium-high heat. Brown the partridge on all sides, 10 minutes. Remove them.

Add the onions and carrot to the remaining oil. Sauté over medium-high heat until the onions begin to brown, 10 minutes. Add the ham, if you're using it, and the garlic. Place the partridge on top of the onions. Sprinkle with the parsley and thyme. Tuck the bay leaves between the birds.

Pour on the brandy, if you're using it, and the wine. Bring to the boil, cover and reduce the heat so the liquid just simmers. Cook the partridge for 25 minutes, then turn them and cook, covered, until very tender, 35 to 45 minutes longer.

Transfer the partridge to a platter. Cook the onions and liquid left in the pan, uncovered, until slightly reduced. Discard the bay leaves and remove the strings from the partridge. Serve with the onion sauce.

PARTRIDGE *with* BEANS

Judías con Perdiz

Y vivieron felices, comieron perdices y a mí no me dieron. And they ate partridge and lived happily ever after. Thus ends many a Spanish fairy tale.

In this dish, beans stretch the servings of partridge, so a single bird, split in half, might serve two. (If you choose to serve half a partridge, split the birds after cooking.) If partridge is not available, use poussin, or turkey thighs. I prefer to cook the beans separately from the partridge, as beans can take well over an hour to cook. You could use tinned cannellini beans (two 420g cans). If you're using dried beans, soak them for at least 6 hours before cooking.

SERVES 4

340g dried cannellini beans, soaked for 6 to 24 hours

1 head of garlic

2 bay leaves

1 fresh rosemary sprig

¼ onion

1 fresh or 2 sun-dried tomatoes

2 teaspoons salt, plus salt for the partridge

2 to 4 partridges, about 350g each

Freshly ground black pepper

4 tablespoons olive oil

250g chopped onion

2 garlic cloves, chopped

1 teaspoon sweet pimentón

2 tablespoons wine vinegar

250ml/scant ½ pint dry white wine

10 peppercorns

Drain the beans and place them in a large saucepan with water to cover. Bring to the boil and skim off the froth.

Slice the top off the head of garlic and place the whole head in the pan with the beans. Add the bay leaves, rosemary, onion, tomato and 1 teaspoon of the salt. Cover and simmer the beans for 30 minutes. Add 150ml/¼ pint of cold water, bring again to the boil, and simmer until the beans are very tender, 30 to 60 minutes more.

Meanwhile, sprinkle the partridge with salt and pepper. Heat the oil in a large cazuela or deep fying pan over low heat. Brown the partridge very slowly, about 10 minutes on the first side. Turn them, then add the chopped onion and garlic. Continue sautéing until the partridge and onions are golden, about 10 minutes.

In a small bowl, mix the pimentón with the vinegar. Add to the partridge with the wine and 250ml/scant ½ pint of water. Add the peppercorns and remaining teaspoon of salt. Cook at a gentle bubble for 30 minutes. Turn the partridge and simmer for 30 minutes more.

Drain the beans, reserving the liquid. Discard the bay leaves and rosemary. Add the beans to the cazuela with the partridge. Slip the skin from the tomato and break it up into the cazuela. Squeeze the cloves of garlic into the partridge. Add 470ml/¾ pint of the bean liquid. Simmer all together for 30 minutes and serve.

SQUABS STUFFED *with* RAISINS, APRICOTS, and WALNUTS

Pichones Rellenos

Once every farmyard had a dovecote. Besides providing an excellent source of guano fertiliser, it yielded tender young squabs (pigeons) for the pot. This squab, stuffed with dried fruit and nuts, is elegant enough for a special dinner party. If squabs are not attainable, substitute poussin.

SERVES 6

35g seedless raisins

85g chopped dried apricots

120ml/scant ¼ pint medium-dry Sherry, such as amontillado or oloroso seco

3 tablespoons olive oil

65g chopped shallot

40g diced serrano ham or bacon

50g fresh breadcrumbs

35g coarsely chopped walnuts

4 tablespoons chopped fresh parsley

Salt and freshly ground black pepper

Pinch of dried thyme

6 squabs or poussin, each about 290g/10 oz

120ml/scant ¼ pint dry white wine

250ml/scant ½ pint chicken stock, home-made (page 94) or fresh stock from the supermarket

3 tablespoons cream

To make the stuffing, combine the raisins and apricots in a mixing bowl and add 3 tablespoons of the Sherry. Allow to macerate for 30 minutes.

Heat 1 tablespoon of the oil in a small frying pan over low heat and sauté half of the shallot until softened, 5 minutes. Add the diced ham and sauté for 1 minute.

Add the sautéed shallot and ham to the raisins and apricots. Add the breadcrumbs, walnuts, parsley, ¼ teaspoon of salt, pepper to taste and the thyme. Combine well.

Clean out the cavities of the squabs. Rinse and pat them dry. Fill the cavities with the stuffing mixture. Skewer the openings closed. Tie the legs together with kitchen string.

Heat the remaining 2 tablespoons oil in a large frying pan over medium heat. Slowly brown the squabs on all sides, 8 to 10 minutes. (Brown them in 2 batches if necessary.) Remove when browned and place in a shallow roasting tin just large enough to hold them.

Preheat the oven to 190°C/170°C fan/GM5.

Pour the white wine over the squabs and place them in the oven, uncovered, until they reach an internal temperature of 71°C, 30 to 40 minutes.

While the squabs are roasting, add the remaining shallot to the oil remaining in the large frying pan and sauté for 3 minutes. Add the stock and remaining Sherry. Bring to the boil, then simmer for 10 minutes.

When the squabs are roasted, transfer them to a serving platter. Remove the skewers and twine. Tent the squabs with foil and keep them warm. Add 4 tablespoons of water to the roasting tin and scrape up any drippings. Add to the frying pan with the stock and Sherry. Bring to the boil, reduce the heat and add the cream. Cook gently for 3 minutes.

Serve the squabs accompanied by the sauce.

. . . y algún palomino de añadidura los domingos . . .

. . . and on Sundays, the addition of some squab
for good measure . . .

WHAT DON QUIXOTE HAD FOR DINNER

QUAIL in 'SLIPCOVERS' of RED PEPPERS

Codornices con Fundas

Red peppers flavour the quail and keep them moist. A sausage stuffing bastes them from the inside out. A single quail does not a dinner make, so serve this as a starter or light supper dish. If you cannot get morcilla sausage, add a spoonful of pimentón and a pinch of ground cloves and cinnamon to the black pudding or pork sausage.

SERVES 6

6 quail, about 170g/6oz each

Coarse salt

2 tablespoons plus 1 teaspoon olive oil

35g finely chopped shallot or onion

170g morcilla, black pudding or pork sausage, casing removed and sausage chopped

50g fresh breadcrumbs

6 large red peppers

120ml/scant ¼ pint dry white wine

250ml/scant ½ pint boiling water

Rinse the quail in running water. Drain and pat them dry. Sprinkle with salt to taste.

Heat 1 teaspoon of the oil in a small frying pan over medium heat and sauté the shallot until softened, 1 minute. Add the chopped morcilla and fry for 3 minutes, breaking up the pieces of sausage with a wooden spatula.

Remove the pan from the heat and stir in the breadcrumbs. Stuff the quail with the sausage-crumb mixture, using about 4 tablespoons for each quail.

Heat the remaining 2 tablespoons oil in a frying pan over medium heat and brown the quail on all sides, about 3 minutes. Remove and reserve.

Preheat the oven to 190°C/170°C fan/GM5.

Cut off the tops of the peppers. Scoop out and discard the seeds and membranes.

Working with one quail at a time, tuck the legs against the body and insert each quail, legs first, into a pepper. Place in a baking dish.

Pour the wine and boiling water over the quail-stuffed peppers. Bake them, uncovered, until the peppers are completely softened and the quail tender, about 1½ hours. If the pan liquid cooks away, add 150ml/¼ pint boiling water.

Allow the peppers to stand for 15 minutes. If desired, peel the peppers. Serve them hot, with the pan juices spooned over them.

HUNTERS' RICE *with* RABBIT

Arroz al Cazador

When is a paella not a paella? When it's cooked in a *perol,* a deep two-handled frying pan with flared sides, instead of in a shallow paella pan. A flat-bottomed wok makes a perfect perol. Hunters in the field cook the rice and wild rabbit over a campfire. As farm-raised rabbit from the butcher's shop is more likely to be available, I suggest adding mountain herbs for a subtle 'wild' flavour. A hunter's version might include wild asparagus and wild cardoons or artichokes. In this recipe I have used cultivated asparagus and artichokes.

Rabbit is naturally very lean, so it profits from cooking with juicy chorizo sausage. If not available, you could use pork sausage plus a heaped teaspoon of pimentón. A tender, young farm-raised rabbit will cook in the time the rice cooks, but, should you have wild rabbit or a substantially larger rabbit, you will need to simmer it for 15 to 20 minutes in the liquid before adding the rice.

Please resist the urge to stir the rice! Once rice and pieces of rabbit are distributed in the pan, let them cook undisturbed. Stirring breaks up the rice grains and makes them sticky. It is permissible, though, to shake the pan to keep the contents from sticking to the bottom.

Trim the artichokes immediately before adding them to the frying pan so they don't darken. They do not need to be rubbed with lemon.

✺ SERVES 5 TO 6

1 rabbit (roughly 1kg/ 2½lbs), cut into 6 pieces	¼ teaspoon saffron threads
Salt and freshly ground black pepper	6 peppercorns
4 tablespoons olive oil	4 baby artichokes or 1 medium artichoke
75g chopped green pepper	230g thin spears of green asparagus, chopped
6 garlic cloves, chopped	2 bay leaves
2 Spanish chorizo links (140g), preferably soft, casing removed and sausage chopped	1 fresh rosemary sprig
	1 fresh thyme sprig
175g chopped tomato	380g Spanish round-grain rice

Sprinkle the pieces of rabbit generously with salt and pepper and allow to come to room temperature, 1 hour.

Heat the oil in a deep casserole or sauté pan over medium heat and brown the rabbit, turning the pieces to brown lightly on both sides, about 8 minutes. Remove the rabbit.

Add the green pepper, garlic and chorizo to the pan and sauté for 3 minutes. Raise the heat and add the tomato. Fry for 3 minutes more.

Crush the saffron in a mortar with the peppercorns. Stir in 4 tablespoons of water and allow to infuse.

Snap off the outer leaves of the artichokes and trim away the top two-thirds of the leaves. Cut baby artichokes in half; cut a medium artichoke into eighths. Add the artichoke to the pan with the asparagus, bay leaves, rosemary and thyme. Add 1 litre/1½ pints of water and bring to the boil. Return the rabbit to the pan. Add 1 teaspoon salt and the saffron-pepper water. Stir in the rice.

Cook over fairly high heat for 10 minutes. Reduce the heat to medium-low and cook until the rice is al dente, 8 to 10 minutes longer. Cover the pan with a lid or foil and allow to rest for 10 minutes before serving. If convenient, remove the bay leaves and rosemary and thyme sprigs before serving.

RABBIT with FIGS and MUDÉJAR SPICES

Conejo con Higos al Estilo Mudéjar

Toledo, evocative and a little mysterious, sits on a hill over the River Tajo (Tagus). Still enclosed by ancient walls and monumental gates, the old town of narrow cobbled streets preserves much of its mediaeval character. Inhabited over the centuries by Romans (the ruins of a Roman circus, one of the largest of the empire, lies just outside the walls), Visigoths (at least one church originally was Visigothic), Sephardic Jews (two synagogues remain in the old Jewish quarter), Arabs and Berbers (a tenth-century mosque is preserved), and Christians, who built an astonishing cathedral and dozens of convents and monasteries, Toledo is at once monumental and intimate.

The Muslim Moors took Toledo in 712. When King Alfonso VI wrested control of the city from them in 1085, many of the Moors opted to stay under Christian dominion. Called *Mudéjars* – meaning 'permitted to remain' – they had an enormous influence on architecture, building churches, synagogues and civic buildings in the graceful Mudéjar style, with its low towers, horseshoe arches, plaster, tile and wood decorations. The Toledo School of Translators flourished, bringing together Arab, Hebrew and Latin scholars who translated Greek philosophy, Persian literature and Arabic medicine into Latin and Spanish.

The Mudéjar influence permeated the style of cooking as well, bringing exotic spices from Eastern lands into Spanish cooking. This rabbit dish, subtly sweet and sour, perfumed with cinnamon, clove, anise and saffron, is a delicious example. If rabbit is not an option, make it with bone-in chicken breasts.

Serve the rabbit with rice or couscous and Minted Carrots (page 256). A Syrah wine from Dominio de Valdepusa would complement the spices in the rabbit dish.

4 tablespoons honey (preferably rosemary honey)

4 tablespoons Sherry vinegar (if unavailable, use Sherry or red wine vinegar)

One 2.5cm/1in piece fresh ginger, cut in half

5 peppercorns

5 coriander seeds

¼ teaspoon mustard seeds

⅛ teaspoon aniseeds

One 2.5cm/1in cinnamon stick

1 clove

12 dried figs, stems removed

⅛ teaspoon saffron threads, crushed

4 tablespoons olive oil

4 tablespoons blanched almonds

3 garlic cloves, peeled

1 rabbit, about 1kg/2 to 2½lbs, cut into 8 pieces

½ medium onion, chopped

120ml/scant ¼ pint dry white wine

Salt and freshly ground black pepper

Combine the honey, vinegar, ginger, peppercorns, coriander, mustard seeds, aniseeds, cinnamon and clove in a saucepan with 350ml/12 fl oz of water. Bring to the boil, then simmer for 5 minutes. Remove from the heat and add the figs. Cover and let them macerate for at least 2 and up to 24 hours.

Add 4 tablespoons of warm water to the saffron and let it steep for at least 15 minutes.

Heat the oil in a cazuela or sauté pan over medium heat, and fry the almonds and garlic until light golden, about 1 minute. Skim them out and reserve.

Add the rabbit pieces to the hot oil and sauté over medium heat until lightly browned on all sides, about 8 minutes. Add the chopped onion and continue sautéing.

Put the fried almonds and garlic in a blender with the wine and process to make a smooth paste.

With a slotted spoon, remove the figs from the spiced liquid and reserve them. (Don't worry if some spices cling to the figs.) Strain the liquid and reserve it. Discard the spices. Add the liquid to the rabbit with the saffron. Stir in the almond paste. Season with salt and pepper to taste. Cover and simmer for 30 minutes. Add the figs to the rabbit and cook until the rabbit is tender, another 15 to 20 minutes.

HUNTER'S STEW *with* HARE

Liebre a la Cazadora

While rabbit is 'white meat', hare is definitely red meat. Wild mushrooms, thyme and brandy add to the 'wild' flavour. You could make this recipe with beef stewing steak, increasing the cooking time to 2½ hours.

Serve the braised hare with noodles and a side of Chard Sauté (page 251). Accompany with a red *reserva* wine from Valdepeñas.

SERVES 4

1 hare, 1 to 1.5kg/2½ to 3 lbs, cut into 6 to 8 serving pieces

Salt and freshly ground black pepper

3 tablespoons olive oil

190g chopped onion

6 garlic cloves, chopped

85g diced bacon

¼ teaspoon ground allspice

½ teaspoon dried thyme

4 tablespoons brandy

120ml/scant ¼ pint dry red wine

2 tablespoons chopped fresh parsley

200g sliced fresh mushrooms, such as porcini (ceps) or oyster

Sprinkle the pieces of hare with salt and pepper to taste and allow to stand at room temperature for 30 minutes.

Heat the oil in a heavy frying pan over medium heat. Add the pieces of meat and brown them slowly on all sides, 10 minutes. Add the onion, garlic and bacon and continue frying for 5 minutes.

Sprinkle with the allspice, thyme, brandy, wine and parsley. Add 120ml/scant ¼ pint water. When the liquid begins to bubble, cover, lower the heat and cook slowly for 30 minutes.

Turn the pieces of hare. Add the mushrooms and cook for 45 minutes more, or until the meat is fork-tender.

SHEPHERD'S STEW *with* GAME *or* TURKEY

Gazpachos de Pastor

If you're wondering what turkey is doing in gazpacho, take note that this stew is gazpacho*s* – plural – not to be confused with Andalusian cold soup (although the origin of the name is the same, as *gazpacho* refers to fragments of bread). Gazpachos is an ancient dish, with its roots in the pastoral life of La Mancha. Shepherds tending their flocks far from villages cooked whatever wild game they could shoot or bring down with a slingshot, sometimes with foraged leaves and wild mushrooms. It was stewed over a wood fire and embellished with *torta*, an unleavened campfire bread that thickened the stew and served as a dinner plate.

Over the years, gazpachos has been domesticated, prepared in home kitchens with chicken and farm-raised rabbit, as well as game. A commercial version of the torta is sold in La Mancha today. It's a crisp flatbread, about 38cm/15in in diameter, that looks all the world like matzo on steroids!

Homemade torta is soft and pliable when fresh off the griddle. It's delicious dipped in olive oil as a breakfast bread. But it quickly goes stale. Break it into pieces before adding to the stew, where it cooks like pasta. If you don't want to prepare the homemade version, substitute matzo or water biscuits.

I prefer dark-meat turkey to game. But you could use chicken or rabbit as well. I've added chard in place of wild salad leaves and oyster mushrooms to impart a woody taste. If you're using bone-in turkey, cooking time will be 2 hours or more. Chicken, partridge or rabbit will cook much faster.

SERVES 6

FOR THE TORTAS

270g plain flour, plus flour for rolling out the dough

½ teaspoon salt

270ml / ½ pint hot water (60°C)

Olive oil for the griddle

Combine the flour and salt in a mixing bowl. Make a well in the centre and pour in the hot water, 2 tablespoons at a time, gradually stirring the flour into the water to make a soft dough.

Gather the dough into a ball.

Divide the dough into 4 equal pieces and roll each into a ball. Knead each ball on a lightly floured board until smooth and stretchy, about 1 minute. Place the balls in a large bowl, cover with clingfilm and a dampened towel (the dough shouldn't touch the clingfilm), and allow to stand at room temperature for 1 hour and up to 4 hours. The dough won't rise.

Roll out each ball on a floured surface to a 20cm/8in circle, about 3mm/⅛in thick. Place the circles on a lightly floured baking sheet. Prick them all over with a fork.

Heat a flat griddle or large cast-iron frying pan over medium heat and brush lightly with oil. Place a torta on the griddle and cook until it is blistered and lightly browned on the bottom, about 1½ minutes. Turn and cook the other side for 1 minute. Transfer to a pan and cover with a dry cloth. Cook the remaining tortas in the same manner.

Cool the tortas, covered with a cloth. They can be eaten fresh or be allowed to dry and then broken into pieces to cook with the stew.

FOR THE STEW

3 tablespoons olive oil

1½ to 2kg/3 to 4lbs turkey legs and thighs

1 head of garlic

½ medium onion, sliced

2 teaspoons salt

¼ teaspoon dried thyme, crumbled

2 bay leaves

1 fresh rosemary sprig

10 peppercorns

3 cloves

100g sliced oyster mushrooms

174g peeled, seeded and chopped tomatoes

1 teaspoon sweet pimentón

75g chopped chard (optional)

6 sheets (150g) matzo or 4 tortas, broken into pieces

Heat the oil in a very large deep frying pan or a flat-bottomed wok over medium heat. Brown the turkey pieces, turning them to brown all sides, 8 to 10 minutes. Transfer the turkey to a large casserole.

Peel off the papery outer layers from the head of garlic. Slice off the top of the head, leaving the cloves attached at the root. Add the head of garlic and the onion to the oil remaining in the frying pan and sauté them for 3 minutes. Tip the pan so the oil drains to one side while you skim out the garlic and onion, and add them to the casserole. Leave the oil in the frying pan.

Add 2 litres/3½ pints of water to the casserole with the turkey. Add the salt, thyme, bay leaves, rosemary, peppercorns, cloves and mushrooms. Bring to the boil, cover and cook slowly until the turkey is very tender, turning the pieces occasionally, about 2 hours.

Lift the turkey out of the stock and reserve. Discard the bay leaves and cloves. Reserve the stock with the mushrooms.

Heat the oil that was left in the frying pan. Add the tomatoes and fry over high heat for 5 minutes. Stir in the pimentón, chard if you're using it, and 1.2 litres/2 pints of the reserved stock and mushrooms. Bring to the boil and simmer for 15 minutes. Any stock remaining in the casserole can be reserved for another use.

Strip the turkey from the bones, discarding the skin, bones and tendons. Use kitchen scissors to cut the chunks of meat across the grain into pieces. Reserve.

Add the pieces of matzo to the frying pan and cook until soft (10 minutes for matzo, 15 to 18 minutes for home-made torta).

Add the cut-up turkey to the stew. Stir to combine and heat thoroughly, 10 minutes.

Meat

In La Mancha you can drive for miles on minor roads and never pass another car. On these back roads you will frequently see the standard signpost for a livestock crossing – a sign with a cow. Except, rarely will you actually see a cow. Livestock in La Mancha means sheep. Sheep, sometimes goats, and more sheep. They graze on stubbled fields on the plains; they spread across hillsides; they huddle in the shade of a solitary tree. Accompanied by a shepherd and his dogs, the flocks of sheep are a timeless symbol of La Mancha life.

Sheep are raised both for meat and to produce milk for cheesemaking. In an age of synthetic textiles, the wool is no longer valued as it was in bygone days. Several breeds of sheep are raised in La Mancha, but the Manchega breed is especially valued, both for its meat and for milk production. It is the only milk allowed in the production of authentic Manchego cheese. Lamb from this breed that has the special label 'Denominación Específica Cordero Manchego' is finished in barns on natural feeds and slaughtered before the age of three months. It is wonderfully tender meat, whether roasted or braised. Also much appreciated is baby suckling lamb, slaughtered at thirty-five days. Where this is available, a whole shoulder or leg of the tiny lamb makes one serving. In Spain, lamb is the most favoured choice for the festive family dinner on Christmas Eve.

There are, indeed, cattle in La Mancha and some very fine veal and young beef. There are pigs too, both of the generic variety and of the famed Iberico breed that makes especially succulent ham. La Mancha has a long tradition of customs and recipes associated with the *matanza*, annual pig slaughter, when families get together to make sausages and hams. One such dish is *sopa de cachuela*, a heavy-duty stew with tripe and pork liver, which might be served to the helpers at a *matanza*. I haven't included the recipe for cachuela because, if you haven't slaughtered a hog, a whole pig liver may not be easy to come by. But here are many recipes for slow-cooked stews and braises, quick-cooking cutlets and nicely flavoured roasts. Recipes for small game, both furred and feathered, appear in the poultry chapter. But I've placed a recipe for venison here because it works equally well with beef.

BRAISED VEAL 'LARDED' with OLIVES and SALT PORK

Ternera Mechada con Aceitunas y Tocino

According to the dictionary, *ternera* means 'veal'. However, in Spain *ternera* means young beef from a year-old bull, unless the word is followed by a qualifier such as *lechal,* 'milk-fed'. The meat has very little marbling, so it benefits this method of cooking, threaded with lardons – strips of fat – and slow-braised in aromatic wine sauce.

A special tool exists for 'larding' meat. It's a pointy tube that inserts the strip of fat through the length of meat. I don't own one, so I do what most home cooks do: use a knife to cut slits in the meat and fingers to insert the lardons. Freezing the strips of fat makes it easier to poke them into the slits.

A shoulder joint is best for this slow-cooked casserole. (However, see the variation, in which a rump joint is roasted medium-rare.) If the shoulder joint comes already rolled and tied, do not untie it. This manner of larding and braising is also used for large cuts of boned pork such as a shoulder blade joint.

The meat can be braised several hours to one day in advance. Cool, then refrigerate it, covered. Refrigerate the strained sauce separately. Before serving, remove and discard the congealed fat from the surface of the sauce. Thinly slice the meat and reheat in a little of the sauce.

SERVES 8

85g/3 oz salt pork or bacon in one piece

35g pimiento-stuffed olives, finely chopped

2 garlic cloves, crushed

2 tablespoons chopped fresh flat-leaf parsley, plus chopped parsley for garnish

Salt and freshly ground black pepper

Pinch of dried thyme

1½kg/3½lbs boneless veal shoulder joint

1 tablespoon olive oil

1 large onion, quartered and sliced

1 carrot, chopped

350ml/12 fl oz dry white wine

1 bay leaf

Cut one third of the salt pork into ½ cm/¼in strips. Place them in one layer on a sheet of clingfilm and freeze them for at least 30 minutes.

Finely chop the remaining salt pork. Combine it with the chopped olives, half of the garlic, 1 tablespoon of the chopped parsley, salt and pepper to taste, and the thyme.

Place the meat on a work surface. With a sharp knife, cut deep slits lengthways through the meat, spacing the gashes regularly on the meat's surface. With the tip of a knife or fingers, push as much of the olive paste as possible into the slits.

Removing 3 or 4 frozen 'sticks' of salt pork from the freezer at a time, insert one into each slit. Continue, filling all of the slits. Use any remaining pieces of salt pork to plug the gashes.

If the meat is not already tied, tie it with butcher's string to hold the larding in place and shape the joint. Wipe off any of the olive paste clinging to the meat's surface and sprinkle the meat with salt and pepper. Let it stand at room temperature for 30 minutes.

Preheat the oven to 160°C/140°C fan/GM3.

Heat the oil in a lidded cazuela or heavy casserole over medium heat. Brown the roast, turning it to brown all sides. On the last turn, add the onion and carrot to the pan and let it brown.

Add the wine and 120ml/scant ¼ pint water, the remaining garlic, remaining tablespoon of parsley, bay leaf and any unused olive paste. Bring to the boil, then reduce the heat so the liquid just simmers. Turn the joint to moisten both sides. Cover tightly and place in the oven.

After 45 minutes, turn the joint and continue braising until the meat is very tender when tested with a fork, about 1 hour and 15 minutes more.

Transfer the meat to a chopping board and let it rest for at least 15 minutes. Pour the cooking liquid through a sieve into a saucepan, pressing hard on the solids. Discard the solids. Skim off the fat.

Thinly slice the meat with a sharp knife and place on a heated serving platter or individual plates. Heat the sauce until it begins to boil. Spoon some of it over the sliced beef and pass the rest separately. Garnish the meat with a little chopped parsley.

VARIATION: *Use a boned rump, topside or silverside joint, all of which are quite fine-grained, instead of the shoulder joint. Insert the olive paste and salt pork as directed. After browning the meat, place the meat and liquid, uncovered, in a preheated 180°C/160°C fan/GM4 oven. Roast until medium-rare, to an internal temperature of 60°C, about 1 hour, depending on the shape and thickness of the meat. Remove and allow to rest before slicing very thinly. Boil the remaining liquid to reduce slightly, then skim the fat off and strain.*

STUFFED VEAL ROLL

Aleta de Ternera Rellena

Brisket or breast is a cut of veal that benefits from slow braising. For this casserole the brisket is opened up, spread with minced meat, carrots, eggs and olives, then rolled. When sliced, the meat shows nuggets of orange, white, green and red.

Have the butcher remove visible fat and membranes from the brisket and then cut it open horizontally through the middle so the slab of meat opens like a book ('butterflying' it). Trim the meat to make an approximate rectangle.

SERVES 12

2 to 2.2kg/4½ to 5 lbs boneless beef or veal brisket

450g/1lb minced pork

30g salt pork or fatty bacon, chopped

2 garlic cloves, finely chopped

1 shallot, chopped

¼ teaspoon freshly grated nutmeg

Pinch of ground cloves

½ teaspoon freshly ground black pepper

1 teaspoon salt

4 tablespoons chopped fresh parsley

4 tabelspoons dry white wine

3 carrots

2 hard-boiled eggs

12 pimiento-stuffed olives

2 tablespoons olive oil

½ onion, sliced

1 tomato, quartered

2 bay leaves

250ml/scant ½ pint dry Sherry

700g turnips, peeled and halved (optional)

Open the meat and pound it with a meat mallet to an even thickness.

Combine the minced pork, salt pork, garlic, shallot, nutmeg, cloves, pepper, salt, parsley and white wine in a bowl. Mix thoroughly and allow the mixture to stand for 30 minutes.

Cook 2 of the carrots in water to cover until tender. Drain, saving the water. Cut the cooked carrots in half lengthways. Cut the eggs in half lengthways.

Spread the pork mixture in a thin layer to within 5cm/2in of the edges of the open brisket. Lay the carrots in 2 rows parallel to the short sides of the meat and press them into the minced pork. Place the eggs, cut side down, in a row down the middle. Make a line of olives on either side of the eggs.

Starting on a short side, roll up the brisket, enclosing the stuffing. Tie it well, criss-crossing at intervals with kitchen string.

Preheat the oven to 180°C/160°C fan/GM4.

Heat the oil in a cazuela or heavy casserole over medium heat. Brown the brisket on all sides. Slice the remaining carrot and add to the meat with the onion, tomato, bay leaves, Sherry and 180ml/about ¼ pint of the reserved carrot water. Heat on the hob until the liquid begins to simmer. Cover with foil or a lid and place in the oven.

Let the meat cook for 1 hour. Remove from the oven and carefully turn the meat. If you're including turnips, add them to the cazuela with the meat. Cover and return to the oven until the meat is fork-tender, about 1½ hours more. If necessary, add water or stock so that there is always at least 5cm/2ins of liquid in the bottom of the roasting tin.

Transfer the meat to a platter. Tent it with foil and allow to stand 30 minutes. Transfer the turnips to a serving bowl.

Skim the fat from the liquid remaining in the pan. Discard the bay leaves. Purée the remaining liquid and vegetables in a blender, then pass it through a sieve, pressing hard on the solids. Reheat the sauce in a small saucepan.

Remove the strings from the meat. Slice the meat into 1cm/½in slices and arrange on a serving platter. Drizzle with some of the sauce and pass the rest separately. Serve the turnips alongside the meat.

BEEF *or* VENISON ESCALOPES *in* ADOBO

Filetes de Ciervo en Adobo

In Los Yébenes, a hunting area south of Toledo, I enjoyed the way venison was prepared by Taller Gastronómico, a company that distributes gourmet game products. First marinated in an adobo, it was thinly sliced and quickly pan-grilled so the meat was just cooked through and still juicy. I have exchanged the venison for beef in this recipe. If possible, use some smoky pimentón de la Vera in the adobo mixture (see Sources). While not essential, it adds a wonderful smoky dimension to the meat. Use this adobo spice rub also with shoulder of pork or pork loin. The piece of meat also can be roasted instead of sliced and pan-grilled. Roast to an internal temperature of 60°C for medium-rare, 60 to 70 minutes. Allow to stand for 10 minutes before slicing the meat as thinly as possible.

SERVES 6

900g/2 lbs boneless beef or venison, such as topside or silverside

5 garlic cloves, peeled

2 tablespoons smoked pimentón

2 teaspoons dried oregano

½ teaspoon dried thyme

½ teaspoon ground cumin

½ teaspoon ground coriander

2 tablespoons coarse salt

2 tablespoons chopped fresh parsley

4 tablespoons white wine vinegar

1 tablespoon olive oil, plus oil for the frying pan

¼ teaspoon black peppercorns

2 bay leaves

Place the piece of beef or venison in a container. Purée the garlic in a blender with the pimentón, oregano, thyme, cumin, coriander, salt, parsley, vinegar and oil to make a smooth paste. Coat the meat with the paste. Sprinkle with the peppercorns and tuck the bay leaves under the meat. Cover tightly and refrigerate. Marinate the meat for at least 24 and up to 72 hours, turning it twice a day.

Slice the meat across the grain 1cm/⅜in thick. Brush a griddle or heavy frying pan with oil and heat it until very hot. Grill the escalopes in 2 or 3 batches until they are browned on one side, 1 minute. Turn them and brown the reverse side, 1 minute.

'ALTOGETHER' VEAL *or* BEEF STEW

Tojunto

This dish comes from Almagro, in the southern part of Castilla–La Mancha, and can be made with veal, beef, pork, chicken or rabbit. All the ingredients are put to cook together – hence the name, *tojunto*, or *todo junto,* meaning 'all together'. Supposedly this allowed the women of Almagro to get on with their lacemaking (they make very pretty lace), the shepherd to keep the cheesemaking going, and the hunter in the fields to have a meal ready when he returned to camp. Rump steak is a good cut for this slow-cooked stew.

SERVES 4

1 onion, quartered and sliced

1 green pepper or 2 mild green long peppers, cut into 2½cm/1in pieces

1 large tomato or 3 plum tomatoes, peeled and cut into eighths

2 garlic cloves, chopped

1 large carrot, peeled and quartered

4 medium potatoes, peeled

680g/1½lbs boneless veal or beef, cut into 4cm/1½in pieces

Pinch of ground cloves

Freshly ground black pepper

2 bay leaves

¼ teaspoon saffron threads, crushed

1 teaspoon sweet pimentón

120g green beans in 2½cm/1in pieces

2 teaspoons salt

4 tablespoons olive oil

120ml/scant ¼ pint dry white wine

Chopped fresh parsley for garnish

Place the onion, pepper, tomato and garlic in a cazuela or casserole. Add the carrot, potatoes and meat. Sprinkle the meat with cloves and pepper to taste. Tuck the bay leaves around the meat.

Combine the crushed saffron and pimentón in a small bowl. Add 4 tablespoons of water and stir to dissolve. Pour the liquid over the meat. Place the green beans on top. Sprinkle with salt. Pour on the oil and wine plus 300ml/½ pint of water. Cover the cazuela or pot and bring to the boil. Reduce to a simmer and cook, without stirring, until the meat is very tender, 2 to 2½ hours. Allow to stand for 10 minutes before serving garnished with chopped parsley.

HEARTY BEEF STEW *with* SAUSAGE

Carcamusas

This hearty beef stew, a dish from Toledo, improves if prepared a day in advance and reheated. However, potatoes are best if cooked shortly before serving, so cook them separately and add to the stew when it is reheated.

SERVES 6

1kg/2¼lbs boneless stewing beef, such as skirt, shin or rib

4 tablespoons olive oil

1 cup chopped green pepper

1 medium onion, chopped

6 garlic cloves, 3 chopped and 3 sliced

260g peeled, seeded and chopped tomato

300ml/½ pint dry white wine

¼ teaspoon black peppercorns

1 teaspoon salt

1 bay leaf

4 tablespoons diced serrano ham or bacon

170g Spanish chorizo, preferably soft

170g morcilla sausage, or black pudding (optional)

125g frozen peas

1 roasted and peeled red pepper, cut into strips

6 small potatoes (60g), peeled and cooked

¼ teaspoon chilli flakes

½ teaspoon dried oregano

1 teaspoon sweet pimentón

Cut the beef into 2.5cm/1in cubes. Heat 3 tablespoons of the oil in a heavy frying pan over high heat. When the oil is smoking, add the beef. Allow it to brown on one side, 2 minutes, then turn the meat. Add the green pepper, onion and chopped garlic. Fry for 3 minutes. Add the tomato and fry for 2 minutes.

Add the wine and 250ml/scant ½ pint of water. Season with peppercorns, salt and bay leaf. Bring to the boil, cover and reduce the heat so the stew just simmers. Cook for 1 hour.

Add the ham, chorizo and morcilla if you're using it. Return to the boil, reduce the heat, and simmer until the beef is very tender, about another hour.

Add the peas and strips of roasted pepper. Cook, uncovered, for 10 minutes. Add the cooked potatoes and heat.

Heat the remaining tablespoon of oil in a small frying pan over medium heat. Add the sliced garlic, chilli flakes and oregano and fry until the garlic is golden, about 1 minute. Remove the pan from the heat and stir in the pimentón plus 3 tablespoons of liquid from the stew.

Cut up the sausages (kitchen scissors work well). Serve the stew, sausage and cooked potatoes with the fried garlic mixture drizzled on top.

BEEF-STUFFED PEPPERS *with* CHUNKY TOMATO SAUCE

Pimientos Rellenos con Salsa de Tomate

Stuffed peppers in a fresh tomato sauce deliciously celebrate summer. In Spain, the peppers might be thin-skinned green frying peppers or fat peppers. Green ones are preferred for stuffing, but red ones add a nice sweetness to the dish. If you are using peppers, don't slice off the tops, but cut around the pepper's stem, leaving a small opening for stuffing. You can use minced beef, as in this recipe, or a combination of beef and pork. I like to use minced chicken thighs in place of beef.

SERVES 4

4 large peppers, green and/or red	¼ teaspoon freshly grated nutmeg
Roughly 1kg tomatoes (about 6)	Pinch of ground cloves
2 slices bread	Freshly ground black pepper
Milk or water for soaking the bread	4 tablespoons chopped fresh parsley
1 egg, beaten	450g minced beef
150g finely chopped onion (about 1 large)	4 tablespoons chopped serrano ham or pancetta
3 garlic cloves, 2 chopped, and 1 very finely chopped	1 tablespoon plain flour
	4 tablespoons olive oil
2 teaspoons salt	¼ teaspoon ground cumin

Remove the stems and seeds from the peppers. Bring a large saucepan of water to the boil and blanch the tomatoes until the skins split, about 1 minute. Drain and let them cool, then peel the tomatoes. Cut them into wedges or small chunks.

Soak the bread in milk until softened. Squeeze out the liquid and discard. Crumble the bread into a mixing bowl.

Remove 1½ teaspoons of the beaten egg and reserve in a saucer. Add the remaining egg to the bread. Add 4 tablespoons of the finely chopped onion and the finely chopped garlic. Stir in 1 teaspoon of the salt, the nutmeg, cloves, pepper to taste and parsley. Add the minced beef and chopped ham. Combine the mixture well. Stuff the peppers with the meat mixture.

Dip the open ends of the peppers in the reserved beaten egg, then into the flour.

Heat the oil in a deep frying pan over medium heat. Fry the peppers, floured side down. Add the rest of the onion and garlic and turn the peppers to let them fry slowly on all sides, about 8 minutes. Add the tomatoes, cumin, remaining teaspoon of salt, and pepper to taste. Bring to the boil, cover the frying pan, and simmer for 45 minutes, turning the peppers occasionally. Remove the lid and cook for another 20 minutes, until the pepper skins are shrivelled and the tomato sauce is reduced.

Cut the peppers in half lengthways and arrange on a serving plate. Spoon the sauce over them.

MEAT-STUFFED AUBERGINES SPICED *with* NUTMEG

Berenjenas Rellenas

Use minced beef, pork, lamb or chicken for this tasty stuffed aubergine, spiced with freshly grated nutmeg. With a salad on the side, it makes a light luncheon or supper dish.

SERVES 6

3 medium aubergines (about 350g each)

3 tablespoons olive oil

35g chopped bacon

1 medium onion, chopped

4 garlic cloves, chopped

450g minced beef

1 teaspoon salt

Pinch of freshly grated nutmeg

Freshly ground black pepper

120ml/scant ¼ pint Tomato Sauce, home-made (page 26) or tinned

60g Manchego, grated

Preheat the oven to 190°C/170°C fan/GM5.

Remove and discard the stems and leaves from the aubergines, then cut them in half lengthways. Slash the flesh at 4cm/1½in intervals. Place the aubergines in a single layer on a baking tray and brush with 2 tablespoons of the oil. Bake until fork-tender, about 20 minutes.

While the aubergines are baking, heat a tablespoon of oil in a large pan over medium heat and sauté the bacon for 1 minute. Add the onion and garlic and fry for 3 minutes. Add the minced beef and continue frying over high heat, breaking up the meat, until it is browned, 2 to 3 minutes. Add the salt, nutmeg, pepper to taste the tomato sauce, and 120ml/scant ¼ pint water. Bring to the boil, then reduce the heat and simmer, covered, for 20 minutes.

When the aubergines are tender, scoop out the flesh and reserve the shells. Add the flesh to the meat in the frying pan. Uncover the pan and cook for 5 minutes more, or until most of the liquid has cooked away. Arrange the aubergine shells in a single layer on a baking tray. Spoon the meat filling into the shells. Top with the grated cheese. Add enough water to cover the bottom of the pan.

Bake, uncovered, until the cheese is melted and the filling bubbling. Allow to stand for 10 mins.

THE CUTTING EDGE — AN ALBACETE TRADITION

The 23cm/9in chef's knife, made of forged molybdenum-vanadium stainless steel, feels just right in hand, light but balanced. It slices effortlessly through an onion. Roberto Arcos holds the knife with respect. He made it. Not personally. It is one of seventy thousand pieces of cutlery and kitchen utensils manufactured daily at his factory in Albacete. The plant produces high-quality professional and kitchen knives that are sold worldwide.

The company dates back to 1875, when Sr. Arcos's great-grandfather, Gregorio Arcos Aroca, set up a knife-making workshop in Albacete.

'My great-grandfather made *navajas* [folding pocket knives] and rustic knives for country and hunting,' said Sr Arcos. 'They were all made artisanally. My grandfather later began to mechanise the workshop,' By the 1950s and 60s, with massive movement of people to the cities, demand for hunting knives had decreased. 'My father decided to change production to domestic knives. We're still expanding our range of both professional and home kitchen knives,'

The line of cutlery includes speciality items, such as a 25cm/10in flexible blade designed especially for thinly slicing serrano ham from the bone.

'The thinner the slice, the more aromatic the ham,' said Sr. Arcos. There are also thin and flexible ridged knives for thinly slicing salmon, Japanese-style knives, serrated knives for slicing tomatoes, fish scalers, filleting and boning knives.

Butchers and fishmongers use Arcos knives. Professional chefs use Arcos knives. Karlos Arguiñano, a well-known Spanish chef, uses them on his television cooking show. Home cooks use Arcos knives.

The Arcos plant, with cutting-edge technology – literally and figuratively – employs about three hundred people and twenty-five robots.

Programmed machines cut the blades from strong forged steel. The molybdenum and vanadium alloy improves hardness, which is a measure of a knife's tensile strength, resistance to corrosion and ability to hold an edge. The steel blades are next tempered in furnaces at high temperatures to harden and strengthen them. Two stones hone the edges. A white-cloaked robot looking like a witch wields the blades in a mesmerising sequence of sharpening. Polishing follows before the blades are inserted into handles.

Knife handles are variously hard plastic, soft plastic, or different woods, depending on the knife design (and, ultimately, price). The top line of Arcos professional chefs' knives has handles of tough polyoxymethylene, making them exceedingly resistant to wear, but those destined for butchers, who use knives all day long, have soft handles for ease of use. The tang – the sheath of metal that extends the full length of the handle – is completely encased in the soft coating for a seamless handle, more comfortable for prolonged use in a butcher's shop or abattoir.

The knives receive a final sharpening before passing quality control and moving to packaging. Here a line of women puts the final polish on the knives before they are packaged. Smoothing the blades with polishing cloths, they look at risk of slashing themselves. The plant foreman acknowledged that workers can never become overconfident in the handling of sharp instruments. Working with knives requires respect.

Albacete, whose name derives from the Arabic *al basit,* meaning 'flat lands', lies on the extreme south-east of the La Mancha plain. Though not nearly as well known as the other provincial capitals of Castilla–La Mancha – Toledo, Cuenca, Ciudad Real and Guadalajara – Albacete is, surprisingly, larger than any of them.

The city has a long and illustrious history of knife making. Archaeological digs have turned up iron knives and pincers from the Celtiberian and Phoenician eras from before the fourth century B.C. Arabs brought their honed skills to the region during their domination, dating from the eighth century. By the fifteenth century occasional mentions of Albacete's knife trade appeared in documents. By the second half of the sixteenth century records show a developing artisanal business in scissors, daggers, swords and knives. A hundred years later, Albacete began to stand out, with most of the workshops located in a single street. By the eighteenth century, the city's craftsmen were considered the best cutlers in Spain, displaying a high level of quality and great artistry. Besides superior blades, artisans crafted beautiful handles of bone, horn, inlaid silver and gold. The nineteenth century saw a setback, as French products invaded the national market. This also was the beginning of a separation between the small, artisanal shop and the industrialised factory such as the Arcos family business. Albacete still has small workshops producing hand-made pocket knives and hunting knives.

PORK CHOPS in GARLICKY SAUCE

Chuletas de Cerdo al Ajo Manchego

This dish can be made with pork chops or pork casserole meat. The chops are juiciest if browned, removed from the pan while the vegetables cook, and then returned to the pan to finish cooking. However, cubes of casserole meat cut from the neck end of the pig can be braised with the vegetables. Garlic added at the end is pungent! I especially like the flavour of bittersweet (*agridulce*) pimentón de la Vera with the pork, though ordinary sweet pimentón can be used.

SERVES 4

4 thick bone-in pork chops (about 900g/2 lbs)

Salt and freshly ground black pepper

3 tablespoons olive oil

1 medium onion, chopped

75g chopped green pepper

700g baking potatoes, peeled and cut into 2½cm/1in pieces

175g peeled, seeded and chopped tomato

½ teaspoon pimentón, bittersweet if available

Pinch of ground cloves

Freshly grated nutmeg

Pinch of dried thyme

3 garlic cloves, peeled

5 tablespoons chopped fresh flat-leaf parsley

Sprinkle the chops with salt and pepper and let them stand for 30 minutes. Heat the oil in a large frying pan over high heat and fry the chops, turning to brown both sides, for 3 to 4 minutes. Remove them from the pan.

Add the onion, green pepper and potatoes and sauté for 5 minutes. Add the tomato and cook for 5 minutes. Add 120ml/scant ¼ pint water, ½ teaspoon salt, the pimentón, cloves, nutmeg and thyme. Cover and cook, stirring occasionally, until the potatoes are tender, 30 minutes.

Return the pork chops and any juices to the pan and reheat gently until the chops are cooked through, 5 to 10 minutes.

Purée the garlic and parsley in a blender with 5 tablespoons of water. Stir into the frying pan and combine with the pan juices. Cook for 5 minutes.

BAKED PORK CHOPS *with* LEMON MARINADE

Chuletas de Cerdo al Horno

Lemon marinade adds a tang to both pork chops and potatoes. Cauliflower or Broccoli with Golden Garlic and Almonds (page 255) is a good side dish.

🌿 SERVES 4

6 garlic cloves, peeled

4 tablespoons fresh flat-leaf parsley

¼ teaspoon dried thyme

1 teaspoon salt

1 teaspoon smoked pimentón

4 tablespoons fresh lemon juice

4 tablespoons olive oil

Freshly ground black pepper

Four 2½cm/1in thick bone-in pork chops (about 900g/2lbs)

700g potatoes, peeled and thinly sliced

2 bay leaves

Combine the garlic, parsley, thyme, salt, pimentón, lemon juice, oil, pepper to taste and 4 tablespoons of water in a blender. Process to make a smooth marinade. Place the pork chops in a single layer on a plate. Pour the marinade over them and turn the chops to coat both sides. Allow to stand at room temperature for 1 hour or refrigerate for up to 4 hours.

Preheat the oven to 190°C/170°C fan/GM5.

Place the sliced potatoes in the bottom of an ovenproof pan or casserole. Place the chops on top with all of the marinade. Cover the pan with foil and bake for 45 minutes. Remove foil and bake for 15 minutes more. Allow the chops and potatoes to stand for 10 minutes before serving.

SPICED PORK LOIN *in* CONFIT

Lomo de la Orza

An *orza* is an earthenware jug or amphora in which, at a traditional *matanza,* hog slaughtering, whole pork loins are placed in a spiced, salty marinade. After the brining, the meat is cooked (whole or sliced), then packed in the orza and completely immersed in lard or olive oil, which seals the meat against bacteria. In cold winter months the pork, a sort of confit, keeps for several months. A few slices of the pork, fried with potatoes in some of the fat from the orza, made very tasty 'fast food' in the traditional Manchegan kitchen.

In modern times, refrigerators and freezers make preserving unnecessary. But the special flavour is enjoyed nevertheless.

Pork loin cooked in this manner makes a great main course for a party because it can be prepared well in advance and served hot or cold. If you're not feeding a crowd, after marinating and cooking the whole loin, cut it into smaller pieces and freeze them with some of the oil in which the loin was cooked.

SERVES **12** TO **18**

1½ to 1.7kg/3½ to 4lbs boneless pork loin

10 garlic cloves, peeled

4 tablespoons coarsely chopped fresh parsley

1 teaspoon ground cinnamon

2 teaspoons freshly ground black pepper

¼ teaspoon ground cloves

¼ teaspoon ground coriander

¼ teaspoon coarsely ground aniseeds

¼ teaspoon caraway seeds

1 teaspoon freshly grated nutmeg

4 tablespoons sweet pimentón

2 bay leaves, broken into pieces

½ teaspoon dried thyme

1 teaspoon dried oregano

120ml/scant ½ pint dry white wine

4 tablespoons coarse sea salt

700ml/1¼ pints olive oil

Pierce the pork loin with a skewer 10 to 12 times on both sides. Place it in a container. If necessary to fit, cut the loin in half.

In a blender, combine the garlic, parsley, cinnamon, pepper, cloves, coriander, aniseeds, caraway, nutmeg, pimentón, bay leaves, thyme, oregano and wine. Blend until smooth.

In a large saucepan, bring 1 litre/1½ pints of water and the salt to the boil. Boil for 1 minute. Add the spice mixture and bring again to the boil. Remove the pan from the heat. Allow to cool, then refrigerate until chilled.

Pour the spiced brine over the pork loin. Cover tightly and refrigerate for 24 hours.

Turn the pork over in the brine and marinate for a further 24 hours.

Remove the pork from the brine, drain well, and pat dry with kitchen paper. Discard the brine.

Place the oil in a saucepan deep enough to hold the pork. Heat until barely shimmering, about 120°C. Very carefully place the pork in the hot oil. (It will not be completely covered in oil.) Keep the oil just bubbling gently around the pork (oil temperature about 90°C). Cover the pan and poach the pork in the oil for 30 minutes.

Very carefully turn the pork over in the oil. Cover and continue cooking for 20 minutes more. Test the meat with an instant-read thermometer. Turn the pork and immediately test the internal temperature again. The pork is done when it reaches 65°C. If not, cover and cook for 10 minutes more, and test again.

Remove the pan from the heat and allow the pork to cool in the oil. Place it in a nonreactive container just large enough to hold it and pour the oil over it. The pork should be completely immersed in the oil. Cover and refrigerate for at least 1 day and up to 1 week.

To serve, slice the pork loin about 1cm/⅜ in thick. It can be reheated in some of the oil or served at room temperature.

PORK FILLETS *with* GLAZED ONIONS

Solomillos de Cerdo con Cebolletas Glaseadas

This is the sort of dish to serve for a special dinner party. Sweet 'raisin' wine glazes the little onions that roast with the meat and makes a luscious sauce. The wine is made from Pedro Ximénez grapes, which are allowed to dry in the sun for several days before vinification, concentrating the sugar and aroma. If this is not to be found, use a muscatel or medium-dry Sherry.

SERVES **8**

2 pork fillets, each about 570g/1¼ lbs

Salt and freshly ground black pepper

1 teaspoon dried thyme

3 tablespoons olive oil

450g small onions (18 to 20)

250ml/scant ½ pint sweet wine such as Pedro Ximénez

2 tablespoons Sherry vinegar (if unavailable use red wine vinegar)

Sprinkle the fillets with salt, pepper and thyme, then rub with 1 tablespoon of the oil. Allow them to sit at room temperature for 2 hours.

Peel the onions and cut a small slit in the root end. Cook them in boiling salted water to cover until just tender, about 15 minutes. Remove them with a draining spoon. Reserve the cooking liquid.

Preheat the oven to 200°C/180°C fan/GM6.

Heat the remaining 2 tablespoons oil in a large, heavy frying pan over medium-high heat and brown the fillets on all sides, 6 to 8 minutes. When they are browned, transfer them to a roasting tin just big enough to hold them. Place the onions around the meat. Pour on half of the wine, plus the vinegar and 120ml/scant ¼ pint of the reserved onion-cooking liquid.

Roast for 15 minutes. Turn the onions and baste the meat with some of the liquid in the pan. Roast until a meat thermometer inserted into the centre of the pork registers 65°C, about 10 minutes longer.

Transfer the meat to a platter and cover with foil. Swirl the onions in the syrupy glaze in the roasting pan, then transfer them to a serving plate and keep warm.

Add the remaining wine and 300ml/½ pint of the remaining onion liquid to the roasting tin and cook over medium heat, stirring up the glaze on the bottom, until reduced by half.

Cut the pork into 1cm/½in slices. Accompany with the onions. Drizzle the sauce over and serve.

MACARONI with CHORIZO SAUSAGE

Macarrones con Chorizo

In Spain, just as in Italy, pasta is usually served as a starter, not a main course. Here is an everyday way to prepare pasta. Chorizo provides the flavour 'package'. Cheese on top is optional.

SERVES 4

3 tablespoons olive oil

75g chopped green pepper

1 medium onion, chopped

130g courgettes cut into ½cm / ¼in chunks

1 garlic clove, chopped

170g diced Spanish chorizo, hard or soft

350g chopped tomato

Pinch of dried oregano

Salt and freshly ground black pepper

225g penne pasta

Grated Manchego cheese for serving (optional)

Heat the oil in a deep casserole or cazuela over high heat and sauté the green pepper, onion, courgettes, garlic and chorizo for 10 minutes. Add the tomato, oregano, and salt and pepper to taste. Cook until slightly reduced, about 20 minutes longer.

Cook the pasta in boiling water until al dente (according to directions on the packet, but usually about 8 minutes). Drain the pasta and combine with the sauce. Serve with grated cheese if desired.

BLOODLESS BLOOD SAUSAGE

Morcilla Blanca

Morcilla, blood sausage or black pudding, is one of the most distinctive sausages in the Spanish repertoire of pork products. It adds spiciness to stews with lentils or chickpeas. Variations abound. Some morcilla contains rice and onions, others only onion. In La Mancha it is often made with mashed potato and pumpkin. One version exchanges the onions for apples. Clove, cinnamon and sweet pimentón are the predominant spices.

As pig's blood is not easy to come by, I suggest making white morcilla, using rice and minced pork belly, which is about equal parts lean and fat. You needn't bother with sausage casings. Just wrap the sausages in muslin. This is not a cured sausage, so store it, refrigerated, like any cooked meat. Use within two or three days. If you want to keep the sausage longer, wrap it tightly in clingfilm, place in an airtight container and freeze.

❧ MAKES 6 SAUSAGES, WEIGHING ABOUT 900G/2LBS

2 bay leaves

2 teaspoons salt

65g Spanish round-grain rice

1 medium onion, chopped

700g minced fresh pork belly (uncured pancetta)

2 garlic cloves, crushed

½ teaspoon freshly ground black pepper

1 teaspoon sweet pimentón

½ teaspoon bittersweet smoked pimentón

1 teaspoon dried oregano

½ teaspoon ground cinnamon

¼ teaspoon ground cloves

Grating of fresh nutmeg

⅛ teaspoon crushed aniseeds

1 tablespoon dry white wine

1 egg, beaten

Bring 300ml/½ pint of water to the boil with one of the bay leaves and 1 teaspoon of the salt. Add the rice, cover, and simmer until the water is absorbed, 15 minutes. Remove from the heat and allow to cool. Discard the bay leaf.

Cook the onion in boiling water for 5 minutes. Drain, saving the liquid.

Combine the onion, rice and minced pork belly in a bowl. Add the crushed garlic. In a small bowl, mix the pepper, both kinds of pimentón, oregano, cinnamon, cloves, nutmeg, aniseeds and remaining teaspoon of salt. Sprinkle half of the spice mixture over the pork. Turn the pork mixture over and sprinkle on the rest of the spices.

Add the wine and egg and knead the sausage mixture until thoroughly mixed. Make a 5cm/2in patty. Fry it on both sides in a small frying pan. Cool slightly and taste the patty. Add salt or spices, if necessary.

Cut a double piece of muslin into 3 rectangles measuring 30 × 20cm/12 × 8in. Divide the sausage mixture into three. Spread a sheet of greaseproof paper on the work surface. Roll and pat one-third of the sausage mixture into a log, about 25cm/10in long and 2½cm/1in thick. Place it on one edge of a muslin rectangle and roll the sausage log in the muslin. Tie the ends with kitchen string. Tie the middle of the roll, dividing it into 2 links of sausage. Continue with the remaining two thirds of sausage mix.

Place the reserved onion water, remaining bay leaf and enough additional water in a saucepan deep enough to hold the sausages in one layer. Bring to the boil; add the sausages and cook, covered, for 30 minutes.

Drain the sausages. Hang them in a cool place to dry for 3 hours. Refrigerate the sausages in a covered container and use them within 3 days.

Before serving, remove and discard the muslin. The sausages can be sliced and eaten cold, added to stews and cocidos, or fried.

MORCILLA *with* RAISINS *and* PINE NUTS

Morcilla con Pasas y Piñones

I tasted this at a very old Madrid tapa bar, where it was served with a red wine from Valdepeñas in La Mancha. The morcilla should be one made with rice (such as the white morcilla in the preceding recipe). If you are substituting another type of blood sausage (such as *boudin noir* or black pudding), add about 85g of cooked rice to the frying pan with the sausage. At the tapa bar, the morcilla was served heaped on a platter placed in the centre of the table, accompanied by forks and chunks of bread. We all helped ourselves straight from the platter. At home I serve the morcilla atop salad leaves.

SERVES 4 AS A MAIN DISH OR 6 TO 8 AS A TAPA

2 tablespoons olive oil

4 tablespoons pine nuts

450g morcilla, casings removed and sausage sliced

4 tablespoons raisins

4 tablespoons dry white wine

Salad leaves for serving

Heat the oil in a frying pan over medium-high heat and fry the pine nuts until golden, 30 seconds. Tip the pan so the oil flows to one side and skim out the pine nuts.

Add the morcilla and raisins and fry for 3 minutes. Use a wooden spatula to break the morcilla into smaller pieces. Add the wine and simmer for 5 minutes, until the morcilla begins to sizzle again.

Spoon the hot morcilla onto salad leaves and scatter the pine nuts on top.

SLOW-COOKED PIG'S TROTTERS

Manos de Cerdo Estofadas

I finally 'get it' about pig's trotters, after various experiments in eating them and cooking them. They fall into the same category as snails – the sauce is so delicious that it makes preparing something a little strange, with a weird texture to boot, worth all the trouble. Pig's trotters have a gelatinous texture that either you like or else you don't want to know.

I consulted various recipes for cooking pigs' trotters. Invariably they instructed me to boil the trotters, remove the bones, and cut up the 'meat'.

Well, let me tell you, pig's trotters don't have 'meat'. Meat is, really, muscle, and feet don't have muscle. They have thick skin and gelatinous cartilage. The stock they cook in, which sets up into a firm gelatin, makes a serious soup or sauce. The 'meat', cut into bits and stewed in a flavourful sauce, is unctuous, a little slippery, and ever so delicious. (If you want a meatier version, add 120g of pork shoulder meat to cook with the trotters.) Serve the pig's trotters very hot with lots of fresh bread for sopping up the sauce.

SERVES 4

4 pig's trotters (feet) split in half (1.7 to 2 kg/ 4 to 4½lbs)

2 leeks, white part only

3 carrots

1 dried choricero pepper or 3 ñora peppers (optional)

2 bay leaves

½ teaspoon black peppercorns

3 cloves

1 tablespoon plus ½ teaspoon salt

3 tablespoons wine vinegar

2 tablespoons olive oil

1 medium onion, chopped

3 garlic cloves, chopped

2 tablespoons plain flour

½ teaspoon hot pimentón or pinch of cayenne

1 to 3 teaspoons sweet pimentón

2 tablespoons dry red wine

Chopped fresh parsley for garnish

Put the pig's trotters in a large casserole with water to cover. Bring to the boil, boil for 5 minutes, and drain.

Rinse out the pan and put the trotters in with fresh water to cover. Bring to the boil. Add the leeks, carrots, choricero pepper (if you are using it), bay leaves, peppercorns, cloves, 1 tablespoon of the salt and the vinegar. When the water boils, cover and reduce the heat to a simmer. Cook until the pig's trotters are fork-tender, about 2 hours.

Lift the trotters out of the stock. When they are cool enough to handle, remove all the bones and thick parts of the skin and discard them. Cut the remaining meat, skin and cartilage into bite-sized pieces. Skim out the carrots and choricero peppers and reserve. Discard the bay leaves.

If using the choricero or ñora peppers, split them open and scrape the pulp with the blunt edge of a knife. Save the pulp and discard the skins.

When the stock cools, skim off and discard the fat that rises to the surface.

Heat the oil in a deep frying pan over medium heat and sauté the onion until it begins to brown, 5 minutes. Add the garlic and sauté for 2 minutes.

Remove the pan from the heat. Stir in the flour. Add the pulp of the choricero peppers plus the hot pimentón and 1 teaspoon of sweet pimentón. If not using the choricero peppers, stir in 1 tablespoon of sweet pimentón.

Gradually stir in 450ml/¾ pint of the stock in which the trotters cooked. Add the wine and the remaining ½ teaspoon salt. Return the pan to the heat and cook, stirring, until the sauce thickens. Return the reserved meat to the sauce. Simmer, covered, for 30 minutes.

Slice the reserved carrots and add to the sauce. Heat. Serve the trotters with the sauce very hot, garnished with chopped parsley.

NOTE: *Choricero and ñora peppers are dried sweet peppers. The choricero is long and skinny; the ñora is round and plum sized. They are available at shops that specialise in products from Spain (see Sources). If not available, use additional pimentón in the recipe.*

LAMB ROASTED with SAFFRON POTATOES

Cordero en Rustidera con Patatas

A *rustidera* is a shallow roasting pan, big enough to hold a whole baby lamb that is cut into pieces and combined with potatoes, onions and tomatoes. The giant casserole is carried to a large baker's oven to roast. This version uses leg of spring lamb and can be roasted in a regular oven. Choose a small leg, weighing 1.6 to 1.8kg / 3½ to 4lbs. Use a roasting pan, an oval cazuela, a tian or an ovenproof casserole pot big enough to hold the lamb. Ideally you should be able to serve the lamb in the pan in which it roasts.

SERVES 6

One 1.8kg / 4lb leg of lamb, excess fat removed

Salt and freshly ground black pepper

80ml olive oil

900g / 2lbs baking potatoes, peeled and cut into ½cm / ¼in slices

1 large onion, cut in half and thinly sliced

1 green pepper, cut into strips

3 tomatoes (about 450g), sliced

4 tablespoons chopped fresh parsley

½ teaspoon saffron threads

2 cloves

10 black peppercorns

½ teaspoon ground cinnamon

3 garlic cloves, crushed

3 bay leaves

450ml / ¾ pint dry white wine

Sprinkle the lamb with salt and pepper and allow to come to room temperature.

Preheat the oven to 200°C / 180°C fan / GM6.

Pour half the oil into the bottom of a roasting tin or cazuela. Layer the sliced potatoes, onion, green pepper and tomatoes in the pan, sprinkling with salt and parsley.

In a mortar or spice grinder, grind together the saffron, cloves and peppercorns. Add 4 tablespoons of hot water and allow to stand for 10 minutes. Stir in the cinnamon and crushed garlic. Pour the spice mixture over the potatoes. Tuck the bay leaves into the layered vegetables. Pour on the wine. Place the leg of lamb on top. Pour the remaining oil over the lamb.

Reduce the oven temperature to 180°C/160°C fan/GM4 and roast the lamb until the potatoes are fork-tender and an instant-read thermometer inserted in the thickest part of the lamb registers 60°C for medium, about 1 hour. (If you prefer rare, place the pan with potatoes, uncovered, in the oven for 30 minutes before placing the lamb on top of it. Roast the lamb for about 30 minutes, to an internal temperature of 52°C.)

Transfer the lamb to a chopping board. Allow to rest for 10 minutes, then carve the meat off the bone. If roasted in a cazuela that can be served at table, arrange the meat on top of the potatoes. Otherwise, use a wide spatula to transfer the potatoes and other vegetables to a serving platter, discarding the bay leaves, and place the meat on top.

VARIATION: *Substitute 1.6kg/3¼lbs lamb shanks for the leg of lamb. Place the lamb and vegetables in a preheated 200°C/180°C fan/GM6 oven for 30 minutes. Reduce the heat to 180°C/160°C fan/GM4. Cover the roasting tin with a lid or heavy-duty foil and bake until the meat is well done and very tender, about 1½ hours.*

LEG OF LAMB ROASTED *with* MEDITERRANEAN HERBS

Pierna de Cordero Asado con Hierbas

One of the glory dishes of Castilian cooking is spring lamb roasted in a wood-fired oven. Rubbed with lard and a few herbs, placed in a cazuela on a bed of onions and laurel (bay) leaves, it emerges with crisp skin and succulent flesh. I heartily recommend a trip to Spain to sample roast lamb at its best. Should this not be possible, here is a way to roast spring lamb that recalls the flavours of Castile. Look for the smallest possible leg of lamb and trim it of excess fat.

Should you be able to obtain spring lamb (a whole baby lamb weighs 12 to 15 pounds), split it open lengthways and prepare in the same manner as described here. Spring lamb is not served rare, so roast it to an internal temperature of 68°C.

I like crisp-fried Hot Potatoes (page 271) and Artichoke Sauté (page 247) with the lamb. A *crianza* wine with a Vinos de la Tierra de Castilla denomination (see page 350) would be a fine accompaniment.

SERVES 6

1 leg of lamb, about 1.8kg/4lbs

Salt and freshly ground black pepper

1 teaspoon finely chopped fresh rosemary

1 teaspoon finely chopped fresh thyme

4 tablespoons chopped fresh flat-leaf parsley

2 garlic cloves, crushed

1 tablespoon olive oil or lard

1 tablespoon wine vinegar

1 onion, halved and sliced

3 bay leaves

250ml/scant ½ pint dry white wine

Fresh rosemary sprigs for garnish (optional)

Trim the lamb of excess fat. Salt it generously and sprinkle with pepper. Combine the rosemary, thyme, parsley, garlic, oil and vinegar. Spread this mixture on all sides of the meat. Allow to stand for 1 hour at room temperature or 4 to 6 hours refrigerated.

Preheat the oven to 200°C/190°C fan/GM6.

Spread the sliced onion and bay leaves in the bottom of a cazuela or roasting tin and place the leg of lamb on top. Roast it for 30 minutes.

Reduce the oven temperature to 180°C/160°C fan/GM4. Pour the wine and 300ml/½ pint water around the lamb. Roast until the internal temperature, tested with an instant-read thermometer, reaches 60°C for medium-rare meat, about 30 minutes longer. (A larger leg of lamb will take longer to reach this temperature and may require more water added to the roasting pan.)

Transfer the lamb to a carving board and let it rest for 10 minutes. Skim any fat from the pan juices. Discard the bay leaves. Purée the pan juices and onions in a blender.

Carve the meat and arrange on a heated serving platter. Add the juices that collect on the board to the puréed sauce. Serve the lamb with some of the sauce spooned over it and the rest in a jug or gravy boat. Garnish with sprigs of rosemary if desired.

ROAST LAMB with SPINACH and BREADCRUMB STUFFING

Cordero Asado con Relleno

The spinach, pine nuts and raisins in the stuffing make this an especially tasty way to prepare a boned leg of lamb. Don't worry that the slab of meat is somewhat ragged. Tie it at intervals wherever is needed to hold the stuffing in. Once roasted, the meat can be sliced thickly, showing a spiral of stuffing, and arranged onto a platter or individual plates.

SERVES 6

One boned leg of lamb, 1.6 to 1.8kg / 3½ to 4lbs

Salt and freshly ground black pepper

10 to 12 spinach leaves, stems removed

2 tablespoons olive oil

35g / 4 tablespoons pine nuts

35g / 4 tablespoons finely chopped shallot

35g / 4 tablespoons chopped bacon or pancetta

35g / 4 tablespoons raisins

1 tablespoon chopped fresh mint

50g fine fresh breadcrumbs

1 egg white, lightly beaten with 1 tablespoon water

120ml / scant ¼ pint dry white wine

Trim the lamb of excess fat. Lay the meat open on a work surface. With the knife parallel to the surface, slice horizontally nearly all the way through the 2 thickest parts of the meat in order to fold them open, creating an extended slab of more or less equal thickness. Sprinkle with salt and pepper.

Arrange a layer of spinach leaves, shiny side down, on top of the meat.

Heat the oil in a small frying pan over medium-high heat. Toast the pine nuts until golden, 30 seconds. Skim them out and reserve. Add the shallot and bacon to the oil and sauté for 2 minutes. Remove from the heat and add the pine nuts, raisins, mint, breadcrumbs and egg white. Season with salt and pepper. Spread this mixture on top of the spinach leaves.

Starting at the narrowest end, roll the meat up, enclosing the stuffing. Fasten with poultry skewers, then tie well with string to keep it from unrolling.

Place the meat in a bowl just large enough to hold it. Pour on the wine. Marinate the lamb for 2 hours. Turn the meat and marinate for 2 hours more.

Preheat the oven to 200°C/180°C fan/GM6.

Place the lamb in a roasting pan. Pour on the marinating wine and 300ml/½ pint of water. Roast the lamb, basting occasionally with pan juices, to an internal temperature of 60°C for medium-rare, about 70 minutes. Add water as needed so there is always liquid in the bottom of the pan.

Allow the meat to rest for 15 minutes. Remove the skewers and string and slice thickly. Spoon the pan juices over the meat.

HERB-ROASTED KID

Cabrito Asado

This is a speciality of Guadalajara. The herbs and vinegar in the marinade give the meat a delicious flavour. It is best roasted in a large oval earthenware cazuela, but any roasting tin will work fine. If you parboil the unpeeled onions, you can peel them much easier, without tears.

🌿 SERVES 6

2 legs of kid (young goat), about 1.6kg/3lbs 10oz total

4 tablespoons wine vinegar

12 garlic cloves, peeled

1 teaspoon fresh mint

½ teaspoon finely chopped fresh rosemary

½ teaspoon dried thyme

4 tablespoons fresh flat-leaf parsley

1 teaspoon salt

Freshly ground black pepper

1 tablespoon olive oil

12 very small potatoes (about 750g)

12 small onions (350g)

Place the legs in a container large enough to hold them.

In a blender, combine the vinegar, garlic, mint, rosemary, thyme, parsley, salt, pepper to taste, oil and 4 tablespoons of water. Blend until smooth. Rub the herb blend on both sides of the legs. Cover with foil and refrigerate for at least 6 and up to 24 hours, turning the legs at least once.

Peel the potatoes and parboil in salted water for 10 minutes. Drain. Trim the tops and roots of the onions, but do not peel. Parboil them for 2 minutes and drain. When they are cool enough to handle, slip off the skins.

Preheat the oven to 100°C/180°C fan/GM6. Place the legs and all of the herb marinade in a large oval earthenware cazuela or roasting pan. Put the potatoes and onions around the meat. Add 300ml/½ pint boiling water and place the cazuela, uncovered, in the oven. Immediately lower the oven temperature to 150°C/130°C fan/GM2. Roast for 1 hour.

Add 300ml/½ pint of boiling water. Roast until the meat registers 82°C when tested with an instant-read thermometer, about 30 minutes longer. Add water whenever neccessary so that there is always liquid in the bottom of the pan.

Remove from the oven and allow the meat to stand for 10 minutes before carving. Carve the meat off the bones and place on a heated platter with the potatoes and onions. Reheat the pan drippings (adding water if necessary) and serve with the meat.

LAMB STEW in CAZUELA

Cazuela de Cordero

Almost any cut of lamb – neck, shoulder, shank or leg – works for this stew. I prefer the shoulder. I ask the butcher to bone it and then use the bones to make a simple stock that adds so much flavour to the finished dish. If you don't have lamb stock, substitute chicken stock.

SERVES 4

2 tablespoons olive oil

2 medium onions, julienned

700g/1½ lbs boned lamb, cut into 4cm/1½in pieces

4 tablespoons flat-leaf parsley

1 teaspoon sweet pimentón

4 garlic cloves, peeled

180ml/about ¼ pint dry white wine

250ml/scant ½ pint lamb or chicken stock

1 teaspoon salt

Freshly ground black pepper

2 bay leaves

2 carrots, quartered

450g potatoes, peeled and cut into 2½cm/1in pieces

190g fresh or frozen peas

1 tablespoon chopped fresh mint

Heat the oil in a cazuela or casserole over medium-high heat and sauté the onion until softened, 5 minutes. Add the lamb and sauté for 3 minutes longer.

Place the parsley, pimentón, garlic and wine in a blender and purée the mixture. Add to the lamb with the stock, salt, pepper to taste, bay leaves and carrots. Bring to the boil, reduce the heat and simmer, covered, until the meat is tender, about 50 minutes.

Add the potatoes. If you're using large fresh peas, add them now. If using frozen peas or fresh petits pois, add them during the last 5 minutes of cooking. Simmer until the potatoes are tender, about 20 minutes.

Remove the cazuela from the heat and allow to stand for 10 minutes before serving. Sprinkle with the mint.

BRAISED LAMB *with* CHILLIES

Caldereta de Cordero

This rustic dish derives from the shepherds' *caldereta,* or iron casserole, in which meals were cooked over embers. At its most basic, the stew was eaten straight from the pot, with bread for mopping up the gravy. Other versions use either the lamb liver, grilled and mashed, or ground almonds, pine nuts or walnuts to thicken the sauce. A very similar lamb stew is called *cochifrito.*

Keep the lamb covered with liquid as it cooks and, if preparing it in advance, keep the cooked meat completely covered with liquid so that it doesn't darken and dry out.

Ñoras are plum-sized dried sweet chillies. After cooking, the soft flesh is scraped from the insides of the peppers. Mild long green peppers are a possible substitute, although they are not quite as fleshy as the ñora. Otherwise use a spoonful of sweet pimentón. Use only a little hot chilli in addition to the mild. I like to add some smoky Pimentón de la Vera to make up for the shepherds' wood fire smoke.

I serve the lamb and gravy with Potatoes Mashed with Green Garlic (page 270), but rice or couscous would be equally good.

❧ SERVES 6

1.1 to 1.4kg/2½ to 3lbs lamb steaks cut from the leg, with or without bone

Salt and freshly ground black pepper

3 tablespoons olive oil

1 large onion, quartered and sliced

3 ñora peppers or 1 dried long green pepper, stem and seeds discarded (or a spoonful of sweet pimentón)

1 small hot dried chilli, such as cayenne

4 sun-dried tomatoes, sliced

½ red pepper

4 tablespoons chopped fresh flat-leaf parsley

½ teaspoon dried thyme

2 bay leaves

2 heads of garlic, char-roasted (see note page 238) and peeled

250ml/scant ½ pint dry white wine

4 tablespoons blanched almonds

1 teaspoon smoked pimentón (sweet, bittersweet or hot)

Trim off and discard as much fat as possible from the lamb. Sprinkle the meat liberally with salt and pepper and allow to stand at room temperature for 1 hour.

Heat the oil in a large casserole or lidded cazuela over medium heat and sauté the sliced onion until lightly browned, 6 to 8 minutes. Put in the pieces of meat and turn them in the oil for a few minutes. They do not need to brown, only to lose their pink colour. Add ñoras or the long green pepper with the whole dried chilli, tomatoes, pepper, parsley, thyme, bay leaves and peeled garlic cloves.

Add the wine and 700ml/1¼ pints water. Bring to the boil, then cover and simmer until the meat is very tender, 1 to 1½ hours.

Lift the pieces of meat out of the cooking liquid with any vegetables clinging to them and set aside, covered tightly. Skim off the fat from the liquid remaining in the casserole.

Place a sieve over a bowl and pour the liquid through it. Discard the cayenne chilli and bay leaves. Lift out the pieces of ñora. Use a spoon to scrape the pulp from the inside of the ñoras or long pepper. Put the pulp in a blender or food processor (discard the skins). Scrape the pulp from the piece of pepper and discard the skin. Add the pulp to the blender with any pieces of onion, tomato and garlic remaining in the sieve.

> . . . *se fue tras el olor que despedían de sí ciertos*
> *tasajos de cabra que hirviendo al fuego,*
> *en un caldero estaban. . .*
>
> . . . he set off on the trail of the smell wafting from some
> hunks of goat meat bubbling in a casserole over the fire . . .
> SANCHO PANZA AT THE GOATHERDS' CAMP

Add the almonds to the blender with the pimentón and 250ml/scant ½ pint of the strained liquid. Blend or process until the almonds are ground to a smooth paste.

Return the sieved liquid to the casserole and add the almond mixture. Bring to the boil, stirring. Return the lamb to the pot and cook gently for 20 minutes longer.

TO CHAR-ROAST A HEAD OF GARLIC

Spear the head of garlic on a fork or grasp it with tongs (protect your hands with an oven glove) and hold over a gas flame or put under the grill. Turn the garlic until it is charred on all sides. Peel the garlic cloves and rinse in water.

LAMB SHANKS BRAISED *with* BEANS

Cordero Estofado con Alubias

This is a satisfying dish that can be made with any bony cut of lamb – shanks, necks, ribs. If you use shanks, you may wish to strip the meat from the bones after cooking to facilitate serving.

SERVES 4

225g dried cannellini beans, soaked overnight

2 bay leaves

1½ teaspoons salt

2 tablespoons olive oil

4 lamb shanks (about 1.4kg/3lbs)

1½ medium onions chopped

3 garlic cloves, chopped

90g drained tinned diced tomato

1 teaspoon black peppercorns, coarsely crushed

Pinch of ground cloves

½ teaspoon dried thyme

1 fresh rosemary sprig (optional)

Chopped fresh coriander, parsley or mint for garnish

Drain the beans and put them in a large saucepan with 1 litre/1½ pints of water. Bring to a rolling boil. Drain the beans, rinse them in cold water, and return them to the pan. Add 1 litre/1½ pints of water, the bay leaves and 1 teaspoon of the salt. Bring to the boil and simmer for 15 minutes.

Heat the oil in a heavy frying pan over medium-high heat. Brown the lamb shanks on all sides, about 5 minutes. Remove them and reserve. Add the onion and garlic to the pan and sauté until the onion begins to brown, 4 minutes. Add the tomato and sauté for 2 minutes. Add the pepper, cloves, thyme, rosemary if you're using it, remaining ½ teaspoon salt, and 450ml/¾ pint of water and stir.

Add the tomato mixture to the beans with the browned shanks. Bring to the boil, then reduce the heat so the beans bubble very gently. Cover and cook until the beans and lamb are very tender, about 1 hour.

If desired, strip the meat from the bones to serve. Serve the lamb and beans in bowls, garnished with chopped coriander.

LAMB CHOPS SIZZLED *with* GARLIC

Chuletas de Cordero al Ajillo

Calling this by the diminuitive *ajillo,* meaning 'a wee bit of garlic', is rather tongue in cheek. In reality it's a whopping quantity of garlic. I had these delectable lamb chops in Las Pedroñeras, a La Mancha town that bills itself as the garlic capital. I learned that garlic gradually loses its punch. So when made with July's newly picked garlic, the ration of cloves is minimal (one per lamb chop). But later in the year, when the flavour is milder, the number is increased (two to three cloves per chop). I prefer chops cut from the leg for this dish. If you're using rib lamb chops, have them 'frenched', or trimmed of all fat.

SERVES 4

8 to 12 lamb chops(900g/2lbs), cut 1cm/½in thick	10 garlic cloves
Salt and freshly ground black pepper	3 tablespoons olive oil
Pinch of dried thyme	1 tablespoon chopped fresh parsley
	2 tablespoons fresh lemon juice

Sprinkle the chops with salt, pepper and thyme. Cut the unpeeled garlic cloves in half crossways.

Heat the oil in a large frying pan over medium heat. Add the lamb chops and garlic. Brown the chops on one side, about 3 minutes. Stir and turn the pieces of garlic. Turn the chops and brown on the other side, 3 to 4 minutes.

Transfer the chops to a serving platter. Add 2 tablespoons water, the parsley and the lemon juice to the remaining oil and garlic. Heat until sizzling. Pour over the chops and serve immediately.

LAMB ROLL WRAPPED *in* CHARD LEAVES

Rollo de Cordero con Acelga

This is a delicious 'meat loaf' cooked on the hob. Spiced minced lamb braises in a wrap of chard leaves with a surprise in the middle – nuggets of hard-boiled egg. This can also be prepared as individual packages instead of a large roll, in which case you will need three rather than two hard-boiled eggs, allowing ½ egg per package. If the lamb is very lean, it will benefit from the addition of pancetta or bacon. The recipe also works quite well with minced turkey. Potatoes Mashed with Green Garlic (page 270) or plain steamed rice would be a good side dish with the lamb roll and its sauce.

SERVES 6

1 bunch of chard (18 to 24 leaves)

50g fresh breadcrumbs (white or wholemeal)

700g/1½lbs minced lamb

2 garlic cloves, crushed

4 tablespoons chopped fresh parsley

45g diced pancetta or bacon (optional)

4 tablespoons finely chopped onion

4 tablespoons seedless raisins

Pinch of ground cloves

⅛ teaspoon ground cinnamon

Grating of fresh nutmeg

⅛ teaspoon ground coriander seeds

Salt and freshly ground black pepper

2 eggs, 1 separated

2 hard-boiled eggs, halved lengthways

3 tablespoons olive oil

1 medium onion, coarsely chopped

60g diced carrot

175g drained tinned diced tomato

1 tablespoon plain flour

1 teaspoon sugar

180ml/just over ¼ pint dry white wine

1 bay leaf

Cut off the chard stems and discard (or save for another use). Bring a large saucepan of water to the boil and blanch the leaves until just wilted, about 30 seconds. Drain the leaves.

Soak the breadcrumbs in water to cover until softened. Squeeze out the water and put the softened bread in a mixing bowl. Add the minced lamb, garlic, parsley, bacon, finely chopped onion, raisins, cloves, cinnamon, nutmeg, coriander, ½ teaspoon salt, pepper to taste, the whole egg and 1 egg yolk.

With a large wooden spoon (or your hands), mix the meat thoroughly with the other ingredients.

Spread half of the chard leaves, shiny side down, in an overlapping layer on a work surface or on a platter. Divide the meat in half. Pat half of the meat into an oblong (about 23cm/9in). Place the cooked eggs, cut side down, in a row down the middle. Pat the remaining meat on top of the eggs. With your hands, shape the meat into a loaf, sealing in the eggs.

Fold the chard leaves up over the meat roll. Cover with the remaining chard leaves and tuck them under the roll, completely enclosing the meat roll. Pat the roll to firm it. It is not necessary to tie it.

Whisk the egg white lightly with 1 teaspoon water. Place in a shallow pan. Turn the meat roll in the egg white to coat all sides.

Heat the oil in a deep frying pan or casserole big enough to hold the roll. Brown the roll on all sides over medium heat, about 6 minutes. Remove and reserve.

Add the coarsely chopped onion and carrot to the oil and sauté until the onion begins to brown, 5 minutes. Add the tomato and cook over high heat for 3 minutes. Stir in the flour, sugar and ½ teaspoon salt. Add the wine, bay leaf and 120ml/¼ pint of water. Return the meat roll to the frying pan. Bring to a simmer, cover and cook slowly for 35 minutes.

Turn the roll and cook for 35 minutes more. Remove from the heat and let stand for 15 minutes. Use a sharp serrated knife to cut the roll into 2cm/¾in slices. The sauce can be strained or left chunky. Serve it with the meat roll.

Vegetables
and Other
Side Dishes

Vegetables get pride of place at a typical Spanish family meal, making their appearance either as a first course or incorporated into the main dish. A good example is the signature dish of La Mancha, *pisto manchego*, a medley of tomatoes, peppers and courgettes. In La Mancha it's served in small, individual *cazuelitas* as a starter, with crusty bread for dipping. But, if you prefer to serve it as a side dish, go ahead. It makes a delightful accompaniment to roast chicken, grilled lamb chops, grilled fish or pan-fried pork.

Other substantial vegetable dishes, such as Cazuela of Potatoes and Chard, are actually main courses, whether for vegetarian meals or embellished with small quantities of meat, fish or eggs. You'll find they make tasty lunch dishes, as hearty as a bowl of soup.

However you choose to serve these vegetable dishes – as starter or side dish – you will find some enticing recipes and new ways of putting flavours together. A pinch of caraway with aubergine is a revelation!

I've included in this chapter the peasant dishes of *migas*, fried breadcrumbs, and *gachas*, garlicky 'porridge', because, although in La Mancha they are breakfast dishes, they can be served as side dishes too.

Also here are recipes for some spicy pickles that seem to embellish every salad, pâté and relish platter in La Mancha.

MEDLEY OF SUMMER VEGETABLES

Pisto Manchego

You might recognise this dish – a medley of tomatoes, peppers, courgettes and sometimes aubergine – as Provençal *ratatouille*, but *pisto* is authentically La Mancha, very possibly where ratatouille began. Its origins are Moorish – *alboronía* – although in those times it was a slow-cooked stew with onions, aubergine and meat juices.

Pisto is a good side dish with grilled fish, roast meat and chicken. It makes a quick meal when paired with fried eggs (call it breakfast or supper). In La Mancha it is often served as a first course with toast or chunks of bread for dipping in the savoury juices. Pisto also makes the sauce for chicken or lamb (see Chicken with Peppers and Tomatoes, Toledo Style, page 153).

If you prefer a 'refined' version of pisto, roast and skin the green peppers before chopping them. While not absolutely essential, peeling the peppers prevents curls of pepper skin from coming loose in the vegetable medley. Feel free to embellish with favourite herbs and spices. Personally, I like ground cumin and hot pimentón.

SERVES 8

4 tablespoons olive oil	1 teaspoon salt
140g chopped green pepper	Freshly ground black pepper
1 medium onion, chopped	½ teaspoon dried oregano
1 garlic clove, chopped	700g diced courgette (4 medium courgettes)
500g peeled, seeded and chopped tomato	

Heat the oil in a large frying pan over medium heat and sauté the green pepper, onion and garlic until softened, 15 minutes. Raise the heat and add the tomato, salt, pepper and oregano. Cook until the tomato releases juice, 8 minutes.

Add the courgettes and cook, uncovered, until they are tender and most of the liquid has cooked off, about 30 minutes. Serve hot or at room temperature.

VARIATION: *Use half an aubergine and half a courgette in place of the 700g courgette. Sauté the aubergine first with the green pepper, onion and garlic.*

FLAME-ROASTED GARDEN VEGETABLES

Asadillo de la Huerta

This is a wonderful dish to make with end-of-summer tomatoes and peppers from the garden or farmers' markets, but a quick version could be put together with fire-roasted vegetables from the grocery store. In La Mancha *asadillo,* which just means 'roasted', is generally served as a starter, but I like it as a side dish with grilled or roasted meats.

SERVES 6

5 red peppers	1 teaspoon salt
5 large tomatoes (about 900g)	½ teaspoon ground cumin
2 garlic cloves	4 tablespoons olive oil

Roast the peppers in a single layer over charcoal or a gas flame or under the grill, turning to char them on all sides. Roast the tomatoes, turning once, until they are charred in places and the skins are split.

Place the roasted vegetables in a bowl and cover until they are cool enough to handle. Scrape off the charred pepper skins; remove and discard with the stems and seeds. Tear the peppers into strips. Slip the skins off the tomatoes, cut out the stem and core, and chop the tomatoes. Combine with the peppers.

Crush the garlic with the salt in a mortar. Add the cumin. Gradually stir in the oil. Pour over the peppers and tomatoes and combine well. Serve at room temperature.

VARIATION: *To serve hot, heat 1 tablespoon olive oil in a frying pan. Add the roasted and peeled tomatoes and peppers and fry over high heat only until heated through.*

ARTICHOKE SAUTÉ

Salteado de Alcachofas

These artichokes don't get put in lemon-water, so prepare them immediately before cooking so they don't darken. They are delicious as a side dish with roast lamb or chicken but may also be served as a warm salad on top of salad leaves, drizzled with a little Sherry vinegar. The artichokes most commonly found in Spain only reach fist size, even when mature. If you are using very large artichokes, cut them in half and nip out the choke with the tip of a very sharp knife.

✳ SERVES 6

900g artichokes (6 small)
120ml / scant ¼ pint olive oil

Coarse sea salt

Pull off and discard the outer layer of artichoke leaves. Cut off the stems. Use a serrated knife to cut the top two-thirds off the artichokes. Discard leaves.

Begin to heat the oil in a heavy frying pan over medium-high heat. Place the artichoke bottoms on a chopping board, cut edges down. With a sharp knife, cut the bottoms into 3mm/⅛in slices.

Add them to the hot oil as they are cut. Continue slicing until all the artichokes are in the sauté pan.

Fry the artichokes over medium-high heat until they are crunchy-tender, about 3 minutes. Remove them from the oil with a slotted spoon. Drain briefly and sprinkle with salt. Serve hot or at room temperature.

CHEESY ARTICHOKE GRATIN

Gratinado de Alcachofas con Queso

Artichokes with cheese make a substantial vegetable dish that you could serve as a luncheon main course. This dish can also be prepared with cardoons, a vegetable thistle related to the artichoke. While artichokes consist of the thistle's flower bud, cardoons are thick stems, looking like oversized stalks of celery. They need to be peeled, then cooked slowly until very tender.

If you cook the artichokes in a clay cazuela or casserole, they can go from the hob to the oven. Otherwise, transfer the cooked artichokes to a baking dish.

SERVES 4 AS A LUNCHEON MAIN COURSE OR 6 TO 8 AS A SIDE DISH

1 tablespoon fresh lemon juice	60g diced bacon
8 medium-large artichokes (1.4kg)	4 tablespoons dry white wine
3½ tablespoons olive oil	½ teaspoon salt
½ medium onion, chopped	85g coarsely grated Manchego cheese
1 garlic clove, chopped	25g fresh breadcrumbs

Fill a bowl with cold water and add the lemon juice.

To trim the artichokes: cut off the stem close to the artichoke base. Snap off the first 3 layers of leaves (about 12 leaves). Use a sharp knife to slice each artichoke about 3cm/1¼in above it base, discarding all the upper leaves. Cut the artichokes in half. Use the tip of a knife or a melon baller to scoop out and discard the fuzzy choke. Drop the artichoke halves into the lemon water. Artichoke stems can be peeled down to the pale centres and cooked with the prepared artichoke halves.

Heat 3 tablespoons of the oil in a medium casserole or cazuela over medium heat. Sauté the onion, garlic and bacon for 5 minutes.

Drain the artichoke halves. Add them to the casserole and sauté over medium high heat for 5 minutes. Add the wine, salt and 4 tablespoons of water. Cover the pan and simmer until the artichokes are tender, 15 minutes.

Preheat the oven to 190°C/170°C fan/GM5.

Remove the casserole from the hob and uncover. Spread the grated cheese on top. Sprinkle with the breadcrumbs. Drizzle the remaining ½ tablespoon of oil over the crumbs.

Bake until the mixture is bubbling and the crumbs are light golden, 15 minutes. Serve hot.

CASTILIAN GREEN BEANS *with* RED PEPPERS

Judías Verdes a la Castellana

These green beans are so delicious you may want to serve them as a main course. If possible, use flat romano beans; but if unavailable, young stringless runner beans would make a good substitute. Should you choose to use frozen beans, skip the first step, in which the beans are blanched. Tinned or jarred roasted red peppers can be used in this recipe.

SERVES 6

700g green beans, topped and tailed and cut into 5cm/2in lengths

2 tablespoons olive oil

85g diced pancetta, bacon or serrano ham

2 garlic cloves, sliced

Pinch of cumin seeds

Pinch of chilli flakes

½ teaspoon salt

Freshly ground black pepper

3 roasted and peeled red peppers, cut into thin strips

Cook the beans in boiling salted water until crisp-tender, 5 minutes. Drain, saving 120ml/scant ¼ pint of the liquid. Refresh the beans in cold water and drain again.

Heat the oil in a large casserole or cazuela over medium heat. Sauté the pancetta for 2 minutes, until it begins to crisp. Add the garlic and fry until light golden, 1 minute. Stir in the cumin and chilli flakes. Add the beans and sauté over medium heat for 3 minutes. Sprinkle with the salt and pepper to taste.

Stir in the strips of red pepper and half of the reserved bean liquid. Cook, uncovered, over medium heat, stirring occasionally, until the beans are very tender and most of the liquid is cooked off, about 12 minutes. (Add more bean liquid if needed.)

CHARD SAUTÉ

Mojete de Acelgas

Chard is such a satisfying vegetable because, with the leafy greens and substantial stems, it adds up to much more than spinach. In Spain, chard is usually grown huge, with leaves like palm fronds and stems as broad as pork chops.

This typical Manchegan chard dish would typically be served as a starter or a simple supper dish – with eggs folded into the vegetables. I prefer it without the eggs, as a side dish.

SERVES **6**

900g fresh chard

2 tablespoons olive oil

2 garlic cloves, sliced crossways

1 teaspoon pimentón

85g chopped tomato, well drained if tinned

1 teaspoon salt

Freshly ground black pepper

1 tablespoon wine vinegar

Wash the chard, remove strings, if necessary, and chop the leaves and stems. Bring a large saucepan of salted water to the boil and cook the chard until tender, about 10 minutes. Drain, rinse in cold water and drain thoroughly again.

Heat the oil in a frying pan over medium heat and fry the sliced garlic until golden, about 1 minute. Remove the pan from the heat and add the pimentón and tomato. Return to medium heat and cook for 3 minutes.

Stir in the chard, salt, pepper to taste and 2 tablespoons water. Cook until the chard begins to simmer. Stir in the vinegar. Serve hot.

SPINACH with GARLIC, INIESTA STYLE

Espinacas a la Iniestense

Iniesta is a village in the Manchuela region of the province of Cuenca, where the spinach is said to be especially tasty due to being irrigated with saline water. This recipe comes from a study of the culinary heritage of the region by Javier Cuéllar Tórtola and Pedro Pardo Domingo.

SERVES 4 TO 6

700g fresh spinach

3 tablespoons olive oil

1 egg, separated

2 garlic cloves, peeled

½ teaspoon coarse salt

Pinch of ground cloves

Pinch of ground ginger

Freshly ground black pepper

120ml/scant ¼ pint milk

Wash and trim the spinach. Place in a large saucepan over high heat. Cover and steam until wilted, about 5 minutes. Drain in a colander, pressing out as much liquid as possible. Use kitchen scissors to cut up the spinach.

Heat the oil in a large frying pan over medium heat and add the spinach. Toss it in the oil for 1 minute, then add the egg white and stir it around.

Crush the garlic with the salt in a mortar. Add the cloves, ginger, pepper and 2 tablespoons water. Stir this into the spinach.

Beat the egg yolk with the milk and add to the spinach. Cook, uncovered, until most of the liquid cooks away, 10 minutes. Serve hot.

PAN-SAUTÉED CABBAGE *with* CUMIN

Coles Salteadas

Seasoned with garlic and cumin, simple cabbage becomes a delicious side dish. Serve it with pork chops, roast chicken or salmon.

SERVES 6

900g green cabbage

Salt

2 tablespoons olive oil

2 garlic cloves, thinly sliced lengthways

Pinch of cumin seeds

Freshly ground black pepper

1 tablespoon white wine vinegar

Pomegranate seeds (optional)

Slice the cabbage crossways. Bring a large saucepan of salted water to the boil and cook the cabbage until tender, about 10 minutes. Drain and refresh in cold water. Drain well.

Heat the oil in a large frying pan over medium heat and sauté the garlic until light golden, 1 minute. Add the cumin seeds and sauté for 30 seconds. Stir in the cabbage. Season with pepper and ½ teaspoon salt. Sauté the cabbage until thoroughly heated, 5 minutes. Stir in the vinegar immediately before serving. If desired, scatter a few pomegranate seeds on top of the cabbage.

BATTER-FRIED CAULIFLOWER

Coliflor Rebosada

Served with a piquant tomato sauce for dipping, these titbits of cauliflower make a nice appetiser. Or serve them as a side dish with simple grilled meat or poultry.

𝒳 SERVES **4** TO **6**

Salt

570g cauliflower florets

1 tablespoon finely chopped fresh parsley

1 tablespoon fresh lemon juice

Olive oil for frying (about 370ml / 12 fl oz)

About 70g flour for dredging

¼ teaspoon caraway seeds

⅛ teaspoon cayenne

1 egg

Bring 2 litres/3½ pints of water to the boil with 2 teaspoons salt. Add the cauliflower, bring to the boil again, and cook until crisp-tender, about 5 minutes. Drain, cover with cold water, and drain again. Place the cauliflower in a bowl and sprinkle with the parsley and lemon juice. Toss the cauliflower and allow to stand for 15 minutes.

Heat oil to a depth of ½cm/¼in in a heavy frying pan over medium-high heat until very hot but not smoking. Combine the flour with caraway and cayenne in a shallow dish. In a small bowl, beat the egg with 1 tablespoon water.

Dredge the florets in the seasoned flour, then coat them in beaten egg, and lift them into the hot oil. Fry them, in 2 or 3 batches, until golden on all sides, about 3 minutes. Remove with a slotted spoon and drain on kitchen paper. Sprinkle with salt if desired. Serve hot.

NOTE: *The cauliflower may be prepared 1 hour in advance and reheated in a 200°C/180°C fan/GM6 oven for about 8 minutes.*

CAULIFLOWER *or* BROCCOLI *with* GOLDEN GARLIC *and* ALMONDS

Coliflor o Brócoli con Ajo Dorado y Almendras

You can prepare this vegetable dish with both cauliflower and broccoli. Cook them separately and place them together in a heated serving bowl before spooning the garlic dressing over them both.

SERVES **6** TO **8**

800g cauliflower and/or broccoli

Salt

3 tablespoons olive oil

4 garlic cloves, sliced crossways

1 tablespoon flaked almonds

1 teaspoon sweet pimentón

1 tablespoon wine vinegar

1 tablespoon chopped fresh parsley

Cut the cauliflower and broccoli heads into 5cm/2in florets. Cut the broccoli stem into 5cm/2in pieces by peeling the stem, cutting in half lengthways, and cutting crossways into 5cm/2in pieces.

Cook the cauliflower and broccoli separately in boiling salted water until tender, 10 minutes. Drain, saving 3 tablespoons of the cooking water. Keep warm in a serving bowl.

While the cauliflower and broccoli are cooking, heat the oil in a small frying pan over medium-high heat. Add the sliced garlic and almonds and fry them until they begin to turn golden, about 30 seconds. Remove the frying pan from the heat.

Stir in the pimentón, then immediately add the vinegar and reserved cooking liquid. Add the parsley.

Spoon the garlic and almond dressing over the cauliflower and broccoli and serve immediately.

MINTED CARROTS

Zanahorias con Hierbabuena

Fresh mint adds a sprightly touch to carrots. They are also good as a salad – add a bit of Sherry vinegar to the cold carrots and serve on top of salad leaves with a sprinkling of chopped spring onion.

SERVES 4 TO 6

450g carrots, peeled and thinly sliced

1 tablespoon olive oil

1 tablespoon chopped onion

1 tablespoon pine nuts

1 small garlic clove, finely chopped

1 tablespoon raisins (optional)

1 tablespoon fresh lemon juice

Salt and freshly ground black pepper

1 tablespoon chopped fresh mint leaves

Cook the carrots in boiling salted water until just tender, about 5 minutes. Drain and refresh in cold water. Drain.

Heat the oil in a small saucepan over medium heat and sauté the onion for 2 minutes. Add the pine nuts and garlic and sauté for 2 minutes more. Add the carrots and raisins, if you're using them, and sauté until the carrots are heated through, about 2 minutes. Stir in the lemon juice and season with salt and pepper. Remove from the heat and add the mint leaves.

BROAD BEANS *with* ESCAROLE (BROAD-LEAVED ENDIVE) *and* MINT

Cazuela de Habas

Springtime is so fleeting! Tender broad beans, spring onions and mint come and go. Salad leaves such as endive bolt to seed with the first hot days. Here is a dish to celebrate the season. It makes a fine side dish to serve with lamb.

If small broad beans are freshly picked and shelled, their outer skins are perfectly edible. Only dry boad beans or old beans need to be blanched and then skinned.

SERVES 6

2 tablespoons olive oil

350g shelled broad beans

55g chopped spring onion

1 fresh mint sprig

Shredded escarole (broad-leaved endive) or Cos lettuce(6 to 8 large leaves)

1 teaspoon salt

1 tablespoon white wine vinegar

Chopped fresh mint for garnish

Heat the oil in a cazuela or heavy casserole pot over low heat. Add the broad beans, onion and mint. Cook, uncovered, stirring occasionally, for 20 minutes.

Remove the mint. Add the salad leaves, salt, vinegar and 4 tablespoons of water. Cover and simmer for 15 minutes. Serve garnished with chopped mint.

SAUTÉ OF FRESH PEAS and CARROTS

Salteado de Guisantes con Zanahorias

Made with sweet, freshly shelled garden peas, this dish is exceptional. In Spain it might be served as a first course, with a garnish of chopped egg. But it makes a good side dish, with fish, chicken or meat.

You will need about 1.5kg of peas in their pods to make 250g or so of shelled peas. Frozen peas can be substituted. Other vegetables – broad beans, chopped asparagus, green beans – can be used in place of peas, although cooking time may need to be adjusted.

SERVES 4

2 tablespoons olive oil	1 tablespoon chopped fresh parsley
70g diced carrot	Pinch of dried thyme
85g diced serrano ham or bacon	½ teaspoon salt
½ medium onion, chopped	Freshly ground black pepper
1 garlic clove, chopped	2 tablespoons chopped spring onion
40g diced red pepper	1 hard-boiled egg, chopped (optional)
250g fresh or frozen peas	

Heat the oil in a cazuela or medium frying pan over medium heat. Add the carrot, ham and onion and sauté for 5 minutes. Add the garlic and red pepper and sauté for 2 minutes longer.

Add the peas to the pan and sauté them for 3 minutes. Season with parsley, thyme, salt and pepper to taste. Add 120ml/scant ¼ pint water. Bring to the boil, cover and simmer until the peas are tender, about 5 minutes. (Some peas may require longer cooking. If so, add more water and simmer them until tender.)

Remove the cover and cook for 1 minute, until most of the liquid is cooked away.

Serve immediately, garnished with spring onion and, if desired, chopped egg.

MARKET DAY IN ALCÁZAR DE SAN JUAN

Monday is *mercadillo,* street market day, in Alcázar de San Juan, a town in the very heart of La Mancha. From Roman times this was a crossroads for legionnaires and for trade. The Arabs followed the Romans, bequeathing the town the first part of its name, Alcázar, meaning 'fortress', although nothing remains of the Arab fortifications. After the reconquest by Christian kings, the town was repopulated by the military order of San Juan, the Knights of St John. Thus the second part of the name. In the thirteenth century, King Sancho IV declared Alcázar de San Juan a market town. In more recent history, Alcázar emerged as an important railway hub. Today it is a thriving centre of agribusiness – wine (the offices of the regulating board for DO La Mancha wine are located in Alcázar), cheese (one of the country's biggest cheese producers is here) and fresh produce from market gardens.

Every Monday vendors spread out their wares across dozens of open-air stalls on the edge of town. Most of them are selling shoes and underwear, baby clothes and tea towels, pots, pans and screwdrivers. But just past a trailer with cages of live baby chicks, ducks, and turkeys dyed fluorescent pink, yellow and purple begin the food stands.

A prickly smell that tickles the taste buds announces the pickle sellers. Their stalls have vats of brine-cured olives, pickled aubergine, pickled onions in several colours and sizes and pickled peppers, both hot and sweet.

The seller of *chucherías,* children's sweets in a riot of different colours and shapes – pink and green sugar chews, gumdrops, foil-wrapped caramels, lemon balls, strawberry twists, liquorice sticks – scoops the sweets into bags and weighs them on an old-fashioned balance scale. Next to his stand is one selling *frutos secos,* all types of dried fruits and nuts. There are five kinds of almonds (whole, shelled, skinned, toasted, fried and salted); hazelnuts, walnuts, peanuts, pine nuts, toasted chickpeas; *pipas,* sunflower seeds; dried chestnuts, edible acorns, figs, dried apricots (called *orejones,* little ears); prunes, raisins, honey. A nearby spice seller has wooden boxes heaped with pungent spices and aromatic herbs, both culinary and medicinal. Bunches of thyme hang above the table. Thyme flavours the olives gathered in the autumn to be home-cured in brine.

On the back loop of stalls is the farmers' market. (No fresh meat or cheese is sold at the Monday market.) Mercedes Martín sells farm produce at the market with her two brothers, Julián and Jesús. They also have a stall in the Alcázar municipal market, bringing produce from the family farm in nearby Herencia. On one September morning Mercedes had two kinds of aubergine, green beans, spinach, tomatoes, peppers, courgettes, pumpkin, cauliflower, spinach, chard, peppers, garlic, leeks, cabbages, carrots, potatoes, melons, watermelons and plums. Only apples, pears and some other fruits came from outside the region.

She proffered slivers of melon for tasting. Juicy and sweet, it was a delight. The melon grown here is a variety known as *piel de sapo,* 'toad skin'. It has dark green, hard, ridged skin and pale yellow flesh. It's commercialised under the protected label of Indicación Geográfica Protegida Melón de la Mancha.

Mercedes also had sun-dried tomatoes – *tomatillas* – from the farm.

'Split them in half, put them in the sun for one week,' she said. 'The sun of La Mancha is powerful. Add a couple of sun-dried tomatoes to a slow-cooked stew,' she suggested.

She also had strings of skinny dried sweet peppers plus hot chillies.

The dried peppers, she said, go into *tiznao,* a favourite La Mancha dish of roasted peppers, onions and cod. A customer filling her market basket at Mercedes' stall offered her recipe for white beans cooked with the dried peppers, sun-dried tomatoes, onion, pig's trotter and jowls. Julián, Mercedes' brother, said the *guindillas,* dried chillies, were an essential ingredient in the sauce for cooking snails.

And those tiny aubergines? 'In Almagro they pickle them,' offered another shopper, 'but I cook them whole with tomatoes and cumin.'

An elderly man was picking out some freshly dug potatoes. 'These will be good in a *mojete* with asparagus and mushrooms,' he said. *Mojete* is a vegetable stew served soupy, for dunking bread into. He also bought some spinach, to be sautéed in olive oil with garlic, then scrambled with eggs.

A pretty young woman carrying a huge bouquet of yellow and white flowers selected gemlike plums in green, pink and violet. The local greengage plums were in their moment of glory, juicy, tart and sweet.

By half past one in the afternoon, the constant stream of shoppers had lessened. It was time to pack up the merchandise and the portable tables and head back to the farm.

AUBERGINE *with* TOMATO *and* CARAWAY

Berenjena Guisada con Alcaravea

In Alcázar de San Juan this is prepared with a variety of tiny green aubergine, cooked whole. Caraway seed, a spice used in several La Mancha dishes, adds an interesting flavour. You could substitute cumin seed. Serve the aubergine with lamb chops or roast chicken.

SERVES 6

2 medium aubergines (about 700g)

2 teaspoons salt

1 bay leaf

2 tablespoons olive oil

2 garlic cloves, chopped

250g peeled, seeded and chopped tomato

⅛ teaspoon caraway seeds

Freshly ground black pepper

2 teaspoons fresh lemon juice or wine vinegar

Chopped fresh mint or parsley for garnish

Peel the aubergines and cut into 2cm/¾in cubes. Bring 1 litre/about 1½ pints of water to the boil with 1½ teaspoons of the salt and the bay leaf. Add the aubergine and cook until barely tender, 3 to 4 minutes. Drain. Discard the bay leaf.

Heat the oil in a large frying pan over medium heat. Add the garlic and sauté until golden, 1 minute. Raise the heat to high, add the aubergine and tomato, and sauté for 1 minute. Season with caraway, pepper and the remaining ½ teaspoon salt. Reduce the heat and cook until most of the liquid has cooked away, 10 minutes.

Remove from the heat and stir in the lemon juice. Sprinkle with chopped mint to serve.

BAKED AUBERGINES *with* CHEESE

Berenjenas con Queso al Horno

This easy dish can cook alongside a roast. The spices and wine turn the slow-roasted aubergines sweet and sticky. The aubergine skins serve as a vessel to hold the roasted aubergine and are not meant to be eaten. While authentic Manchego is best, you could substitute Parmesan, Gruyère or pecorino.

⁂ SERVES 8

4 medium aubergines (about 1.4kg)

Salt

4 tablespoons olive oil

¼ teaspoon ground cinnamon

Pinch of ground cloves

Pinch of ground ginger

Grating of fresh nutmeg

Pinch of dried oregano

Freshly ground black pepper

250ml/scant ½ pint dry white wine

170g Manchego, grated

Cut off and discard the stems and leaves from the aubergines. Cut each aubergine in half lengthways. With a sharp knife, make deep cuts in the flesh lengthways and crossways. Salt the aubergines and leave them, cut side down, to drain for 1 hour.

Preheat the oven to 180°C/160°C fan/GM4.

Rinse the aubergines in water, drain well, then pat dry with kitchen paper. Place the aubergine halves, cut side up, in a single layer in a roasting tin. Drizzle with the olive oil. Combine the cinnamon, cloves, ginger, nutmeg, oregano and pepper to taste. Sprinkle the spices over the aubergine. Bake for 15 minutes.

Pour the wine over the aubergines. Return to the oven for 15 minutes. Turn the aubergines cut side down and bake for 30 minutes longer, or until they are fork-tender.

Turn cut side up again and spoon the pan juices over the aubergines. (If the pan is dry, add about 4 tablespoons of water.) Spread the grated cheese on top of the aubergine halves. Return to the oven and bake until the cheese is melted and lightly browned, 12 to 15 minutes. Serve hot.

FRIED AUBERGINE *with* A DRIZZLE OF HONEY

Berenjena con Miel

Salty fried aubergine paired with sweet, sticky honey makes a tantalising combination of flavour and texture. In Spain, the aubergine slices, heaped on a platter, are served as a tapa or starter.

SERVES 4 TO 6

2 medium aubergines (700g)

Salt

About 130g plain flour for dredging

About 700ml/1¼ pints olive oil for frying

2 teaspoons honey

Peel the aubergines and cut them crossways into 4mm/³⁄₁₆in thick slices. Layer them in a bowl, sprinkling liberally with salt. Allow to stand for 1 hour.

Rinse the aubergine slices in water and drain. Dredge them in flour and shake off the excess.

Heat 1cm/½in oil in a large frying pan until almost smoking. Working in 2 or 3 batches, add slices of aubergine to the oil. Fry them, turning once, until golden, about 1 minute per side. Remove and allow to drain on kitchen paper.

Heap the aubergines on a platter and drizzle with the honey. Serve hot.

CHAR-GRILLED AUBERGINE *with* LEMON DRESSING

Berenjena a la Parilla con Aliño

These grilled aubergines are the perfect accompaniment to a barbecue meal. They can be served hot off the grill but are even better if the dressing is allowed to soak in for 30 minutes. The tangy lemon dressing is also good tossed with cooked green beans.

SERVES 6

3 medium aubergines (about 1 kg)

Salt

5 tablespoons olive oil, plus oil for the grill

2 tablespoons fine dry breadcrumbs

2 garlic cloves, chopped

Pinch of chilli flakes

5 tablespoons fresh lemon juice

4 tablespoons chopped fresh parsley

½ teaspoon dried oregano

Cut off the stems and leaves from the aubergines. Cut each aubergine in half lengthways. Make 2 to 3 slashes in the flesh side. In a large bowl, combine 1½ litres/2½ pints of water with 1½ tablespoons salt. Place the cut aubergine in the brine and place a saucer on top to keep them submerged. Allow to stand for at least 1 hour and up to 3 hours.

While the aubergine are soaking, prepare the dressing. Heat 5 tablespoons of olive oil in a small frying pan over medium heat. Add the breadcrumbs, garlic, ½ teaspoon salt and the chilli flakes and stir until they begin to turn golden, about 2 minutes. Immediately add the lemon juice and 4 tablespoons of water. Stir until the sauce thickens and emulsifies. Remove from the heat and allow to cool for 5 minutes. Stir in the parsley and oregano.

Drain the aubergines and discard the water. Light the barbecue. When the coals are medium-hot and uniformly covered with grey ash, brush both sides of the aubergine halves with oil. Set them skin side down on the grill and grill for 5 minutes. Turn the aubergines cut side down and grill until they are tender when tested with a skewer and the surface is golden brown, about 5 minutes.

Transfer the aubergines to a platter and spoon the dressing over them. Serve hot or at room temperature.

PAN-GRILLED VEGETABLES

Verduras a la Parrilla

This assortment of pan-grilled vegetables makes a good starter, in place of a salad. Use either a ridged grill pan or a flat griddle. Cooking time will vary for each vegetable, depending on thickness, but all should cook in 8 minutes or less. Grill the aubergine until very tender, but allow asparagus and onion to stay somewhat crisp. These vegetables are so delicious with nothing more elaborate than extra virgin olive oil. However, if you like, serve *ajiaceite,* garlic sauce (page 115), as an accompaniment.

SERVES 4

1 medium aubergine (about 350g)

1 medium courgette (about 350g)

Coarse sea salt

4 tablespoons olive oil

1 red pepper

8 asparagus spears

1 onion

4 mushrooms, such as portobello, oyster or porcini (ceps)

1 firm plum tomato, quartered

4 garlic cloves

1 tablespoon plus 1 teaspoon extra virgin olive oil

Fresh parsley or basil sprigs for garnish

Peel the aubergine and cut off the stem end. Cut lengthways into 2cm/¾in thick slices. Place in a shallow pan. Trim the ends of the courgette and slice it lengthways into 1cm/½in thick slices. Place in a single layer in the pan. Sprinkle the aubergine and courgettes on both sides with salt. Let them stand for 1 hour. Drain the aubergine and courgette in a colander for 15 minutes. Pat dry.

Wipe out the shallow pan. Spread the aubergine and courgette slices in it. Brush them on both sides with oil.

Cut the pepper into quarters, discarding the stem and seeds. Use a vegetable peeler to shave the outer skins from the asparagus. Slice the onion 1cm/½in thick. Spread the pepper, asparagus, onion, mushrooms, tomato and unpeeled garlic in another shallow pan and brush them with oil.

Brush a ridged grill pan or flat griddle with oil and heat until very hot. Cook each of the vegetables until tender, turning slices with tongs to grill both sides. Aubergines will need about 8 minutes; courgettes, 6; asparagus, 8; onion, 5; mushrooms, 8; and tomato, 3.

Arrange slices of each vegetable on 4 plates. Sprinkle with the coarse salt and drizzle 1 teaspoon extra virgin olive oil over each serving. Garnish with parsley or basil. Serve warm or at room temperature.

Mirad, señor doctor; de aquí adelante,
no os curéis de darme a comer cosas regaladas,
ni manjares exquisitos, porque será sacar a mi estómago
de sus quicios, el cual está acostumbrado a cabra,
a vaca, a tocino, a cecina, a nabos y a cebollas. . . .

Look, Doctor, from now on, don't even think about feeding me cakes, nor fancy foods, because you'll just upset my stomach, which is used to goat meat, beef, salt pork, jerky, turnips and onions. . . .

SANCHO PANZA, COMPLAINING ABOUT THE FOOD
HE IS SERVED AS GOVERNOR OF AN ISLAND

BRAISED TURNIPS *with* PIMENTÓN

Nabos Guisados al Pimentón

These turnips go nicely with roast turkey or roast pork. Smoky pimentón de La Vera gives them a special nuance.

SERVES 6

570g turnips

½ red pepper

2 tablespoons olive oil

1 garlic clove, sliced crossways

1 teaspoon sweet pimentón, preferably smoked

Chilli flakes

Pinch of dried oregano

½ teaspoon salt

1 tablespoon Sherry vinegar

Peel the turnips and cut them into 5cm/2in pieces. Cut the pepper into 5cm/2in strips. Heat the oil in a frying pan or cazuela over medium heat and sauté the turnips until lightly browned, 5 minutes. Add the pepper and garlic and sauté for 2 minutes longer.

Remove the pan from the heat and stir in the pimentón, chilli flakes, oregano, salt and vinegar. Add 300ml/½ pint water. Return the pan to the heat. Bring to the boil, cover and simmer, turning the turnips occasionally, until they are very tender and most of the liquid has cooked away, about 35 minutes.

MUSHROOM *and* POTATO STEW

Guisado de Setas y Patatas

La Mancha is Spain's biggest producer of cultivated mushrooms.

A real forager might return to the kitchen with two or even three varieties of wild mushrooms. (*Níscalos, Lactarius sanguifluus* and *setas de cardo, Pleurotus eryngii*, are the most common.) But, if your foraging takes place at the supermarket, that's fine too. You can select several varieties if you like, or make this stew with just one – woody portobellos and shiitakes, delicate chanterelles or oyster mushrooms. A satisfying vegetarian main dish.

SERVES 6

5 tablespoons olive oil

½ medium onion, chopped

2 garlic cloves, 1 chopped, 1 crushed

2 bay leaves

700g sliced mushrooms (can be a mixture)

1 teaspoon sweet pimentón

¼ teaspoon saffron threads, crushed (optional)

40g chopped red pepper

90g peeled and chopped tomato

1.4kg baking potatoes, peeled and cut into 4cm / 1½in chunks

120ml / scant ¼ pint dry white wine

2 teaspoons salt

2 tablespoons chopped fresh parsley

Pinch of hot pimentón for garnish

In a cazuela or deep sauté pan over high heat, heat the oil and sauté the chopped onion, chopped garlic, bay leaves and mushrooms for 5 minutes, or until the mushrooms begin to sizzle. (Some varieties of mushrooms will release more liquid and take longer to cook.)

Stir in the pimentón, saffron if you're using it, red pepper, tomato, potatoes and wine. Continue to cook over high heat for 10 minutes.

Add 250ml / scant ½ pint water and the salt. Bring to the boil, cover the cazuela and simmer for 20 minutes. Add the crushed garlic to the stew. Uncover and cook until the potatoes are tender, about 10 minutes more. Let stand for 5 minutes before serving. Sprinkle with the parsley and pimentón.

CAZUELA OF POTATOES *and* CHARD

Patatas con Acelgas en Cazuela

The distinctive flavours of chard, leeks and fennel meld nicely with potatoes in this dish, which goes especially well with fish. Bake it in a flameproof cazuela or gratin dish. A topping of grated Manchego is optional.

Leftovers make an admirable cold dish. Spike the potatoes and chard with fresh lemon juice and serve with a sprinkling of chopped spring onion and parsley.

SERVES 6 TO 8

3 tablespoons olive oil

900g baking potatoes

230g chard stems and leaves, chopped

50g chopped leek

Freshly ground black pepper

¼ teaspoon fennel seeds

1 teaspoon salt

2 tablespoons wine vinegar

1 garlic clove, crushed

45g grated cheese (optional)

Preheat the oven to 180°C/160°C fan/GM4. Oil the cazuela.

Peel the potatoes and slice them 6mm/¼in thick. Mix together the sliced potatoes, chopped chard and leek and spread in the cazuela. Sprinkle with pepper, fennel seeds and salt.

In a small bowl, combine the remaining oil, the vinegar, crushed garlic and 120ml/scant ¼ pint water. Pour this mixture over the vegetables.

Cover the cazuela with foil. Set the cazuela over medium heat on the hob until the liquid begins to bubble. Then place it in the oven and bake for 30 minutes.

Remove the foil, add the grated cheese if desired, and return to the oven for 15 minutes.

Allow the vegetables to sit for 10 minutes before serving.

POTATOES MASHED *with* GREEN GARLIC

Palotes con Patatas

Palotes are garlic scapes – stems with flower buds – that are removed from the garlic plants so the bulbs develop more fully. Green garlic shoots or spring onions can be used in this recipe in place of scapes. Serve this dish with poached eggs if desired. This recipe comes from Las Pedroñeras, a village in Cuenca famed for its garlic.

SERVES 6

900g baking potatoes

3 tablespoons olive oil

40g chopped scapes, green garlic shoots or spring onions

1 garlic clove, chopped

1 teaspoon sweet pimentón

Chilli flakes

½ teaspoon salt

Freshly ground black pepper

Peel the potatoes, cut them into pieces and cook them in boiling salted water until very tender. Drain the potatoes, saving 250ml/scant ½ pint of the liquid.

Heat the oil in a heavy frying pan over medium heat and gently sauté the chopped garlic shoots and garlic for 5 minutes. Remove the pan from the heat and stir in the pimentón and chilli flakes.

Return the frying pan to the heat and add the drained potatoes. Chop and mash them in the oil until almost puréed. Stir in half of the reserved potato water, the salt and pepper to taste. Keep stirring and mashing the potatoes, adding as much of the remaining liquid as needed to make a mixture the consistency of mashed potatoes. A few lumps in the potatoes are fine.

HOT POTATOES

Patatas Bravas

These potatoes are hot as in spicy. Accompanied by a chilli spiced tomato sauce, they are the *patatas bravas* that originated in the Madrid tapa bar Café Brava. This version, without the sauce, is good served alongside steak, roast lamb, grilled chicken or fried fish.

The potatoes can be peeled and cut several hours in advance. Leave them covered with water. Then drain and pat them dry on tea towels. Fry the potatoes in olive oil for the best flavour. If using extra virgin oil, select one of the Picual variety blends, for they are especially stable at high temperatures. After the oil has cooled, strain it and reserve in a cool dark place for a second use.

SERVES 4 TO 6

900g baking potatoes, peeled and cut into 2½cm / 1in cubes

About 1 litre / 1½ pints olive oil for frying

½ teaspoon ground cumin

1 teaspoon salt

Cayenne to taste

Pat the potatoes dry. Heat the oil in a large, deep straight-sided frying pan to a depth of 1 to 2cm / ½ to ¾in. When the oil is shimmering and almost smoking (180°C), add the potatoes. Fry them, turning occasionally, until they are golden brown and tender when pierced with a skewer, about 12 minutes.

Remove the potatoes to a bowl lined with kitchen paper. Sprinkle them with cumin, salt and cayenne. Serve immediately.

HASH BROWN POTATO CAKE

Hartatunos

The Spanish name of this dish, *hartatunos*, means 'fill the rascals up'. It makes a good side with roast meat or game stews.

SERVES 6

4 tablespoons olive oil

700g peeled potatoes in 5mm/¼in thick slices

45g diced bacon

1 garlic clove

1½ teaspoons sweet pimentón

⅛ teaspoon cayenne

½ teaspoon salt

Freshly ground black pepper

Pinch of cumin seeds

Six 1cm/½in thick baguette slices

1 fresh mint sprig for garnish

Heat the oil in a large heavy frying pan over medium heat. Add the potatoes and bacon. Cut a slit in the unpeeled garlic and add it whole to the pan. Cook the potatoes, turning them frequently, for 10 minutes. Don't let them brown. As the potatoes begin to soften, use the edge of a spatula to begin breaking them into smaller pieces. Continue cooking and breaking up the potatoes until they are completely tender and lightly browned, about 15 minutes more.

Remove the frying pan from the heat. Tip the pan so the remaining oil drains to one side. Lift out the potatoes, bacon, and garlic with a spatula and reserve them.

Stir the pimentón, cayenne, salt, pepper to taste and cumin seeds into the oil remaining in the pan. Add 4 tablespoons of water and stir to blend the spices well. Add 4 tablespoons more water. Place the baguette slices in the pan and return it to medium heat. Break up the pieces of bread with the edge of a spatula. Cook until the bread begins to dry and toast.

Return the potatoes, bacon and garlic to the frying pan. Cook, tossing the mixture together for 3 minutes. Discard the garlic. Press the potato-bread mixture into a round, flat cake, 20 to 23cm/8 to 9in in diameter. Firm the edges with a spatula. Cook until browned. Loosen the potato cake with a spatula. Invert it onto a serving plate, cut it into wedges and garnish it with the mint.

THAT SPECIAL TOUCH –
EXTRA VIRGIN OLIVE OIL

In my kitchen cupboard are four or five bottles of different extra virgin olive oils from several regions of Spain. That's in addition to the 'house' olive oil, my everyday cooking oil.

It's such a pleasure to have a palette of flavours to choose from. When I want nuances of flavour, I dab and dribble from my collection of fine oils. Sometimes I know exactly what flavour I'm looking for to complement a dish. Other times I relish experimenting, sampling the range of possibilities.

I love the Spanish way of drizzling a little extra virgin olive oil over a finished dish – cooked vegetables, grilled fish, sliced cold meat. It lends style and, by varying the chosen oil, changes the focus of a dish. Simple grilled salmon takes on different hues as you splash through the spectrum from sweet and fruity Hojiblanca to almondy Arbequina to peppery Picual.

Olive oils from Spain are not usually single varietals. In most regions the oil is blended to combine the best characteristics of several varieties. For example, Arbequina is prized for its delicate, almondy flavour, but it is somewhat unstable (prone to oxidation). Picual, fruity and somewhat bitter, is remarkably stable, even at high temperatures. When blended with Picual, Hojiblanca lends a sweetness that balances the bitterness.

Olive oil is the single cooking fat in my kitchen – no butter or margarine, no lard, no vegetable shortening, no other vegetable oil. So, I use it in quantity. Yes, on breakfast toast, on popcorn, in cakes and pies, as well as in every single Spanish dish I cook. Happily, I live at the source, so this is not an extravagant gesture. While olive oil is more expensive than most vegetable fats, I feel it's worth the price. I know it has healthful benefits, but it's mainly about taste. I'm willing to pay the price.

My 'house' oil is local, pressed at a town several miles away. Over the Christmas holidays and during the first couple weeks of January, I pick my own olives and haul them to a weighing point. An operator weighs my sacks and gives me a ticket. At the end of the season of *recolección,* I return and find out how many litres of oil I've earned.

Because it is the fruit of my own labour, I am careful to store it properly and use it within a year. No lingering half-empty olive oil bottles in my cupboard! (Keep extra virgin olive oil moderately cool and – and most importantly – protected from the light.)

I also collect olive oil on my travels in Spain, so I can sample many terroirs. In the United Kingdom you might not have available the huge selection that I do in Spain, but you should find in speciality shops that there some of the absolute best in quality from various regions.

I find more and more organic olive oils available, and I use them as much as possible. But I haven't switched completely. For one thing, the bulk of the virgin oil I use is my local one, which comes from growers of all sorts. And, of course, organics off the shelf are more expensive.

SHEPHERDS' GARLIC-FRIED BREADCRUMBS

Migas del Pastor

Shepherds in the field prepare this simple dish with stale bread and bits of salt pork, cooked in a large frying pan over a wood fire. They eat it straight from the pan. During the *vendimia,* grape harvest, sweet grapes accompany the *migas*. In this rendition raisins replace the grapes. Their sweetness makes a nice counterpoint to the garlic and salty sausage. Pomegranate seeds could be used instead.

The technique of making migas is simple – soak the diced bread (start preparations at least eight hours before serving), then fry it slowly in oil until crumbly and crunchy, chopping it as it fries into very small crumbs.

Migas make a delicious breakfast served with fried eggs or a side dish with roast meat or grilled pork chop.

SERVES 4

450g day-old bread in 1cm / ½in dice

1 teaspoon salt

5 tablespoons olive oil

85g diced pancetta or bacon

1 Spanish hard chorizo (60g), casing removed and sausage chopped

8 garlic cloves

⅛ teaspoon cumin or caraway seeds

Chilli flakes

½ teaspoon sweet pimentón

4 tablespoons raisins or pomegranate seeds

Place the diced bread in a bowl. Stir the salt into 180ml / just over ¼ pint warm water. Sprinkle the bread with the water, tossing to dampen the bread evenly. Place the bread in a tea towel that has been dampened. Tie the bread tightly and allow to stand for 8 hours or overnight.

Heat the oil in a deep frying pan over medium heat and fry the pancetta and chorizo for 2 minutes. Skim out and reserve.

Lightly crush the garlic cloves to split the skins, but do not peel them. Add to the oil in which the pancetta fried. Add the cumin, chilli flakes to taste, and bread.

Fry the bread over medium heat, turning it frequently. Keep cutting the bread with the edge of a wooden spatula, gradually reducing the cubes to loose crumbs. Cook until the crumbs are lightly crunchy, 20 minutes.

Add the pimentón, raisins, and reserved pancetta and chorizo. Cook for another 2 minutes and serve.

VARIATION: *Fry the breadcrumbs as directed, omitting the pancetta, chorizo, garlic and spices. Serve them in bowls with thick drinking chocolate (page 365) poured over.*

CHICKPEA PORRIDGE

Gachas

This is a hearty breakfast for a winter's day. Served to the helpers at a hog slaughtering, it would probably incorporate chunks of fried liver, and the liquid used might be the stock in which the blood sausages were cooked.

Gachas makes a good side dish with fried meat, sausages or roast chicken, or it could be served as a dip, a sort of Spanish hummus. In La Mancha it is made with *harina de almorta*, vetch flour. This adaptation switches legume flours, using chickpea flour instead of vetch (vetch refers to a number of species of leguminous plants which include the broad bean).

SERVES 4

3 tablespoons olive oil

85g diced unsmoked bacon or pancetta

4 garlic cloves

250g chickpea flour

1 tablespoon sweet pimentón

2 teaspoons salt

1 whole clove

⅛ teaspoon ground cumin

Freshly ground black pepper

1 teaspoon dried oregano

1 litre / about 1½ pints water or stock

Chopped fresh parsley or coriander for garnish

Heat the oil in a cazuela or pan over medium-high heat and fry the diced bacon until crisped, about 1½ minutes. Skim it out and set aside. Peel 2 of the garlic cloves, add to the oil and fry until golden, about 30 seconds. Remove and reserve. Give the other 2 cloves a light blow with a mallet to split the skins and put them in the oil with the skins still on.

Stir in the chickpea flour. Stir it for a minute to toast it slightly, but do not let it scorch. Remove from the heat and stir in the pimentón.

In a blender, combine the first 2 garlic cloves you fried and set aside, along with the salt, whole clove, cumin, pepper to taste and oregano with 160ml / ¼ pint of the water. Blend until smooth.

Stir it into the chickpea flour. Add 160ml/¼ pint more of the liquid and stir to dissolve the lumps.

Put the cazuela back on the heat and continue stirring. As the porridge thickens, continue to add liquid, 160ml/¼ pint at a time, stirring continuously, until all the liquid is incorporated, about 15 minutes. The mixture should have the consistency of whipped potatoes.

Serve the porridge hot, sprinkled with the reserved bacon bits and parsley.

NOTE: *The gachas can be reheated in a microwave. Beat in additional water to thin it before heating.*

POLENTA *and* CRUNCHY CROÛTONS

Gachasmigas Manchegas

Serve this with fried eggs for a sturdy farmer's breakfast, as a base for grilled portobello mushrooms, or as a side with grilled or roasted meat. As in the previous recipe, Manchegan *gachas* are made with a fine flour from the legume vetch. In this version, polenta (cornmeal) stands in for vetch.

SERVES 4 TO 6

4 slices bread, diced

170g fatty pork, such as pork belly or jowls

4 tablepoons plus another 2 tablespoons olive oil

1 tablespoon sweet pimentón

Pinch of cayenne

150g coarse cornmeal or polenta (not instant)

1 litre / about 1½ pints boiling water

Pinch of ground cloves

¼ teaspoon caraway seeds

1 teaspoon salt

Cut the bread and pork into 1cm/½in cubes. Heat 4 tablespoons of oil in a heavy frying pan over medium-high heat. Fry the bread and pork until browned and crisped, about 2½ minutes. Remove and reserve.

Add the remainig 2 tablespoons of oil to the pan. When the oil is hot, remove the pan from the heat and stir in the pimentón and cayenne. Add the polenta. Return the pan to the heat and add the boiling water, cloves, caraway and salt.

Cook the polenta over low heat, stirring frequently with a wooden spoon. It is cooked when it begins to pull away in a mass from the bottom of the frying pan, about 20 minutes.

Serve the polenta topped with the croûtons and pork bits.

PICKLED AUBERGINE, ALMAGRO STYLE

Berenjenas de Almagro

Almagro is a beautiful town, with a Plaza Mayor enclosed by graceful old buildings, one of which houses the Corral de Comedias, a sixteenth-century theatre. The famous pickled aubergine are made with tiny (5cm/2in) round green aubergines. Speared on short lengths of wild fennel, they are prepared whole, with the stem and some of the calyx attached. The aubergines are served as a tapa. You pick them up by the stem and eat the whole aubergine.

This is an adaptation of the classic Almagro recipe. It is not meant to be a conserve, so keep it, refrigerated, for up to three weeks. It's a good relish with roast lamb. If you serve the aubergines as an aperitif, spear the pieces with cocktail sticks.

MAKES 4 CUPS

2 medium aubergines (900g)	1 tablespoon ground cumin
Salt	½ teaspoon fennel seeds
2 tablespoons sweet pimentón	¼ teaspoon ground cinnamon
½ teaspoon cayenne	5 tablespoons white wine vinegar

Peel the aubergines. Cut them lengthways into quarters, then slice crossways into 4cm/1½in wedges. In a large saucepan, bring 2 litres/3½ pints of water with 3 tablespoons salt to a rolling boil. Have ready a pan of iced water. Add the aubergines to the boiling water. When the water returns to the boil, cook the aubergine for 2 minutes. Drain and plunge into the iced water. When it is cooled, drain well.

In a bowl, combine the pimentón, cayenne, cumin, fennel, cinnamon and ½ teaspoon salt. Stir the vinegar into the spices until smooth. Add this mixture to 350ml of water in a saucepan. Bring to the boil and cook for 1 minute. Add the aubergine and bring to the boil again. Remove the pan from the heat.

Place the aubergine and liquid in a heatproof bowl or jar. Cover tightly. When cool, refrigerate. The aubergine will be ready to eat in 24 hours.

PICKLED MUSHROOMS

Setas en Escabeche

When people living in the country pick wild mushrooms, they have ways of preserving them, by drying and by pickling. This recipe, while not a real preserve, makes a tasty mushroom pickle that goes well with grilled meat or fish or as an addition to salads or soup. Oyster mushrooms work especially well, but you can use any variety of wild or cultivated mushroom. Slice thick ones crossways to an even thickness.

MAKES 1 PINT

450g oyster mushrooms

¼ onion, sliced from stem to root

2 garlic cloves, julienned

4 tablespoons red pepper, julienned

One 2.5cm/1in piece dried red chilli

1 strip lemon zest

⅛ teaspoon black peppercorns

⅛ teaspoon dried thyme

Pinch of celery seeds

1 bay leaf

4 tablespoons extra virgin olive oil

4 tablespoons Sherry vinegar

2 teaspoons salt

Rinse the mushrooms and drain. Trim away hard stems. Cut large mushrooms into 2 or 3 pieces.

Place the onion, garlic, pepper, chilli, lemon zest, peppercorns, thyme, celery seeds, bay leaf, oil, vinegar, salt and 450ml/¾ pint of water in a saucepan. Bring to the boil and cook for 5 minutes.

Add the mushrooms to the pan. Bring again to the boil, then simmer, uncovered, until the mushrooms are very tender, about 30 minutes.

Let the mushrooms cool in the liquid for 30 minutes. Ladle them into a glass jar or other container. Add enough of the pickling liquid to cover them completely. Cover the container and allow to marinate, refrigerated, for at least 24 hours. Keeps for up to 2 weeks.

To serve, drain the mushrooms from the liquid and serve at room temperature.

SCARLET-PICKLED ONIONS

Cebolletas Escarlatas

In La Mancha, any presentation of pâté comes garnished with scarlet pickled onions. Coloured with red beetroots, the onions make a nice contrast to smooth and unctuous foods such as pâté, but they also add colour to salads. Pickled garlic is another spicy relish. Cloves of white garlic are pickled in the same manner as onions, but without the beetroot to colour them.

Soaking the whole onions in brine makes it easier to slip off the skins – and fewer tears, too.

MAKES ABOUT 1 LITRE / 2 PINTS

700g small (4cm/1½in) yellow or white onions (about 32)

1½ tablespoons coarse salt

1 medium beetroot (140g), peeled and quartered

4 cloves

350ml/12 fl oz red or white wine vinegar

Sprinkle the onions with ½ tablespoon of the salt and cover with water. Let soak for 3 hours. Drain the onions. Peel them, trimming the root ends and cutting a thin slice off the tops.

Place the onions in a bowl and add water to cover. Sprinkle with another ½ tablespoon of the remaining salt. Allow the onions to soak for 24 hours. Drain and rinse them.

In a saucepan, combine the remaining salt, quartered beetroot, cloves, vinegar and 530ml/ 18 fl oz of water. Bring to the boil and cook for 5 minutes. Add the onions and cook gently for 10 minutes.

Skim out the beetroot and discard (or reserve for another use).

Ladle the onions into sterile jars and pour the pickling liquid over them. Seal tightly. Wipe the jars clean and allow to cool.

Refrigerate the jars of pickled onions. The onions will be ready to eat in 5 days. They keep, refrigerated, for up to 3 months.

Biscuits, Cakes, Pastries and Puddings

In every village where I stop, I make a point of visiting the local pastry shop to sample the specialities. Every town seems to have its beloved festive biscuits or favourite pudding or confection rooted in tradition. In Valdepeñas I discovered *mostillo*, a sweet made during the grape harvest from boiled-down grape must. In Almagro, on the festival of All Saints and All Souls, I tasted 'saints' bones', edible reliquary of marzipan with cream filling. In Toledo convents I bought sweets from the *torno*, turnstile, where cloistered nuns sell their confections. In La Roda I sampled the town's famed *miguelitos*, flaky pastries with a cream filling. My collection of recipes (and my waistline) kept expanding at an alarming rate.

I have included recipes for the most authentic cakes, puddings and other sweets of La Mancha, many of which come from the region's rich heritage of Arab and Sephardic cooking. Here are also some new takes using La Mancha ingredients. Saffron ice cream is a winner.

CINNAMON-WINE RINGS

Roscos de Vino

The olive oil makes a crispy biscuit, not too sweet. The soft dough is easy to knead. You will hardly need any flour on the board, as the oil content keeps the dough from sticking. Serve the rings with coffee, tea or sweet wine.

MAKES 24

430g plain flour plus more for the board

3 teaspoons baking powder

½ teaspoon ground cinnamon

250ml/8 fl oz mild-flavoured olive oil

120ml/4 fl oz dry white wine

4 tablespoons granulated sugar

1 teaspoon grated lemon zest

1 teaspoon sesame seeds, toasted

Pinch of salt

About 5 tablespoons icing sugar for dusting

Preheat the oven to 180°C/160°C fan/GM4.

Sift together the flour, baking powder and cinnamon.

Combine the oil, wine and granulated sugar in a mixing bowl and whisk to blend. Add the zest, sesame seeds and salt. Stir in the dry ingredients to make a soft dough.

Turn the dough out on a lightly floured board and knead until the dough is shiny, about 4 minutes.

Divide the dough into 24 walnut-sized balls. Roll each ball into a rope, about 15cm/6in long and 1cm/½in thick. Pinch the ends together, forming a ring. Place the rings on baking sheets lined with baking parchment or non-stick silicone liners.

Bake in the middle of the oven, changing the position of the sheets once, until the rings are lightly golden, 15 to 20 minutes.

Cool the rings on a rack. Sift icing sugar over them.

ALMOND RINGS

Melindres

Here is a variation on Toledo marzipan. Formed into tiny rings, this sweet is especially appreciated as presents.

One egg white makes enough glaze for a double batch of *melindres*. If preferred, use ½ egg white, 60g icing sugar and 1½ teaspoons lemon juice for the glaze.

MAKES THIRTY 5CM/2IN RINGS

230g unsweetened ground almonds

200g plus 2 tablespoons granulated sugar

1 egg white

125g icing sugar, sifted

1 tablespoon fresh lemon juice

Combine the almond meal and granulated sugar in a blender or food processor and blend until very smooth. Add 8 to 10 teaspoons of water, 1 teaspoon at a time, processing until the almond mixture forms a smooth mass that sticks together. Turn it out onto a marble slab or cool work surface and knead briefly.

Preheat the oven to 150°C/130°C fan/GM2.

Divide the almond mixture into balls about the size of a pecan. Roll each one into a rope, 12cm/4½in long and about 1cm/⅜in in diameter. Bend the rope to make a circle, pinching the ends together. (If the rope breaks, just pinch together the broken bits.) Place the rings on a baking sheet lined with baking parchment or a non-stick silicone liner.

Bake the rings for 12 minutes. Cool them on a rack.

Combine the egg white and sifted icing sugar. Beat at high speed for 3 minutes. Add the lemon juice and beat for 2 minutes longer.

Dip the rings into the egg white glaze. Use a skewer to drag the rings through the egg white. Lift the rings out and let the excess drip off. Place them on a baking sheet and return to the oven for 10 minutes. Remove and cool the rings on a rack.

MARZIPAN — A SWEET TRADITION IN TOLEDO

Sor Sagrario and Sor Isabel, two nuns of the Cistercian Order, sit behind a table just inside the massive doors to the sixteenth-century convent of Santo Domingo el Antiguo in Toledo's historic old town. They sell admission tickets to the convent's church, which contains an altarpiece and paintings by Toledo artist El Greco, whose tomb is in the church. The nuns also sell marzipan and other sweets, all prettily packaged, that they make in the convent kitchen.

'We put on aprons over our habits,' said Sor Sagrario. *Orar y trabajar,* pray and work. 'We say the rosary while we work in the kitchen.'

At the San Antonio convent, on the edge of the Jewish quarter, Franciscan sisters also confect a variety of sweets. Two nuns tending the shop explain that the *corazones* – hearts of marzipan with an egg yolk cream filling – are made from a very old convent recipe. At another convent cloistered nuns sell the sweet marzipan from a *torno,* a turnstile. Customers approach the grilled window and place their order with a nun inside a cage like a bank teller.

Etymologists have never traced how the word *marzipan* – *mazapán* in Spanish – came into current language. If they could, they might be able to explain the origins of this delectable sweet. One theory is that the word derives from the Arabic *mauthabán,* meaning 'seated king', because, supposedly, the bars of marzipan were stamped with a logo of a king on a throne. As Islamic people generally did not use the human image in pictures, this seems to stretch the point. But, undoubtedly, marzipan devolved from an Arabic sweetmeat, for the Arabs introduced the cultivation of both almonds and sugar to Spain after their domination of Iberian lands in 711.

But marzipan making may also come from Sephardic Jewish confectionery traditions. Toledo had an important Sephardic community during the Moorish reign and after. When in 1492 the Catholic kings, Ferdinand and Isabella (the same monarchs who conquered the last Moorish kingdom of Granada and funded Columbus's scheme to sail west to find the Spice Islands), proclaimed the expulsion of the Jews from Spain, many converted rather than flee. The *conversos* took many of their customs, traditions and foods with them into Christianity, even into the convents. Those who fled Spain took their Spanish customs with them to other parts of the world. Sephardic Jewish families in many parts of the world today still serve marzipan for holidays and on festive occasions such as weddings and bar mitzvahs.

In Toledo the art of confecting marzipan was kept alive in convents. Cloistered nuns prepared the sweet almond treat as gifts to their benefactors, usually members of the nobility. In another legend, marzipan was invented by nuns as a substitute for bread in a time when invading troops had destroyed wheat fields. Mazapán looks a lot like bread dough: *masa* – dough – and *pan* – bread.

In the shadow of Toledo's grand cathedral is the *obrador* or workshop of restaurateur Adolfo Muñoz. His master *pastelero*, confectioner, Julián de Haza, rolls out a slab of marzipan – 50 per cent almonds, 50 per cent sugar – breaks off little pieces and with sleight of hand, a sculptor's nimble fingers, shapes them into tiny mice, snails and swans. With a tiny hooked knife, he incises eyes, noses, scales and tails. Once dried, they will be glazed with colours.

Julián moves on to larger works – the *anguila* or eel, the most typical marzipan confection of Toledo. He starts with a simple spiral pattern. The marzipan paste is shaped and cut to fit the pattern. He dimples it with his fingers. The filling is spread on top – half 'angels' hair', a sweet pumpkin jam, and half *yema*, candied egg cream mixed with marzipan. Julián rolls out a top slab of marzipan paste, using his hands to form it over the base. He cuts away the excess with a sharp knife. With his fingers he makes indentations to form the scales. With edible silver balls and candied fruits tucked into the coils, this is one of the most emblematic sweets of a Spanish Christmas.

At the family table, Adolfo explains, the eel is cut into small portions, starting from both the tail and the head, so that everyone gets a piece with both fillings.

Why eels? Adolfo says it's because the confectioners wanted to imitate nature – the eels in the River Tajo, snails, birds.

Next Julián prepares trays of *delicias*. These are little circles of marzipan paste folded over an egg yolk filling. After drying, they are brushed with egg, placed on wooden trays and baked in a very hot oven (300°C) for two minutes. They emerge glazed a rich brown.

Adolfo's workshop produces marzipan almost daily. Some goes to the restaurant, some for banquets catered by the restaurant (for a wedding, Julián shapes a massive marzipan book, inscribed with the names of the bride and groom). Artisanal marzipan is made from two varieties of sweet almonds, the oval Largueta, which contributes intense aroma, and the round Marcona, exceptionally rich in oil. Spanish marzipan does not contain bitter almonds.

Marzipan is traditional for Christmas celebrations everywhere in Spain. The sumptuous supper on *Nochebuena,* Christmas Eve, usually begins with prawns and other shellfish, proceeds through a whole baked fish and continues to roast baby lamb. With a dozen or more family members in attendance, dinner reaches the high point of the evening with the appearance of a silver tray with delicacies of marzipan and other sweets. Some of the family will go off to church for midnight mass celebrating the birth of the Christ child; others to the *discoteca* to dance until dawn, while the youngest may, finally, head to bed. But all ardently adhere to traditional observances: Nochebuena is family and sweet marzipan.

LEMON BISCUITS

Pelusas

These light-as-a-feather biscuits are typical of El Toboso, the village that was the home of the fictional Dulcinea – 'Sweetie' – Don Quixote's ladylove. The recipe was given to me by the Clarisa nuns at the San Benito monastery in El Toboso. The sisters make this and other sweets to sell to visitors. Their recipe calls for thirteen dozen eggs, nine kilos of flour, five kilos of sugar and five litres of oil! I have downsized just a bit. The biscuits are pressed together, two by two. They keep well stored in an airtight container. Place parchment paper between the layers so the biscuits don't stick to each other.

MAKES 30 BISCUITS

4 eggs

2 egg yolks

200g granulated sugar

180ml / 6 fl oz mild-flavoured olive oil

1 teaspoon grated lemon zest

1 teaspoon anisette (optional)

470g sifted plain flour

125g sifted icing sugar

Preheat the oven to 200°C/180°C fan/GM6.

Separate one of the eggs and combine the 3 remaining whole eggs and 3 yolks in a mixing bowl with the granulated sugar. Beat on high speed until thickened and very pale, about 5 minutes. Beat in the oil, lemon zest and anisette if you're using it. Fold in the flour, mixing thoroughly.

Transfer the biscuit mixture to a piping bag fitted with a 1cm/½in nozzle. Pipe the batter in 7½cm/3in circles onto baking sheets lined with baking parchment or non-stick silicone liners. (Or simply spoon the batter onto lined baking sheets.)

Bake for 5 minutes and rotate the baking sheets. Bake until the edges of the biscuits are golden and a biscuit springs back if pressed in the centre, 4 to 5 minutes longer. Remove the baking sheets from the oven and let them cool right on the baking sheets.

Beat the remaining egg white until stiff. Beat in the icing sugar. Dribble squiggles of icing over the biscuits. Allow to dry.

CHEWY WALNUT BISCUITS

Mostachos de Nuez

This macaroon-type biscuit from La Mancha is remarkably similar to *mustachudos,* a walnut sweet found in Sephardic cooking. Probably they share common roots in the Arabic-influenced pastries of mediaeval Spain.

MAKES FORTY-EIGHT 5CM/2IN BISCUITS

340g walnuts

3 eggs, separated

¼ teaspoon fresh lemon juice

½ teaspoon grated lemon zest

½ teaspoon ground cinnamon

150g sugar

2 tablespoons plain flour

Blend the walnuts to a medium-fine consistency in a food processor.

Preheat the oven to 180°C/160°C fan/GM4.

Beat the egg whites until stiff and beat in the lemon juice. Reserve. Combine the lemon zest and cinnamon in a small bowl.

Beat the yolks and sugar until light, 1 minute. Stir in the flour and the ground walnuts.

Fold half of the egg whites thoroughly into the walnut mixture. Fold in the remaining whites.

Lightly oil baking sheets. Using 2 teaspoons, drop mounds of the walnut mixture 5cm/2in apart on baking sheets. The mixture will spread out as it bakes.

Bake until the rims of the biscuits are brown, 20 minutes. Place the sheets on racks to cool. Use the edge of a spatula to loosen the biscuits once they are cooled.

BIGGER-THAN-SPONGE FINGERS

Tortas de Alcázar de San Juan

Maybe these should be called 'macho-fingers'. They are sponge fingers with muscle! In Alcázar de San Juan, the town where they originate, the biscuits are baked in ovals, 13 × 9cm/5 × 3½in. A light, fat-free sponge biscuit, they are delightful with coffee, tea or hot chocolate. They also are combined with custard sauce for a typical dessert, *natillas* (page 320).

❧ MAKES 16 BISCUITS

4 eggs at room temperature

40g sugar

½ teaspoon vanilla extract

115g plain flour, sifted

Pinch of salt

Preheat the oven to 200°C/180°C fan/GM6. Line baking sheets with baking parchment.

Beat the eggs and sugar at high speed until very pale, thick and doubled in volume, about 6 minutes. Beat in the vanilla. Sift a third of the flour and the salt over the eggs and fold it in with a spatula. Repeat with the remaining flour.

Spoon or pipe the batter onto baking sheets to make 13cm/5in ovals. Bake until lightly golden on the edges. The biscuits are done when, if pressed in the centre, the sponge springs back, 10 to 12 minutes.

Allow to cool. Loosen the biscuits from the parchment and press them together, two by two.

COCONUT BISCUITS

Cocos

This recipe comes from the Clarisa nuns in El Toboso. On the days they bake Lemon Biscuits, which require numerous egg yolks (page 290), they follow with these coconut biscuits to use up the whites. The potato in the mixture helps keep the biscuits moist and chewy.

MAKES **60** BISCUITS

1 small baking potato (115g)

4 tablespoons milk

3 egg whites at room temperature

1 large egg at room temperature

280g sugar

285g grated unsweetened coconut

3 tablespoons plain flour

⅛ teaspoon bicarbonate of soda

Pinch of salt

Peel and quarter the potato and cook it in boiling water until tender, about 6 minutes. Drain. Mash the potato until smooth and beat in the milk.

Preheat the oven to 220°C/200°C fan/GM7.

In a large mixing bowl, beat the egg whites, egg and sugar until almost doubled in volume, 5 minutes. Beat in the mashed potato and beat for 2 minutes more.

Place the coconut in a bowl, sift the flour, bicarbonate of soda and salt over it, and toss to combine.

Fold the coconut lightly into the egg mixture. Place in 4cm/1½in mounds on baking sheets lined with baking parchment. Bake in the top of the oven until lightly golden on top, about 10 minutes. Turn off the oven and leave the biscuits 10 minutes longer. Allow to cool before removing from the baking sheets.

ORANGE-SCENTED LARD BISCUITS

Mantecados

These are typical Christmas biscuits in Spain. The holiday coincides with cool weather and the season for hog slaughtering. After the hams are salted and the sausages hung to cure, pork fat is rendered to make pure white lard. Lard makes a tender biscuit, but you could use part butter if preferred. These biscuits keep for up to 3 weeks in an airtight container.

MAKES ABOUT SIXTY 5CM/2IN BISCUITS

450g lard or a mixture of lard and butter

200g plus 2 tablespoons granulated sugar

3 egg yolks

2 eggs

1 teaspoon grated orange zest

120ml/4 fl oz fresh orange juice

900g plain flour, plus flour for rolling out the dough

65g chopped almonds (optional)

2 tablespoons icing sugar

Cream the lard in a large mixing bowl until fluffy. Beat in 200g of the granulated sugar, the egg yolks and one of the whole eggs. Add the orange zest and juice. Using a large wooden spoon, gradually stir in the flour. Turn the dough out on a lightly floured board and knead it only until the flour is thoroughly combined with the lard. Cover with clingfilm and refrigerate the dough for at least 4 and up to 24 hours.

Preheat the oven to 190°C/170°C fan/GM5. Line 2 baking sheets with parchment.

Divide the dough into quarters. With a floured rolling pin, roll out one piece of dough 1cm/½in thick. Cut into 5cm/2in circles or squares and place them on the baking sheets. Gather scraps of dough together and roll out again. Roll and cut the remaining dough.

Beat the remaining whole egg with the remaining 2 tablespoons sugar. Brush the tops of the biscuits with the egg mixture. If using, sprinkle almonds on the surface and lightly press them into the dough.

Bake until the tops of the biscuits are golden, about 25 minutes. Cool them before sifting icing sugar over them.

WALNUT CAKE

Torta de Nueces

This recipe is of Sephardic origin. Not overly sweet, it makes a lovely teacake.

SERVES 12

180g walnuts

115g butter

250ml/8 fl oz milk

280g granulated sugar

400g plain flour

3 teaspoons baking powder

Pinch of salt

2 eggs

1 tablespoon grated orange zest

Icing sugar for sprinkling

Finely chop the walnuts in a food processor. Butter and flour a 23cm/9in springform tin.

Combine the butter, milk and granulated sugar in a saucepan and heat until the butter is melted and the sugar dissolved. Cool slightly.

Sift together the flour, baking powder and salt.

Preheat the oven to 180°C/160°C fan/GM4.

Beat the eggs in a mixing bowl. Beat in the butter mixture. Beat in the orange zest. Beat in the flour mixture. Fold in the chopped walnuts.

Pour the cake batter into the prepared tin. Bake until a skewer comes out clean, about 50 minutes.

Cool the cake on a rack for 10 minutes. Release the sides of the pan and cool the cake completely. Sift icing sugar over the top.

SPONGE SANDWICH with APRICOTS and MARZIPAN, TOLEDO STYLE

Bizcocho de Toledo

Here's a cake that starts out absolutely simply – a *bizcocho,* or sponge cake – which is so typical in Spanish homes. It goes a long way back in history – it was called *pan de españa,* 'Spanish bread', by Sephardic Jews. The basic sponge cake is delightful with nothing more than fresh fruit – a perfect base for strawberries, for example. Soaked in wine-laced syrup, it becomes *bizcochos borrachos,* 'drunken cakes'.

This very fancy cake puts together layers of simple sponge with apricots, cream filling and a topping of almond marzipan. In the original Toledo cake, the filling is made with *yema,* an egg-rich cream consisting of a dozen egg yolks! In my modification, the cream filling requires only a fraction of the eggs.

Almond marzipan, so typical of Toledo, is simple to make at home. Ideally, you start with freshly shelled almonds, blanched (and skinned), then ground. You won't need all of the almond paste for the cake, so call in the kids, who will enjoy shaping this sweet almond play-dough.

The cake is finished with a criss-cross decoration made by caramelising sugar with red-hot rods. Use metal skewers heated over a gas flame. Carefully lay them across the surface until the sugar bubbles. If this seems like too much trouble (or danger), simply serve the cake without this flourish.

You will have not only more marzipan than you need for one cake but also more syrup and cream filling.

SERVES 12

FOR THE SPONGE CAKE

115g plain flour

4 large eggs at room temperature

90g sugar

1 teaspoon grated lemon zest (optional)

Preheat the oven to 180°C/160°C fan/GM4. Butter a 20cm/8in springform tin, dust it with flour and tap out the excess.

Sift the flour into a bowl.

Place the eggs in a large mixing bowl with the sugar and beat at high speed until the mixture thickens, becomes very pale in colour and more than doubles in volume, about 6 minutes. Beat in the lemon zest if you're using it.

Sprinkle 4 tablepoons of the sifted flour over the egg-sugar mixture and fold it in with a rubber spatula. Continue adding flour 4 tablespoons at a time until all is incorporated.

Pour the batter into the springform tin and bake until a skewer inserted in the centre comes out clean, about 30 minutes. Cool the cake in the cake tin, on a rack.

FOR THE APRICOT-BRANDY SYRUP (MAKES 250ML/8 FL OZ)
340g apricots
200g sugar
1 strip lemon zest
3 tablespoons brandy

Chop the apricots coarsely. Rinse them and reserve.

Combine the sugar and lemon zest with 250ml/8 fl oz water in a saucepan. Bring to the boil and simmer for 2 minutes. Add the apricots and simmer for 10 minutes.

Pour the apricot syrup through a strainer into a heatproof bowl. Discard the lemon zest and reserve the apricots. Add the brandy to the syrup and set aside. You will need only half of the syrup for the cake; save the remaining syrup for another use.

FOR THE MARZIPAN TOPPING
280g blanched almonds
240g sugar
1 egg white, lightly beaten
1 egg yolk, mixed with ½ teaspoon water

Grind the almonds with the sugar in a food processor, blender, coffee grinder, spice grinder or grain mill to make a paste that – with the addition of egg white or a little water – can be kneaded and moulded until the consistency of very fine meal. Place in a mixing bowl and combine with the egg white. Turn out onto a pastry board and knead the mixture until smooth, 2 minutes.

Preheat the oven to 260°C/240°C fan/GM10.

Roll out the marzipan on a sheet of clingfilm to a thickness of 1cm/½in. Cut an 20cm/8in round to fit the top of the cake. Place it on baking parchment on a baking sheet. Use the remaining marzipan to mould flowers, rabbits, mice, etc., to decorate the cake. Or save it for another use.

Brush the marzipan round and any moulded pieces with the egg yolk. Place in the oven for 3 minutes. Remove and let the marzipan cool.

FOR THE CREAM FILLING (MAKES 450ML/¾ PINT)	2 egg yolks
450ml/¾ pint milk	1 egg
1 strip lemon zest	100g sugar
33g cornflour	

Place 350ml/12 fl oz of the milk in a saucepan with the lemon zest and bring to the boil. Remove from the heat and discard lemon zest.

Combine the cornflour with the remaining milk, stirring until smooth.

Beat the yolks and egg in a heatproof mixing bowl with the sugar. Add the cornflour and milk mixture.

Whisk the hot milk into the egg mixture. Strain into a clean pan. Place over a pan of boiling water and cook the egg mixture, whisking constantly. It will thicken in about 2 minutes. Continue cooking and whisking for 3 minutes more.

Remove the pan from the heat and whisk occasionally as it cools, for 10 minutes. Spread the filling while warm.

You only need 250ml/8 fl oz of the cream filling for this cake, which is half of this recipe. Freeze the rest, thawing and then blending it smooth in a blender before using it, and you'll have enough for another cake.

2 teaspoons icing sugar

Remove the sponge cake from the springform cake tin. Use a serrated knife to split the sponge cake in half horizontally. It helps to mark the halfway point by sticking cocktail sticks into it as a guide for the slicing knife.

Place the bottom half of the cake on a serving plate. Spoon 120ml/4 fl oz of the apricot-brandy syrup over it.

Spread the bottom layer with 250ml/8 fl oz of the cream filling. Spread the reserved apricots on the cream filling, reserving a few for the garnish.

Place the top of the sponge cake over the cream filling.

Top the cake with the round of marzipan. Spoon icing sugar in a grid across the top of the marzipan.

Heat steel pokers or metal skewers until red hot. Lay them across the surface of the marzipan to caramelise the sugar and create a criss-cross pattern. Let the cake cool. Use a brush to remove any excess sugar.

Decorate the cake with the marzipan flowers, mice, rabbits and reserved pieces of apricot.

'LITTLE MICKEYS'
(PASTRY SQUARES *with* PUMPKIN CREAM FILLING)

Miguelitos con Crema de Calabaza

The little town of La Roda (Albacete province) is renowned for these delectable flaky pastry squares with a cream filling. They were invented by a local baker who named them after his appreciative friend, Miguelito ('little Mickey'). The original puff pastry was made not with butter but with lard, which produces a wonderfully flaky pastry. Frozen puff pastry is easier. I've changed the cream filling for one with cinnamon-spiced pumpkin. If you can't find tinned pumpkin, one kilo of pumpkin, steamed until tender, makes approximately 450ml/¾ pint of purée.

⁂ MAKES 18 PASTRY SQUARES

8 tablespoons milk

28g cornflour

2 egg yolks

450ml/¾ pint pumpkin purée

100g granulated sugar

½ teaspoon ground cinnamon

Pinch of ground cloves

1 teaspoon grated lemon zest

One 500g block frozen puff pastry, thawed and cut in half

2 tablespoons icing sugar

For the pumpkin cream filling, combine 4 tablespoons of the milk with the cornflour in a small bowl and stir until smooth. Stir the egg yolks in a separate bowl. Add the milk and cornflour mixture.

Combine the remaining milk with the pumpkin purée and granulated sugar in a saucepan over medium heat. Heat, stirring, until the mixture begins to bubble, about 3 minutes.

Stir some of the hot pumpkin mixture into the egg and cornflour mixture, then whisk the egg into the pan with the pumpkin.

Place the pan over boiling water and cook, stirring, until the custard thickens and is smooth, 5 minutes. Add the cinnamon, cloves and lemon zest.

Cool to room temperature. (The cream can be prepared up to a day in advance and kept covered and refrigerated. Bring to room temperature before spreading.)

Preheat the oven to 220°C/200°C fan/GM7.

For the pastry squares, flour your work surface and roll out each half block of pastry to about 23 × 23cm/9 × 9in. Use a sharp knife or pastry cutter to cut each sheet of puff pastry into nine 7cm/3in squares. Place them 2½cm/1in apart on a baking sheet and bake for 5 minutes. Lower the oven temperature to 190°C/170°C fan/GM5 and bake until the pastry is golden, 20 to 25 minutes.

Transfer the pastries to a rack to cool.

When cool, split the pastries in half horizontally, using the tip of a knife to separate the layers. Spread the bottoms thickly with pumpkin cream and press the tops on lightly to sandwich the cream.

Sift icing sugar over the tops of the pastries.

WALNUT TURNOVERS *with* HONEY GLAZE

Empanadillas de Nueces

These delicious pastries appear on both La Mancha and Sephardic festive menus. The honey glaze stays somewhat sticky. Separate the turnovers with greaseproof paper so they don't stick together.

꙰ MAKES 36 TURNOVERS

FOR THE PASTRY

270g plain flour, plus flour for rolling out the pastry

⅛ teaspoon salt

2 tablespoons sugar

2 eggs, beaten

5 tablespoons olive oil

FOR THE FILLING

210g walnuts

4 tablespoons sugar

2 teaspoons ground cinnamon

Pinch of ground cloves

5 tablespoons raisins

1 egg

FOR THE GLAZE

70g honey (4 tablespoons)

150g sugar

1 teaspoon fresh lemon juice

To make the pastry, combine the flour, salt and sugar in a mixing bowl. Make a well in the centre and pour in the eggs and oil. Stir the flour into the egg mixture little by little, making a soft pastry dough.

Gather the pastry together and turn out onto a lightly floured board. Knead very briefly to combine. Place in a bowl, cover with clingfilm, and refrigerate for 2 hours.

While the pastry is resting, prepare the filling. Blend the walnuts, sugar, cinnamon and cloves in a food processor. Add the raisins and egg and process until uniformly chopped (not puréed).

Preheat the oven to 180°C/160°C fan/GM4.

Divide the pastry in half. Roll out one piece of pastry on a floured board to 3mm/⅛in thickness.

Use a pastry cutter to cut into 7cm/3in circles. Place a teaspoonful of the walnut mixture on each round. Fold over and crimp the edges together with a fork. Place the turnovers on a lightly oiled baking sheet. Gather scraps of pastry to roll out again.

Roll out the remaining pastry, fill, and fold the turnovers in the same manner.

Bake the turnovers until golden brown, about 25 minutes. Transfer them to a rack to cool.

For the glaze, combine the honey, sugar, lemon juice and 120ml/4 fl oz water in a small pan. Bring to the boil and cook for 5 minutes.

Working with 5 to 6 turnovers at a time, dip them into the honey syrup in the pan, turning them to coat both sides. Skim them out and place on a rack. Continue dipping turnovers in the syrup, keeping the syrup over low heat.

When all of the turnovers have been dipped, raise the heat and boil the remaining syrup for 2 to 3 minutes to reduce. Spoon it over the tops of the turnovers. Allow them to cool.

SWEET BREAD ROLL

Pan Dulce

I enjoyed this lovely sweet bread in the village of Quintanar de la Orden, where it is called *borrachos.* But never did I find out why it had that name, which means 'drunken'. Various sweets in the Spanish repertoire are called *borrachos,* because they have wine or spirits in their dough or else are soaked in wine syrup. But this bread has not a trace of alcohol. Could it be that only a drunk might have folded the dough over on itself into a twisted shape? Or is *borrachos,* perhaps, a corruption of *brioche?*

The same dough, studded with candied fruits and with a trinket baked in it, can be used for *roscón de reyes,* Three Kings' Day cake, served on January 6. The roscón is usually split and filled with whipped cream.

Sugar makes the dough very sticky. Using a large wooden spatula, stir as much flour as possible into the dough. Then use one hand to knead in the remaining flour, keeping one hand clean. Before turning the dough out, lightly oil the board and your hands. Knead the dough, brushing the board with additional oil to prevent the dough from sticking.

※ MAKES 2 LOAVES, SERVING 16 TO 20

200g sugar	180ml/6 fl oz oil
120ml/4 fl oz warm water (43°C)	1 teaspoon grated lemon zest
One 7g sachet dried yeast	350ml/12 fl oz very hot water
1½ teaspoons salt	¼ teaspoon saffron threads, crushed (optional)
900g plain flour, sifted	1 egg yolk
2 eggs	

Reserve 2 tablespoons of the sugar for the bread topping. Place 1 teaspoon of the remaining sugar in a small bowl. Add the warm water to the sugar and sprinkle the yeast over it. Allow to stand for 10 minutes, until bubbly.

Place the remaining sugar in a large mixing bowl. Add the salt and 400g of the flour and mix. Make a well in the centre of the flour.

Beat the whole eggs in a bowl. Beat two-thirds of the oil into the eggs with the lemon zest. Pour the very hot water over the saffron, if you're using it, and allow to infuse for 3 minutes.

Add the egg mixture, saffron water and yeast to the flour in the mixing bowl. Beat the batter with an electric mixer or wooden paddle for 5 minutes. Cover the bowl with a dampened cloth and place in a warm, draught-free place to ferment for 1 hour, to make a sponge batter.

Place the remaining oil in a shallow bowl.

Stir the sponge batter. Begin stirring in the remaining of flour. When the dough is too stiff to stir, dip a hand into the oil and knead the dough with one hand. Lightly oil the board and turn the dough out. With oiled hands, knead the dough for 10 minutes, until it is smooth and very elastic. Shape into a ball. Oil a clean bowl. Place the dough in the bowl and turn it to coat all sides lightly with oil.

Cover with a damp cloth and allow to rise until almost doubled in volume, 2 hours.

Preheat the oven to 190°C/170°C fan/GM5.

Knock back the dough and divide it into 2 equal balls. Roll out one ball into a large oval, about 30 × 60cm/12 × 24in and ½cm/¼in thick. Brush the surface with oil. Prick all over with a fork. Fold the short ends to the middle, overlapping them so the dough resembles an envelope. Roll the envelope out with a rolling pin to seal, making a flattened loaf. Transfer the dough to a baking sheet sprinkled with ½ teaspoon flour.

Roll out the second ball of dough. Brush the surface with oil and repeat the process, pricking all over with a fork again, and folding the ends to the middle, overlapping them. Roll out again to seal the folds. Transfer to a baking sheet sprinkled with ½ teaspoon flour.

Beat the egg yolk with 1 teaspoon water. Brush the tops of the two loaves with the yolk. Sprinkle them with the reserved 2 tablespoons sugar.

Bake the bread in the middle of the oven, changing the position of the baking sheets after 15 minutes. The bread is done when it is golden on top and it sounds hollow if tapped on the bottom, 35 to 40 minutes.

VARIATION: *Roscón de Reyes. The one who finds the tiny trinket baked in this cake, served for the Feast of the Three Kings, January 6, is assured a year's good fortune.*

Prepare the dough as directed. Instead of rolling out the dough, insert a metal or other non toxic, heatproof trinket or coin in each ball. Shape each ball into a ring by flattening the ball, then inserting a finger in the centre and gently easing the dough outward to create a hole in the centre. Stuff the hole with crumpled foil and place on a baking sheet.

Brush with beaten egg yolk, sprinkle the top with flaked almonds and decorate with candied fruits. Sprinkle with sugar and bake until browned.

SWEET POTATO BUNS

Tortas de Boniato

Sweet potatoes give a lovely colour and moistness to these buns. Serve them with cream cheese and marmalade for breakfast or split crossways and filled with sliced turkey for a very special lunch.

You will need about 230g mashed sweet potato. You can use leftover cooked sweet potato. If your leftovers have been spiced, that's fine; but if the potatoes have been sweetened, eliminate the sugar from the bread recipe.

MAKES **12 LARGE BUNS**

1 medium sweet potato (400g), peeled and cut into pieces

One 7g sachet dried yeast

120ml/4 fl oz olive oil, plus oil for the bowl and baking sheets

2 eggs

5 tablespoons sugar

1 teaspoon salt

⅛ teaspoon aniseeds (optional)

350ml/12 fl oz warm milk (43°C)

900g plain flour, plus flour for kneading

1 egg yolk

1 tablespoon plus 1 teaspoon milk

Cook the sweet potato in boiling water to cover until fork-tender. Drain, reserving 120ml/4 fl oz of the water.

Cool the cooking water to 43°C. Place in a small bowl and sprinkle the yeast over it. Allow to stand until bubbly, 10 minutes.

Mash the sweet potato or put through a ricer. Stir the 120ml/4 fl oz of oil into it.

Beat the eggs in a large mixing bowl with 2 tablespoons of the sugar, the salt and the aniseeds if you're using them. Add the sweet potato, yeast and warm milk. Use a large wooden spoon to stir in about 800g of flour. Knead in the remaining flour.

Turn the dough out onto a floured board and knead until smooth and shiny, 5 minutes. Sprinkle the board with additional flour as needed to keep the dough from sticking. Gather the dough into a ball.

Oil a large clean bowl. Place the dough in the bowl, turning it to coat all sides lightly with oil. Cover the bowl with a damp cloth and place in a warm place until the dough has doubled in volume, about 2 hours.

Lightly oil 2 baking sheets and dust them with flour.

With a floured hand, knock back the dough. Knead briefly on a floured board. Divide the dough into 12 balls (about 155g each). Roll or pat them into discs about 12cm/5in in diameter and 1cm/½in thick. Place on the baking sheets. Cover the buns with cling film and set in a warm place to rise for 1 hour.

Preheat the oven to 200°C/180°C fan/GM6.

Combine the egg yolk with the milk and brush the tops of the buns with it. Sprinkle them with the remaining 3 tablespoons sugar.

Bake the buns in the middle of the oven, rotating the sheets after 10 minutes, until they are golden on top and sound hollow when tapped on the bottom, 18 to 20 minutes.

Cool the buns on wire racks.

CRISPY LEAVES

Hojuelas

The fried dough that Cervantes refers to, called *frutas de la sartén,* or 'fruits of the frying pan', are typical sweets in areas of Spain such as La Mancha and Andalucía, where olive oil reigns supreme. The simple dough, flavoured with aniseeds and sesame, is rolled out and shaped into rings, twists, ears, leaves, rosettes and turnovers, fried until golden in olive oil, then dipped in boiled honey or sugar syrup.

Some popular fried pastries, such as *flores,* flowers, require special iron moulds for shaping the dough. But these 'leaves' – really just strips of dough – are simple to prepare.

Francisca Mompó in Quintanar de la Orden served me these crisp fried pastries when I visited her to chat about recipes. She says she makes a double batch of the dough and keeps it in the refrigerator, frying up each day only enough to serve to her painting class, grandchildren or visitors.

MAKES ABOUT 36 LEAVES

5 tablespoons mild-flavoured olive oil

1 slice lemon

1 teaspoon sesame seeds

270g plus 2 tablepoons plain flour

1 egg

1 egg yolk

¼ teaspoon salt

2 tablespoons rum, brandy or anisette

4 tablespoons fresh orange juice

120–180ml/about ¼ pint olive oil for frying

5 tablespoons granulated sugar

1 tablespoon icing sugar

Heat the mild-flavoured olive oil in a small pan over medium heat with the lemon slice until the lemon begins to sizzle. Remove from the heat and strain the oil. Add the sesame seeds to the hot oil. Allow to cool.

Place the flour in a mixing bowl and make a well in the centre.

Beat together the egg, yolk, salt, rum and orange juice. Pour into the well in the flour. Mix the flour gradually into the liquid ingredients to make a soft dough. Turn out on a pastry board and knead for 5 minutes. Pat into a ball, cover with clingfilm, and allow the dough to rest at room temperature for 2 hours. (The dough may be wrapped and refrigerated for up to 3 days. Bring it to room temperature before rolling it out.)

Divide the dough into 2 pieces. Leave one covered. Break off pieces of dough and roll into 2½cm/1in balls. Roll them out very thinly, until almost transparent, into rectangles or ovals. Alternatively, roll out the dough into a large rectangle, approximately 25 × 45cm/10 × 18in, and cut strips on the diagonal, 6 × 9cm/2½ × 3½ in.

Place a medium frying pan over medium-high heat. Add enough oil to cover the bottom to a depth of 3mm/⅛in. When the oil is hot but not smoking, fry the leaves, 2 or 3 at a time, until golden on both sides, about 40 seconds per side.

Drain each batch briefly on kitchen paper. Then transfer them to a tray and sprinkle with granulated sugar. Continue frying the remaining strips of dough, replenishing the oil as needed.

Once cooled, serve the leaves dusted lightly with icing sugar.

. . . dos calderas de aceite, mayores que las de un tinte servían de freír cosas de masa, que con dos valientes palas las sacaban fritas y las zambullían en otra caldera de preparada miel.

. . . two cauldrons of oil bigger than a dyer's vat served to fry doughnuts that were scooped out golden from the oil with two awesome paddles and plunged into another kettle of honey syrup.

DON QUIXOTE AND SANCHO PANZA
WATCHING COOKS PREPARING SWEETS FOR
THE WEDDING FEAST FOR RICH MAN CAMACHO

ANISE-FLAVOURED DOUGHNUTS

Rosquillas

These doughnuts are especially loved at Christmas time. Neighbours get together to pool resources to make hundreds of them, sufficient to last the twelve days of Christmas. Working in tandem, one shapes the doughnuts, and the other drops them into the hot oil and skims them out. If you're on your own in the kitchen, cut all the doughnuts and place them on a baking sheet. Then proceed with the frying. If you don't have a doughnut cutter, cut rounds with a pastry cutter and improvise another tool (such as a thimble, bottle cap or round end of a piping bag nozzle) to cut out the centre hole.

You will be surprised by how little oil is absorbed in frying the dough – that is, if you use olive oil.

MAKES **18**

120ml/4 fl oz olive oil, plus oil for deep-frying

½ teaspoon aniseeds

1 teaspoon grated orange zest

720g plain flour

1 tablespoon plus 1 teaspoon baking powder

Pinch of salt

2 eggs

200g sugar

120ml/4 fl oz fresh orange juice

Heat 120ml/4 fl oz oil in a small frying pan until hot but not smoking. Remove from the heat and add the aniseeds. Allow to cool. Stir in the orange zest.

Combine the flour, baking powder and salt.

With an electric mixer, beat the eggs and half of the sugar until thick and pale, 2 minutes. Beat in the oil with aniseeds then the orange juice. With the mixer, beat in 250g of the flour mixture.

Using a wooden spoon, stir in the remaining flour to make a soft dough. Turn out onto a board and knead briefly to thoroughly mix the flour into the dough. Cover with clingfilm and allow to stand at room temperature for at least 1 hour and up to 3 hours.

Roll the dough out to a thickness of 1cm/⅜in. Cut rings using a 6½cm/2½in doughnut cutter. Gather holes and scraps and roll out and cut the remaining dough.

Place enough oil in a deep, heavy frying pan to measure 2½cm/1in deep (about 1.2 litres/2 pints). Heat the oil until shimmering hot but not smoking (180°C). Carefully slide the doughnuts, 5 or 6 at a time, into the oil. Don't crowd them. Turn them to brown both sides. Remove when golden brown, after about 3 minutes. Continue frying the remaining doughnuts, modulating the heat so the oil doesn't smoke.

Drain the doughnuts on absorbent paper and dredge them in the remaining sugar. Allow to cool before serving.

ALMOND FRITTERS

Tortillitas de Almendras

If you love almonds, these fritters are for you. Serve them like biscuits, to be eaten out of the hand. They keep very well in an airtight container.

If possible, grind blanched almonds immediately before preparing these fritters. If you purchase ground almonds, store in the refrigerator to prevent rancidity of the oil-rich nuts.

MAKES ABOUT TWENTY-FOUR 4CM/1½IN FRITTERS

140g finely ground almonds

2 teaspoons plain flour

¼ teaspoon ground cinnamon

Pinch of salt

2 eggs, separated

1 tablespoon granulated sugar

1 teaspoon fresh lemon juice

About 160ml/¼ pint olive oil for frying

1 tablespoon icing sugar

Combine the almonds, flour, cinnamon and salt in a mixing bowl. Add the egg yolks and mix thoroughly.

Place the egg whites in another mixing bowl and beat at high speed until stiff. Beat in the granulated sugar, then the lemon juice.

Mix half of the egg whites with the almond mixture. Fold the remaining whites into the almonds.

Heat the oil in a medium frying pan over medium-high heat until hot but not smoking (180°C). Drop teaspoonfuls of the almond mixture into the oil, flattening them slightly with the back of a spoon or wooden spatula. Fry until golden brown, then turn to brown the reverse side, about 1½ minutes total.

Drain on kitchen paper and allow to cool. When cool, sift icing sugar over the fritters.

PUFFS OF WIND (FRITTERS)

Buñuelos de Viento

Food as entertainment – that's what these fritters are. A bunch of friends and neighbours get together to make *buñuelos*. They are typically seen at fiestas and are delicious accompanied by thick hot chocolate (page 365). They are best enjoyed the same day they are made.

To double the recipe, use twice the amount of milk, butter, salt, sugar and flour, but only 3 eggs.

MAKES 24 4CM/1IN PUFFS

120ml/4 fl oz milk or water

1 teaspoon aguardiente de anís or anisette (optional)

30g butter

Pinch of salt

1 tablespoon sugar

65g plus 2 tablespoons plain flour

2 eggs

About 1 litre/1½ pints olive oil for frying

Icing sugar for dusting

Combine the milk, anisette if you're using it, butter, salt and sugar in a saucepan. Bring to a boil and swirl the liquid to melt the butter.

Add all of the flour and stir hard with a wooden spoon until the paste thickens and comes away from the sides of the pan.

Remove from the heat and beat in 1 egg until it is completely absorbed. Add the second egg and beat until the batter is smooth.

Place oil in a heavy frying pan to a depth of 2½ cm/1in and heat to 180°C (shimmering but not smoking). Drop teaspoonfuls of the batter into the hot oil, using a second spoon to push the batter off. The balls of batter will bob to the surface of the oil and turn themselves over. Remove the puffs when golden brown, 2 to 3 minutes.

Drain on kitchen paper. When cool, sift icing sugar over the puffs.

FIGGY FRITTERS

Buñuelitos de Higos

These sweet fritters would make a delightful breakfast treat. They should be enjoyed the same day they are made.

✳ SERVES 6 TO 10

225g small dried figs, such as Calimyrna

65g plain flour

⅛ teaspoon salt

½ teaspoon bicarbonate of soda

¼ teaspoon grated lemon zest

120ml/4 fl oz milk

300–400ml/½–¾ pint olive oil for frying

2 teaspoons icing sugar

Wash the figs and drain on kitchen paper. Use kitchen scissors to snip out the stems. Cut the figs in half if they are small or quarters if they are larger.

Combine the flour, salt and bicarbonate of soda in a mixing bowl. Add the lemon zest and milk and stir to make a light batter. Add the figs to the batter and mix well.

Place oil in a heavy frying pan to a depth of 1cm/½in. Heat until the oil is hot but not smoking (180°C). Scoop spoonfuls of batter into the hot oil. Turn the fritters as they brown, frying them for about 1 minute.

Drain on kitchen paper. Sift icing sugar over the fritters. Serve warm or at room temperature.

SWEET TOASTS

Torrijas

These toasts are much like 'French toast', but in Spain they are served as dessert, not breakfast. Everywhere in La Mancha, *torrijas* are absolutely essential during Holy Week and Easter holidays. I wonder if this derives from the Jewish tradition of using up all of the *hametz*, or leavened bread, before Passover – the springtime festival that usually coincides with Holy Week. Possibly *conversos*, converts to Christianity, brought with them to a new religion some of the customs of the former.

SERVES **6**

12 slices stale bread (350g)	2 eggs, well beaten
450ml / ¾ pint milk	4 tablespoons olive oil
100g sugar	1 teaspoon ground cinnamon
1 strip lemon zest	1 tablespoon sugar, or 2 tablespoons honey
4 tablespoons red or white wine	mixed with 1 tablespoon water

Place the slices of bread in one layer in a pan.

In a saucepan over medium heat, heat the milk with the 100g sugar and the lemon zest until the sugar is dissolved. Remove from the heat and add the wine to the milk. Pour this liquid over the bread and allow to stand until the liquid is absorbed, about 10 minutes. Discard the zest.

Place the beaten eggs in a dish. Heat some of the oil in a large, heavy frying pan over medium-high heat. Dip the slices of bread into the egg on both sides. Fry them until browned on both sides, about 2½ minutes total. Transfer to a platter.

When all the bread slices are fried, sprinkle them with cinnamon and either the sugar or the honey that has been boiled with water for 1 minute. Serve the toasts hot or cold.

SWEET CINNAMON DUMPLINGS *in* CARAMEL SAUCE

Rellenos Dulces con Canela

This is the sort of homespun dessert that children love. And it's a great way to use up stale bread. Typical of Cuenca, these bread-based dumplings are first fried, then simmered in caramel sauce. In another version the sauce is made with honey and wine boiled down to a syrup.

❧ MAKES ABOUT **24** DUMPLINGS, SERVING **6**

8 to 10 slices stale bread (about 225g)

250ml / 8 fl oz milk

2 eggs

2 tablespoons sugar

¼ teaspoon bicarbonate of soda

½ teaspoon ground cinnamon

⅛ teaspoon aniseeds

120ml / 4 fl oz olive oil for frying

Caramel sauce (recipe follows)

Whipped cream for serving (optional)

Place the bread in a shallow pan. Drizzle with half the milk. Turn the slices and pour on the remaining milk. Allow to stand for 30 minutes, until the bread is softened.

Chop the bread in a food processor with the eggs, sugar, bicarbonate of soda, cinnamon and aniseeds. It does not need to be completely puréed.

Heat the oil in a large frying pan over medium-high heat. Drop the batter by tablespoons into the pan and brown well, about 1½ minutes. Use a spatula to turn the dumplings and brown on the other side, another 1½ minutes. Remove to drain on kitchen paper.

Heat the caramel sauce in a saucepan and add the fried dumplings. Cook them in the sauce for 5 minutes. Remove the dumplings with a draining spoon and allow to cool.

Serve the dumplings drizzled with some of the sauce and accompanied by whipped cream if desired.

CARAMEL SAUCE *Salsa de Caramelo*

Makes 450ml/¾ pint of sauce

200g sugar

1 tablespoon fresh lemon juice

2 teaspoons ground cinnamon (optional)

Place the sugar, lemon juice and 4 tablespoons of water in a heavy saucepan over medium heat. Melt the sugar, stirring. Raise the heat to medium-high and cook the melted sugar without stirring, tilting the pan occasionally, until the sugar turns a medium-dark caramel colour, 8 to 10 minutes.

Remove the pan from the heat and very carefully pour in 450ml/¾ pint of water. The caramelised sugar will bubble and splatter. Add the cinnamon if you're using it. Return the pan to the heat and cook over low heat, stirring to dissolve any lumps of caramel. Sauce will keep, covered and refrigerated, for 6 weeks.

CHRISTMAS ALMOND SOUP

Sopa de Almendras para Navidad

In Toledo, this divine dessert is traditional for the Christmas Eve family dinner. The soup is a thick cream while hot. Cooled, it reaches custard consistency. This recipe makes four generous servings, but, if part of a copious holiday meal, it could be divided between eight small pudding bowls instead of soup bowls. Almond paste can be purchased ready to use. But you can also make your own; see the note following the recipe.

SERVES 4

4 thick slices brioche

225g sweetened almond paste

1 litre / 1½ pints full fat milk

1 strip orange or lemon zest

¼ teaspoon ground cinnamon

Whipped cream for serving (optional)

Preheat the oven to 180°C/160°C fan/GM4.

Place the brioche slices on a baking sheet. Bake them for 8 minutes. Turn the slices and bake for 6 to 8 minutes longer, until golden brown on both sides. Remove from the oven and place a slice in each of 4 shallow soup bowls.

Cut the almond paste into chunks. Dissolve it in half of the milk. (This is quickly accomplished in a blender.) Place the dissolved almond paste in a saucepan and stir in the remaining milk. Add the orange zest. Place over high heat and stir frequently until the soup begins to foam up. Turn the heat to low and simmer, stirring occasionally, for 15 minutes. The soup will thicken to the consistency of heavy cream. Discard the orange zest.

Ladle the soup over the toasted brioche. Sprinkle the cinnamon on top of the soup. Serve hot or at room temperature, accompanied by whipped cream if desired.

NOTE: *To make almond paste, combine 120g of sugar with 120g of ground almonds in a blender or food processor. Blend them. Add 1 tablespoon water to make a paste. The paste can be stored in the refrigerator for up to 2 weeks or in the freezer for up to 3 months.*

CUSTARD PUDDING *with* MERINGUE TOPPING

Natillas

In Alcázar de San Juan, a town in central La Mancha, this pudding is so absolutely simple – warmed sheep's milk is thickened with egg and poured over *tortas,* sponge fingers, then sprinkled with sugar and cinnamon. This custard, which doesn't require sheep's milk, thickens to the consistency of heavy cream. It's luscious poured over sponge fingers or a layer of sponge cake. Traditionally it is flavoured with lemon and cinnamon. However, the milk can be infused with alternative flavours – vanilla pod; orange zest and rosemary; mint. Vanilla custard is particularly good finished with a dribble of chocolate sauce instead of the sprinkled cinnamon. The meringue topping is optional. If you have another use for the egg whites, simply omit it.

SERVES **6**

700ml/1¼ pints milk

One 5cm/2in cinnamon stick

2 strips lemon zest

100g granulated sugar

1 tablespoon cornflour

4 eggs, separated

12 Bigger-Than-Sponge Fingers (page 292) or 24 shop-bought sponge fingers

1½ tablespoons ground cinnamon

2 teaspoons fresh lemon juice

60g icing sugar, sifted

Combine two-thirds of the milk with the cinnamon stick, zest and granulated sugar in a saucepan and bring to the boil. Remove from the heat and strain into a heatproof bowl.

Stir the remaining milk with the cornflour until smooth. Beat in the 4 egg yolks. Whisk in the hot milk. Place the mixture in the top of a double boiler and cook over boiling water, stirring, until it is as thick as cream, 10 minutes.

Place 2 tortas de Alcázar (or 4 sponge fingers) in each of 6 shallow bowls. Spoon the custard over the tortas. Sprinkle with cinnamon. Chill the puddings.

Preheat the oven to 150°C/130°C fan/GM2. Line a baking sheet with baking parchment.

Place the egg whites in a mixing bowl and beat, using clean beaters, at high speed until stiff. Beat in the lemon juice. Fold in the icing sugar and beat at high speed again until combined.

Heap mounds of the meringue on the baking sheet (divide into 6 or 12) and bake until the peaks are golden, 12 minutes. Turn off the oven and allow the meringues to dry in the oven for 30 minutes.

Place a meringue on top of each pudding. (Depending on the size of the meringues, there may be more than required for the 6 puddings.)

MOULDED MANCHEGO CHEESE FLAN
with CARAMEL SAUCE

Bizcochá con Flan de Queso Manchego

This luscious dessert can be made a day or two in advance of a dinner party. A mould is coated in caramel and lined with a layer of sponge cake, brioche or sponge fingers. When the cheese custard is poured in, the cake pieces float to the top. When unmoulded, the cake forms the base of the dessert. Garnish the flan with a few currants or raspberries. Or pair it with quince sorbet (page 343) for a classic combo. Use a large loaf tin, 23 × 13 × 6cm / 9 × 5 × 2½in, for this recipe.

SERVES **8**

200g sugar

140g sponge cake or brioche, sliced 2cm / ¾in thick

250ml / 8 fl oz milk

250ml / 8 fl oz cream

1 bay leaf

1 strip lemon zest

100g Manchego, grated

4 large eggs

1 egg yolk

Place half the sugar and 3 tablespoons of the water in a heavy saucepan. Bring to the boil and stir to dissolve the sugar. Cook without stirring over medium heat, swirling pan occasionally, until the sugar melts and turns a deep golden colour, 4 to 6 minutes. Pour the caramel into the loaf tin, tilting to coat the bottom with the caramel. Cool until the caramel hardens.

Place a layer of the sponge or brioche on top of the caramel in the loaf tin.

Preheat the oven to 180°C/160°C fan/GM4.

Combine the milk, cream, bay leaf, lemon zest and remaining sugar in a saucepan. Bring to the boil, stirring to dissolve the sugar. Remove from the heat. Skim out and discard the bay leaf and zest. Stir in the grated cheese.

Beat the eggs and egg yolk in a heatproof bowl. Beat the hot milk and cheese mixture into the eggs, little by little. Carefully pour the mixture over the cake and caramel in the loaf tin. (The pieces of cake will bob to the top.) Cover the loaf tin with foil.

Set the loaf tin in a larger baking dish. Add boiling water to reach halfway up the sides of the loaf tin, to form a bain marie. Carefully transfer the bain marie to the oven. Bake until a skewer inserted in the custard comes out clean, about 1 hour.

Remove from the oven and transfer the loaf tin to a rack to cool. When cool, loosen the sides with a knife and turn the flan out onto a serving dish. Slice crossways to serve, spooning on some of the caramel sauce.

'FRIED MILK'

Leche Frita

How do you fry milk? First turn it into a thick custard. Served warm, the custard squares are crisp on the outside, creamy on the inside. They may also be served cold, in which case the custard sets up fairly solid.

Traditionally, fried milk is sprinkled with sugar and cinnamon, but at the Restaurante Sucot in Valdepeñas I enjoyed it with a sublime orange syrup (page 326).

A slotted fish slice with a thin, curved edge works well for lifting the custard squares out of the beaten egg and into the crumbs and for scooping them out of the frying oil.

MAKES SIXTEEN 2-IN SQUARES, SERVING 4 TO 8

FOR THE CUSTARD	2 eggs
530ml/18 fl oz milk	45g plain flour
One 15cm/6in strip lemon or orange zest	28g cornflour
One 5cm/2in cinnamon stick	65g sugar

Generously oil a 20cm/8in square cake tin or plastic container.

Place three-quarters of the milk in a heavy saucepan – one which can later serve as the top half of a double boiler – with the lemon zest and cinnamon stick. Bring to the boil. Remove from the heat and let infuse for 5 minutes. Strain the milk into a heatproof jug.

Combine the remaining milk, the eggs, flour, cornflour and sugar in a blender and blend until completely smooth. With the blender running, pour in the hot milk.

Return the custard mixture to the saucepan, using it as the top half of a double boiler and place it over a pan of boiling water. Cook, stirring constantly, until the custard barely begins to thicken. (This happens very rapidly.) Remove it from the heat and beat it hard to prevent lumps from forming. Place the pan over the boiling water again and cook, stirring constantly, for 5 minutes. Remove from the heat and beat the custard until very smooth.

Immediately spread the custard to an even thickness in the cake tin. Cover with clingfilm and refrigerate for at least 4 and up to 24 hours.

TO FRY THE CUSTARD

1 egg

80g fine dry breadcrumbs

About 120ml/4 fl oz olive oil for frying

1½ tablespoons sugar (optional)

1 teaspoon ground cinnamon (optional)

Intensely Orange Syrup (optional; recipe follows)

Cut the custard into sixteen 5cm/2in squares. Beat the egg with 2 teaspoons water in a shallow bowl. Spread half the breadcrumbs in a shallow tray.

Dip each custard square into beaten egg, then lift it out and place it in the breadcrumbs. Sprinkle the remaining breadcrumbs over the custard squares. Shake the tray gently to coat the edges of the custard. Place the breaded custard squares on a baking sheet and refrigerate for at least 30 minutes and up to 4 hours.

Heat the oil in a large, heavy frying pan over medium heat until hot but not smoking. Fry the custard squares, in 2 batches, until browned on both sides, 1 to 2 minutes per side. Transfer them to a tray lined with kitchen paper to drain.

If you're using the sugar and cinnamon, sprinkle them over the fried custard squares while still warm. If you're using the orange syrup, spoon it over the squares immediately before serving. Serve warm or cold.

INTENSELY ORANGE SYRUP *Jarabe de Naranjas*

Slow reduction of pure orange juice makes an intensely flavoured syrup. Spoon it over puddings, sponge cake, ice cream or breakfast toast, or use it in mixing cocktails. Combined with bubbly *cava*, it is sensational.

Makes 350ml/12 fl oz

Zest from 1 orange

700ml/1¼ pints fresh orange juice (from 8 to 10 oranges)

3 tablespoons fresh lemon juice

200g sugar

Cut the orange zest into fine julienne slivers. Blanch the zest in boiling water for 2 minutes. Drain. Blanch again for 2 minutes and drain. Reserve the zest.

Combine the orange juice, lemon juice and sugar in a saucepan. Bring to the boil and skim off the froth from the top.

Finely chop the orange zest. Add it to the pan. Lower the heat so the orange juice bubbles gently. Cook until thickened and reduced by half, about 40 minutes.

Cool the syrup. Store, tightly covered, in the refrigerator. The syrup keeps for several months.

FIGS POACHED *in* VANILLA SYRUP

Higos con Jarabe de Vanilla

These vanilla-scented figs are especially good served with ice cream or whipped cream. They keep well, refrigerated, for up to three weeks. Should any syrup remain, combine it with chilled white wine and pour over ice for delicious wine coolers.

SERVES 8

900g firm, ripe fresh figs (about 5 dozen)

½ vanilla pod

380g sugar

4 cloves

3 tablespoons fresh lemon juice

Wash the figs and nip off the stems.

Split the half vanilla pod lengthways. Place in a large pan with the sugar, cloves, lemon juice and 1 litre/1½ pints of water. Bring to the boil and boil for 2 minutes. Add the figs, bring back to the boil, and cook for 3 minutes.

Remove the figs with a draining spoon and place in a heatproof bowl. Bring the syrup to the boil and cook until reduced by half, about 15 minutes. Pour the hot syrup through a strainer over the figs. Allow to cool, then refrigerate, covered.

Allow the figs to macerate in the syrup for 24 hours before serving.

CINNAMON PUMPKIN SLICES

Hojarascas de Calabaza

Thinly sliced pumpkin fried in oil and sprinkled with sugar makes a surprisingly easy dessert or breakfast treat – sort of like French toast without the toast. (Incidentally, I also love it sprinkled with salt and oregano as a savoury side dish.) Don't expect the pumpkin to be crisp. It should be tender but not overly soft. Use small pie pumpkins in this recipe. If they are not available, substitute acorn or other winter squash.

SERVES 6

¼ small pumpkin (625g)

1 egg, beaten

5 tablespoons plain flour

4 to 5 tablespoons olive oil

1 tablespoon sugar

1 teaspoon ground cinnamon

Scoop out and discard the pumpkin seeds and membrane. Cut the pumpkin crossways into 1cm/⅜in thick slices (approximately 24 slices, 10 × 4cm/4 × 1½in). Pare the slices, discarding the skin.

Place the egg in a shallow dish. Place the flour in a shallow pan. Dip the pumpkin slices in beaten egg, then dredge them in flour, patting off the excess.

Heat the oil in a heavy frying pan over medium heat. Fry a third of the pumpkin slices until speckled brown on both sides, 4 to 5 minutes. The pumpkin should be fork-tender but not overly soft. Remove the pumpkin and drain it on kitchen paper. Continue frying the remaining pumpkin slices in the same manner, adding oil as needed.

Fan the pumpkin slices on a serving dish and sprinkle them with sugar and cinnamon. Serve warm or at room temperature.

QUINCE JELLY

Dulce de Membrillo

Thick enough to cut with a knife, quince jelly (also called *quince paste*) can be served with breakfast breads, makes a delightful addition to a cheese platter and works as appetiser or dessert. The sweetness of the fruit contrasts beautifully with creamy or salty cheeses. Quince jelly is available at speciality food stores. But should you have a windfall of this lovely fruit, here is how to prepare the jelly.

MAKES 1.7KG/3LBS QUINCE PASTE, PROVIDING TWENTY-TWO 2½ × 8 × 4CM/1 × 3¼ × 1IN SLICES.

2 kg quinces (5 or 6)

1 tablespoon fresh lemon juice

About 1 kg/2¼ lbs sugar

Wash the quinces. Place them in a large pan with the lemon juice and water to cover. Bring to the boil and cook over medium heat, covered, until the quinces are easily pierced with a knife, about 30 minutes. Drain, saving 120ml/4 fl oz of the cooking liquid.

When cool enough to handle, peel the quinces and remove the seeds and cores. Purée the fruit in a food mill or food processor, adding the reserved liquid as needed. You should have about 1.3 litres/2¼ pints of purée.

Measure the pureed fruit. For every ¼ pint of purée add ¼ lb of sugar. Place in a heavy saucepan over high heat until it begins to bubble. Continue to cook over medium-high heat, stirring frequently, for 15 minutes. As the mixture begins to thicken, stir constantly so it doesn't scorch on the bottom. Cook until, when stirred, the purée pulls away in a solid mass from the bottom of the pan, 20 to 30 minutes longer. A spoonful dropped on a cold plate should solidify immediately.

Spread the quince jelly to a depth of 4cm/1½in in one or more moulds (an 18 × 28xm/7 × 11in rectangular cake pan is perfect). The quince paste solidifies as it cools.

Once cool, the quince can be cut into smaller portions, each wrapped in clingfilm and foil, and stored refrigerated for up to several months.

Slice 2½cm/1in thick to serve.

MOORISH DELIGHT

Mostillo

This sweet is remarkably similar to the one more commonly known as *Turkish delight*, which in turn is a variation on *halvah*, which, long ago, was also made with thickened grape juice. The Spanish sweet, *mostillo*, derives from the Moorish heritage.

At the *vendimia*, grape harvest, La Mancha is awash in grape juice – *mosto*. Boiled down to a sweet syrup, the juice is thickened with flour and cooked again until it sets almost solid. Spiced with cinnamon, aniseeds and lemon zest, it makes a confection that lasts for many months if stored in a cool place. Another version of the same confection contains no mosto but caramelised sugar syrup.

This small-scale version with nuts isn't made for keeping. Serve it on a dessert tray with cream cheese.

MAKES ABOUT FIFTEEN 4CM/1IN PIECES

1 litre / 1½ pints unsweetened red grape juice

3 strips orange zest

1 strip lemon zest

¼ teaspoon aniseeds

100g sugar

130g plain flour

½ teaspoon ground cinnamon

Blanched almonds, pine nuts or walnut halves

Combine the juice, orange and lemon zest, aniseeds and sugar in a saucepan. Bring to the boil, then cook, uncovered, until reduced to about ¾ pint (about 30 minutes). Strain the juice and discard the zest. Let the juice cool.

Place the flour in a bowl. Stir in the cooled juice 2 tablespoons at a time, mixing very well. Continue stirring to form a smooth paste. Strain the paste to eliminate any lumps.

Place the paste in a saucepan over medium heat. Stirring constantly, cook until the paste comes away from the sides of the pan and is so stiff that it is difficult to stir, about 15 minutes. (Test by putting a spoonful on a plate; turn the plate upside down. If the mixture doesn't fall off, it is done.)

Remove from the heat and stir in the cinnamon. Spread the paste in an 18cm/7in square or round tin or 2 smaller moulds. Use a palette knife dipped in hot water to smooth the top.

Stud the top with almonds or pine nuts or walnut halves, pressed into the surface. Allow to cool completely. Store tightly covered in the refrigerator. The sweet will keep for up to 1 month.

Serve cut into squares or thin wedges.

SWEET POTATOES CANDIED in GRAPE SYRUP

Arrope con Boniatos

Arrope is a syrup produced from boiled-down grape must, which is newly pressed, unfermented grape juice, a commodity much available in La Mancha during the September wine harvest. Various fruits and even vegetables are cooked in the syrup to preserve them.

One La Mancha recipe book (*Recetario Gastronómico de Castilla–La Mancha*, by Enrique García Moreno) gives instructions for making *arrope* from the very beginning:

> *Tread the grapes and strain out the skins and seeds. Put in some firebrands and leave until the following day. Remove the brands and let the must rest awhile. Change it several times from one vessel to another, discarding the sediment. Put the juice to cook, skimming off the scum that rises. Add egg white to the simmering must. When it turns black, strain the juice and return it to cook.*
>
> *Cut a pumpkin into small pieces and put it into* cal viva *[calcium hydroxide, the same substance used to whitewash houses; culinarily known as pickling lime, which hardens the pumpkin so it won't fall apart in the arrope]. Then wash the pumpkin well.*
>
> *When the* arrope *has cooked down to the consistency of honey, add the pumpkin.*

Other fruits and vegetables cooked in *arrope* are melon, aubergine, pears, figs, carrots and sweet potatoes. Sweet potatoes don't need hardening in pickling lime.

As a child I never cared for the candied sweet potatoes that accompanied our holiday turkey dinners. But, moved over to dessert, I think they are lovely. For a real treat, serve these sweet potatoes and their syrup with whipped cream and a scattering of walnuts or with almond ice cream.

꙰ MAKES 1 LITRE / ABOUT 1½ PINTS

2.3 litres / 4 pints unsweetened white grape juice

150g sugar

5 cloves

1 small orange

700g sweet potato in 2cm / ¾in cubes

Combine the grape juice, sugar and cloves in a large, heavy saucepan. Bring to the boil. Reduce the heat to medium so the juice keeps bubbling. Cook until reduced by half, about 1 hour. Skim out the cloves and discard.

Slice the ends off the orange and discard. Cut the orange in half and slice it crossways. Discard any seeds. Add the orange slices to the reduced grape juice with the sweet potato.

Bring to the boil. Cook over medium heat until juice is as thick as syrup and the sweet potatoes are tender, about 40 minutes. Place the hot mixture into 2 sterile 450ml/¾ pint glass jars. Seal and cool. Store, refrigerated, for up to 1 month.

CUENCA-STYLE HONEY-ALMOND NOUGAT

Alajú

This almond sweet, famous in Cuenca, is of Arabic origin and quite similar to *turrón*, another nougat of honey and almonds. Turrón, a speciality of Toledo and of Jijona (Alicante), is usually purchased, but *alajú* is simple to confect at home. So sweet that it is served in slivers, it makes a lovely addition to a sweets tray and a fine present.

The cooked honey and almond mixture is spread between edible paper-thin wafers so that it's not too sticky to pick up. (The wafers can be ordered from specialist baking web sites.) Otherwise, spread it on nonstick baking parchment. Peel off the parchment to cut the nougat. When cool, the nougat is slightly flexible, not hard or brittle.

Walnut halves can be used in place of almonds.

MAKES THREE 12CM/5IN PATTIES, 8 TO 10 SLICES EACH

130g blanched whole almonds

80g fine dried breadcrumbs

Six 12cm/5in diameter wafers (or squares of nonstick baking parchment)

280g honey

1 teaspoon grated orange zest

Preheat the oven to 190°C/170°C fan/GM5.

Place the almonds in a baking tin and the crumbs in another baking dish. Toast them, stirring frequently, until light golden (do not allow to brown), about 14 minutes. Cool the almonds and crumbs.

Arrange 3 wafers on a marble slab or individual china dishes. Have the remaining 3 wafers ready.

Place the honey in a saucepan and position a jam thermometer in the honey. Heat over medium-high heat until the honey bubbles and begins to foam up. Let it cook to the soft-ball stage (115°C), 2 to 3 minutes.

Stir in the almonds. Stir in the breadcrumbs. Cook over low heat, stirring constantly, for 1 minute. Stir in the orange zest.

Spread a third of the honey-almond mixture on each of 3 wafers. Place another wafer on top of each and gently press the patties to spread the filling to an approximate thickness of 1cm/½in. Allow them to cool. The nougat is ready to eat immediately, but it can be kept, wrapped tightly in clingfilm and foil and stored in an airtight container, for up to 3 months.

Use a cleaver to cut the discs of nougat crossways into 1cm/½in slivers. Serve on a sweets tray.

CHOCOLATE-FIG BONBONS

Bombones de Higos con Chocolate

Figs plus chocolate equals divine. This artisanal gourmet product – figs with a chocolate cream filling, bathed in bittersweet chocolate – can be made at home without too much trouble. Don't worry if your bonbons don't have a slick professional finish – they will still taste wonderful. Chocolate-covered figs make great presents. Place them in fluted bonbon papers or simply wrap them individually in tissue paper.

MAKES 75 BONBONS

450g small dried figs, such as Calimyrna

200g plus 2 tablespoons sugar

4 tablespoons brandy

450g bittersweet chocolate, chopped or grated

2 tablespoons extra virgin olive oil

5 tablespoons boiling water

With a sharp knife, cut a slit in the bottoms of the figs, leaving the stems intact.

Combine 700ml/1¼pints of the sugar and 3 cups water in a saucepan. Bring to the boil, stirring to dissolve the sugar. Cook for 3 minutes. Add the brandy, bring back to the boil, and stir in the figs. Remove the pan from the heat and let the figs macerate for 15 minutes.

Drain the figs in a colander, saving the brandy sugar syrup for another use. Spread the figs on a rack and allow to dry in a well-ventilated place for 2 hours.

Prepare the chocolate cream filling. In the top of a double boiler over boiling water, melt 120g of the chocolate. Stir in the olive oil, the remaining 2 tablespoons sugar and the boiling water. Transfer the mixture to a saucepan and place over medium, direct heat and cook, stirring, for 3 minutes. Scrape into a heatproof bowl. Cool the chocolate, then refrigerate.

To stuff the figs with the chocolate cream filling, poke a finger or piece of wooden dowelling into the slit to make a hollow and use the tip of a small knife to push about ⅛ teaspoon of the chocolate cream into the centre. Place each fig on a tray as it is filled. (You may not need all of the chocolate cream. Reserve unused chocolate for another use.) Set aside in a cool place (not the refrigerator) for at least 30 minutes and up to 6 hours.

Place the remaining 330g chocolate in the top of a double boiler. Stir frequently with a wooden spoon until melted. The chocolate is ready when it's warm to the touch but not hot. Dip one fig at a time into the chocolate, rolling it around with a cocktail stick until it is completely coated. Spear the fig with the cocktail stick or use 2 forks to lift it out, letting excess chocolate drip off. Place on a baking sheet lined with greaseproof paper and let sit at room temperature. The sweets are ready when the chocolate hardens completely.

Place the figs in individual bonbon papers or in a box lined with greaseproof paper. They are ready to eat immediately but may be kept, refrigerated, for up to 1 month.

LAVENDER HONEY ICE MILK

Helado de Miel de Espliegas

The provinces of Guadalajara and Cuenca are famed for their delectable honeys. This ice milk is very subtly flavoured with lavender flowers and lavender honey. (The ice milk will be a golden honey colour – not lavender.) You might try variations – sprigs of rosemary with rosemary honey, thyme and thyme honey, orange blossoms with orange blossom honey.

SERVES 6

650ml/about 1 pint full-fat or semi-skimmed milk	1 clove
145g lavender honey	4 egg yolks
12 lavender flowers or 1 tablespoon dried culinary lavender	Pinch of salt

Combine 450ml/¾ pint of the milk with the honey in a saucepan set over medium heat. Heat, stirring, until the honey is dissolved. Remove from the heat and add the lavender flowers and clove. Cover the pan and let the lavender steep for 30 minutes.

Blend the yolks and salt with half of the remaining milk and pour into a clean saucepan. Strain the lavender-infused milk into the egg mixture. Cook over medium heat, whisking, until the custard reaches 82°C, about 5 minutes. Remove from the heat and whisk in the remaining cold milk.

Chill the mixture. Freeze in an ice cream maker according to the manufacturer's instructions.

SAFFRON ICE CREAM *with* PINE NUT PRALINE *and* CHOCOLATE SYRUP

Helado de Azafrán con Guirlache de Piñones y Sirope de Chocolate

La Mancha saffron lends a golden colour and an aromatic, subtly bitter flavour to the rich ice cream. Saffron has a real affinity with chocolate, while the pine nuts provide a crunchy contrast to the smooth cream. Altogether a delightful combination. Ice cream, praline and syrup can all be made several days in advance of serving.

SERVES 8

FOR THE ICE CREAM

450ml / ¾ pint milk

1 strip orange zest

1 teaspoon saffron threads, crushed

6 egg yolks

Pinch of salt

125g sugar

400ml / scant ¾ pint whipping cream or double cream

FOR THE PINE NUT PRALINE

80g sugar

120g pine nuts

FOR THE CHOCOLATE SYRUP (MAKES 180ML/ 6 FL OZ)

115g bittersweet chocolate, broken into pieces

2 tablespoons extra virgin olive oil

120ml / 4 fl oz boiling water

1 tablespoon sugar

Bring the milk and orange zest to the boil. Pour the milk through a strainer into a heatproof bowl and discard the orange zest. Add the crushed saffron to the milk and allow to infuse for 20 minutes.

Beat the egg yolks, salt and sugar in a bowl. Lift off the skin from the top of the milk and beat the warm milk into the yolks. Transfer to the top of a double boiler and cook the custard mixture until foamy and thick enough to coat a spoon. Remove from the heat and allow to cool.

Whip the cream until it holds soft peaks. Fold it thoroughly into the custard mixture and chill.

Freeze the mixture in an ice cream maker according to the manufacturer's instructions.

To prepare the praline, place 3 tablespoons of the sugar and 2 tablespoons water in a heavy frying pan or round-bottomed wok over high heat. Dissolve the sugar, stirring.

When the sugar is bubbling, stir in the pine nuts. Cook, stirring, until the sugar begins to caramelise and adhere to the kernels. Add 2 tablespoons more sugar and stir until it melts and turns golden. Add the remaining sugar and continue stirring and cooking until the pine nuts are coated in caramel.

Spread the mixture out onto an oiled plate or a sheet of baking parchment. Allow to cool. When completely cool, break the praline up into small bits. Store in a covered container for up to 1 week.

To prepare the chocolate syrup, melt the chocolate in the top of a double boiler set over hot water. Stir until smooth. Stir in the oil, then the boiling water, then the sugar.

Transfer the mixture to the saucepan and place it over direct heat and cook, stirring, until it begins to bubble. Cook without stirring for 3 minutes. Remove and cool.

The syrup keeps refrigerated for up to 1 week. It can be reheated in a microwave to bring to pouring consistency.

To serve, allow the ice cream to soften for 20 to 30 minutes. Scoop the ice cream into small bowls. Drizzle with chocolate syrup and scatter the praline on top.

FROZEN FIG MOUSSE

Tarta Helada de Higos

Fig trees grow widely in La Mancha. The dried fruit provides a ready source of sweetness in winter meals. This luscious dessert, combined with honey and cream, makes a grand finale for Christmas dinner. Dessert chefs like to create composite sweets that play off flavours and textures. If you'd like to custom-design your dessert, try the frozen fig mousse with a drizzle or swirl of chocolate syrup (page 339), orange syrup (page 326), caramel sauce (page 318), or Sweet Potatoes Candied in Grape Syrup (page 332). Then add a crisp fried biscuit, such as Crispy Leaves (page 309) or Almond Fritters (page 313). Scatter with pine nut praline (page 339). Very festive.

SERVES 8

225g dried figs
350ml / 12 fl oz boiling water
⅛ teaspoon aniseeds
3 egg yolks
120ml / 4 fl oz milk

90g sugar
2 tablespoons honey
Pinch of ground cloves
350ml / 12 fl oz whipping cream or double cream

Rinse the figs, place them in a heatproof bowl and pour the boiling water over them. Allow the figs to soak for 3 hours. Drain, saving some of the liquid.

Nip out the fig stems with a knife and cut the figs in half. Put the figs in a blender with 120ml / scant ¼ pint of the reserved soaking liquid and the aniseeds. Purée the figs in the blender until smooth. Place the purée in a mixing bowl.

Beat the egg yolks in another bowl. Combine the milk, sugar, honey and cloves in a saucepan. Bring to the boil, stirring to dissolve the honey. Remove from the heat. Whisk the hot milk into the yolks.

Return the milk-yolk mixture to the pan and place over boiling water. Cook over boiling water, whisking constantly, until the mixture thickens, about 4 minutes. The custard will be thick enough to coat a spoon.

Remove the pan from the heat and whisk for 1 minute as the custard cools.

Fold the custard into the fig purée. Chill the mixture.

Chill the whisk beaters and bowl. Once chilled, add the cream and beat until it holds soft peaks. Stir some of the cream into the fig mixture. Then fold the remaining whipped cream thoroughly into the fig purée.

Place the fig-cream mixture in a 20cm/8in springform tin. Cover with clingfilm and freeze for 8 hours, or until the mousse is solid.

The frozen mousse can be removed from the tin, wrapped in clingfilm and foil, and returned to the freezer for up to 2 weeks.

To serve, remove from the freezer at least 10 minutes before serving. Dip a serrated knife into hot water to slice.

VARIATION: *Instead of freezing the mousse, serve it chilled, dolloped into dessert cups.*

QUINCE SORBET

Sorbete de Membrillo

Quince is a full-flavoured, old-fashioned fruit that looks like an oversized, knobbly apple. Somewhere between apple and pear in flavour and texture, the quince has a leathery skin rich in pectin. Cooked with sugar, the fruit sets up as a stiff jelly (also called *quince paste*) that can be cut into slices. (Should you have a windfall of quince, the recipe for Quince Jelly is on page 329.) Imported quince jelly (see Sources) is an easy starting point for this sorbet. Although the fruit has a pleasing graininess, the pectin makes a creamy ice without any fat.

A classic pairing is quince jelly with either aged Manchego or *queso fresco,* fresh white goat cheese. So this sorbet goes especially well with Moulded Manchego Cheese Flan (page 322).

SERVES 8

400g quince jelly

4 tablespoons sugar

1 teaspoon grated orange zest

2 tablespoons fresh lemon juice

Pinch of ground cloves

Allow the quince jelly to come to room temperature.

In a saucepan, combine 600ml/1 pint of water with the sugar. Bring to the boil and simmer for 2 minutes. Add the quince jelly and stir over low heat until it is dissolved. Stir in the orange zest, lemon juice and cloves.

Cool the quince mixture, stirring occasionally, and then chill it. Place in an ice cream maker and process according to the manufacturer's directions. Place the frozen quince sorbet in a container with a tight seal and freeze for at least 2 hours.

Soften the sorbet before serving.

RED WINE GRANITA

Granizado de Vino Tinto

Use an unaged Tempranillo wine for this frosty dessert. A 750ml bottle of wine contains just over 1 pint of liquid. About a third of the bottle of uncooked wine added to the cooked syrup contains just enough alcohol to keep the mix from freezing solid.

SERVES 6

One 750ml bottle red wine

240g sugar

1 vanilla pod

One 12cm/5in strip orange zest

One 12cm/5in strip lemon zest

1 clove

Fresh mint sprigs

Pour all but one third of the wine into a heavy saucepan with the sugar, vanilla, orange zest, lemon zest and clove. Bring to the boil and simmer gently for 10 minutes.

Pour the remaining third of the wine into the cooked wine. Pour through a strainer and discard the solids. Cool the wine.

Place in a 20cm/8in cake tin and freeze for 2 hours. Stir the mixture and return to the freezer. Freeze, stirring every 2 hours. Serve the granita while still slushy. If the mixture freezes solid, break it up and purée in a food processor.

Serve in dessert cups garnished with mint sprigs.

ORANGE ICE

Granizado de Naranja

A *granizado* is an iced drink, served slushy with a straw. But it can also be served frozen, much like Italian granita.

SERVES 6

4 to 5 oranges (to make 350ml/12 fl oz juice)

200g sugar

Fresh mint sprigs for garnish

Remove strips of zest from 1 orange. Grate enough zest from another orange to make 1 teaspoon. Juice the oranges and pass the juice through a fine-meshed strainer.

Place the sugar, strips of zest and 350ml/12 fl oz of water in a saucepan. Bring to the boil and simmer for 5 minutes. Cool. Strain the sugar syrup, discarding the strips of zest. Combine the syrup, orange juice and grated zest.

Pour into a glass or metal pan and freeze for 1 hour. Stir the frozen bits around to incorporate them into the as yet unfrozen liquid and return to the freezer. Repeat the stirring several more times. Transfer to a covered container and freeze.

To serve as an ice, scrape or scoop the ice into dessert cups. To serve as a tall drink, place the ice in a blender with 450ml/¾ pint cold water and blend until slushy. Serve in tall glasses. Garnish the ice or drink with mint sprigs.

Wine and Other Drinks

Nueve meses de invierno y tres meses de infierno. 'Nine months of winter and three months of hell' is how they characterise the climate of Castilla–La Mancha, Spain's central plateau. Blazing-hot summers and freezing winters are hard on people, but good for vines. In this sunny, dry climate, they've never heard of grapes not ripening, as sometimes happens in more northern lands following a cold summer.

This is big wine country. In fact, it is the biggest area of vineyards on earth – about 8 per cent of all land worldwide is planted in vines and almost half of all the vineyards in Spain are within La Mancha. Miles and miles of vineyards keep the landscape verdant through hellishly hot summers.

Wine has been made in the La Mancha region continuously since pre-Roman times. By the nineteenth century, La Mancha wines, in particular those of Valdepeñas, had become the wine of choice for the taverns of Madrid, supplied by muleteers who hauled it to the capital in wineskins. With the coming of the railroad in 1861, a daily 'wine train' delivered carriage-loads of wine to the capital.

The wine of the old days, called *clarete,* was made by mixing quantities of white wine – produced in prodigious quantity – with enough red to give it colour. Having cornered the market in 'ordinary' wine, for most of the twentieth century, winemakers in La Mancha didn't pay much attention to world market trends towards quality wines at higher prices – specifically, aged reds. And growers balked at ripping out white-grape vines and replanting with red-wine grapes.

The 1980s and 1990s brought massive restructuring of vineyards and wineries, with government subsidies to ease the pain of radical change. Acres of Airén white-wine grapes were replaced with red varieties. Relegated to museums are the *tinajas,* huge earthenware vats in which grape must used to be fermented. Wineries replaced them with stainless-steel tanks allowing temperature-controlled fermentation. Underground *cavas,* cellars for keeping wines, were expanded to include oak barrels for ageing wine. Forward-thinking winemakers, with an eye to world markets, pioneered the planting of new grape varietals. Gradually, the tradition-bound regulating boards of the various *denominaciones de origen* have come to allow 'foreign' grapes, such as Cabernet Sauvignon, in winemaking. The region, sometimes likened to a slumbering giant, is taking huge strides towards modern wines, with an emphasis on quality instead of quantity. Big money is being invested in La Mancha by some of the important wineries from other parts of Spain.

🌿 GRAPE VARIETIES

The principal white-wine grape varieties in La Mancha are Airén – the most abundant grape in Spain – and Macabeo. Grown in very small quantities are Verdejo, Merseguera, Albillo, Sauvignon Blanc, Viognier and Chardonnay. Though less and less white wine is made, Airén grapes continue to be important for distillation. The resulting grape spirits are used in *aguardiente,* an anise-flavoured liqueur, and it goes to Sherry bodegas for use in making Brandy de Jerez.

Of red-wine grapes, Tempranillo – also called *Cencibel* in La Mancha – is far and away the most widely used, both in monovarietal and blended wines. Tempranillo is the same grape that has made the fame of La Rioja. It lends itself to fruity young reds and full-bodied oak-aged wines. Other red-wine grapes grown in the region are Garnacha (Grenache), Monastrell, Bobal, Graciano, Cabernet Sauvignon, Merlot, Syrah and Petit Verdot. Blending of varietals opens up opportunities for originality in winemaking.

🌿 DENOMINATIONS OF ORIGIN

Castilla–La Mancha encompasses eight denominations of origin, a designation equivalent to French *appellation contrôlée,* plus the relatively new categories of Vinos de la Tierra de Castilla and Vinos de Pago, or single-estate wines.

DO ALMANSA. Situated on the eastern edge of Albacete province, bordering Valencia, Alicante and Murcia. Whites of Macabeo and Verdejo; reds of Monastrell with Tempranillo.

DO JUMILLA. Centred in the province of Murcia with vineyards in Albacete. Red wines of Monastrell, Tempranillo, Syrah and Cabernet Sauvignon.

DO LA MANCHA. The biggest of the wine regions, it spreads across the provinces of Ciudad Real, Albacete, Cuenca and Toledo. Wineries within this denomination range from gigantic cooperatives to single-estate operations. While Airén for whites and Tempranillo for reds make up most vineyard acreage, Chardonnay, Cabernet Sauvignon and Syrah are allowed.

DO MANCHUELA. Occupies the eastern part of Cuenca and Albacete provinces. Constituted in 2000, the sector has attracted new investments and experimenters. Bobal is the primary grape, but other varieties are being increased.

DO MÉNTRIDA. Situated in the north of Toledo province, bordering Madrid and Ávila. Garnacha has been the preferred varietal, but Tempranillo, Cabernet Sauvignon, Merlot, Syrah and Petit Verdot are grown also. Macabeo and Sauvignon Blanc are the white varieties.

DO MONDÉJAR. Within the province of Guadalajara. White grapes are Malvar and Macabeo; red are Tempranillo and Cabernet Sauvignon.

DO RIBERA DEL JÚCAR. In the south of Cuenca province. The newest denomination concentrated on red wines of Tempranillo, Cabernet Sauvignon, Merlot, Syrah and Bobal.

DO VALDEPEÑAS. A pocket within the huge DO La Mancha, encompassing the lands around the town of Valdepeñas in the south of Ciudad Real province. The wines of this region are, historically, second in popularity only to those of La Rioja. Valdepeñas has huge 'factory' wineries turning out well-made, inexpensive wines, as well as small boutique bodegas making superb wines on a very small scale. White wines of Airén, Macabeo and Chardonnay; rosé (*rosado*) of Tempranillo; and reds of Tempranillo, Garnacha and Cabernet Sauvignon.

VINOS DE LA TIERRA DE CASTILLA. This category was created for wines made within Castilla–La Mancha that don't necessarily fit into one of the denominations. They may fall outside of the geographical limitations; be made of varietals not authorised by the regulating boards; produce yields not authorised; or use techniques in growing or vinification not allowed by the denominations. The intention was to allow winemakers to produce wines that could compete on the world market. Many of the new generation of La Mancha wines carry this label, including some of the most critically acclaimed. Some bodegas make both – wines with a denomination label and another with the Vinos de la Tierra (V.T.) label.

VINOS DE PAGO. *Pago* means an estate, domain, *château*. This denomination is given to single-estate wines that meet stringent quality requisites.

❧ PAIRING WINE WITH FOOD

In most of Spain's wine regions, including Castilla–La Mancha, red-wine vintages are classified as *jóven,* young; *crianza,* slightly aged; *reserva,* aged; and *gran reserva,* long aged. Wines with denomination labels must adhere to minimum ageing requirements. For example, DO Valdepeñas specifies that crianza wines must be aged in oak barrels for at least six months and in bottle for at least eighteen months, and reserva wines must have at least twelve months in barrel and two years in bottle. Traditionally, this has meant that when you buy a bottle of wine, it's ready to drink. You don't have to cellar it and wait for the tannins to smooth out.

Some winemakers, aiming for a world market where crianza and reserva are terms less well understood than in Spain, avoid these classifications. Some of them claim long ageing on oak changes a wine's personality and distorts the fruit. They may label their wines 'aged in oak barrels' and, modelled after the French, allow the consumer to keep the wine in bottle for longer periods.

Drink young wines within a year of the time they are made. Good ones are fruity and fresh, with bright cherry colour. Choose youthful wines to drink with tapas, especially with potato tortilla, meatballs and Spanish sausages such as chorizo; with family meals of lentils, beans, chickpeas or pasta; with paella; with breaded veal or pork escalopes; with roast chicken or turkey. La Mancha's inexpensive young reds are also a good choice for making sangría.

Crianza wines, with just a touch of oak, go especially well with cheese of all sorts, especially aged Manchego. This is also the perfect wine with most meat dishes such as grilled steak or roast pork or lamb. Serve it with a lamb burger or hamburger of choice beef.

A reserva wine, as the word indicates, means 'reserved', a term used in Spanish winemaking to distinguish the finest wines of a vintner's cellar, which are reserved, in bottle, until they are at their optimum for drinking. A reserva wine is made when the grapes in a particular year are of sufficient quality to produce a wine that will improve with ageing. These wines, usually of a deep brick colour, offer complex bouquet and taste. Choose them to accompany dishes such as stewed partridge, venison, duck and beef.

White wines of La Mancha are usually young and simple. Macabeo varietals are rather better than Airén, although either one, when cold-fermented, makes a light and fresh white that, served chilled, accompanies fish and shellfish very nicely. Some winemakers are experimenting with Chardonnay and Viognier, giving them a brief passage through oak to lend sophistication and complexity.

Serve red wines at a cool room temperature. In hot weather, without a controlled-temperature cellar or room air-conditioning, give wines a sixty-minute cooling period in the refrigerator before opening. Crianza and reserva reds need a bit of time in the glass to open up. Some winemakers choose not to clarify and filter their wines. These benefit from being decanted carefully, leaving any sediment behind. Serve most rosés (*rosados*) and white wines well chilled.

❧ CHOICES

As I travelled around La Mancha, I sampled local wines in restaurants and bars. I met winemakers and bought their wines right at the *bodegas,* wineries. I discovered much to like. My personal picks, listed below, include some of the region's priciest bottles ($60 – about £30 in 2007 – and up) and others that are amazing bargains ($3.00 – about £1.50 in 2007). There are many more excellent wines – but I haven't tasted them yet. The bodega's name and location are given first, then the name of one of its wines where it is different from the bodega's name. Incidentally, I just love reading the names of these little towns in La Mancha – Corral de Almaguer, Retuerta del Bullaque, Quintanar de la Orden, Argamasilla de Alba, Mota del Cuervo – any one of which could be *un lugar de la Mancha,* that mysterious someplace in La Mancha where Don Quixote lived.

> Barreda, Corral de Almaguer (Toledo). *Torre de Barreda*; Vino de la Tierra de Castilla.
> Centro Españolas, Tomelloso (Ciudad Real). *Allozo*; DO La Mancha.
> Cooperativa Nuestra Señora del Rosario, El Provencio (Cuenca). *Canforrales*; DO La Mancha.
> Cooperativa Nuestro Padre Jesús del Perdón, Manzanares (Ciudad Real). *Yuntero*; DO La Mancha.
> Cooperativa Tintoralba, Alpera (Albacete). DO Almansa.
> Dehesa del Carrizal, Retuerta del Bullaque (Ciudad Real). Vino de la Tierra de Castilla.
> Dionisos, Valdepeñas (Ciudad Real). *Vinum Vitae*; DO Valdepeñas. Wine made from organic grapes.
> Dominio de Malpica, Malpica del Tajo (Toledo). *Solaz*; Vino de la Tierra de Castilla. Division of the Osborne Sherry company.
> Dominio de Valdepusa, Malpica del Tajo (Toledo). *Emeritus*; Vino de Pago. First-ever denomination for a single-estate wine.

El Vínculo, Campo de Criptana (Ciudad Real). DO La Mancha. Belongs to Alejandro Fernández Tinto Pesquera of Ribera del Duero fame.

Entremontes, Quintanar de la Orden (Toledo). DO La Mancha.

Finca Antigua, Los Hinojosos (Cuenca). DO La Mancha. The bodega is a division of Rioja bodega Martínez Bujanda.

Finca Sandoval, Ledaña (Cuenca). *Salia*; DO Manchuela.

Fontana, Fuente de Pedro Naharro (Cuenca). *Quercus*; DO La Mancha.

J. Santos, La Villa de Don Fadrique (Toledo). DO La Mancha.

Leganza, Quintanar de la Orden (Toledo). DO La Mancha. A division of giant Faustino bodega in La Rioja.

Manuel Manzaneque–Finca Elez, El Bonillo (Albacete). Vino de Pago.

Miguel Calatayud, Valdepeñas (Ciudad Real). *Vegaval Plata*; DO Valdepeñas.

Montalvo Wilmot, Argamasilla de Alba (Ciudad Real). DO La Mancha.

Pago del Ama, Toledo. Vino de la Tierra de Castilla.

Piqueras, Almansa (Albacete). *Castillo de Almansa*; DO Almansa.

S.A.T. Santa Rita, Mota del Cuervo (Cuenca). *Veronés*; DO La Mancha.

Vidal del Saz, Campo de Criptana (Ciudad Real). DO La Mancha.

Viña Albali Reservas, Valdepeñas. DO Valdepeñas. Division of the huge Félix Solís bodega.

MANCHEGAN WHITE WINE SPRITZER

Zurra Manchega

The traditional white wine of La Mancha is made from Airén grapes, the most abundant grape in Spain. Robust, disease-resistant vines yield heavily and produce wines with a pleasant aroma, no complexity, not much keeping power. Low in price, La Mancha whites are perfect for making this refreshing wine spritzer with an intriguing hint of spice. You could use any dry white wine. This drink, called *cuerva* in Albacete, is traditionally made, like a punch, in a large earthenware bowl and served in small earthenware cups.

SERVES 6

65g sugar

Fresh mint sprigs, plus 6 mint sprigs for garnish

1 stick of celery

One 5cm/2in cinnamon stick

1 lemon, sliced

1 orange, sliced

One (750ml) bottle dry white wine, chilled

1 peach, sliced

Sparkling water to taste (300–450ml / ½–¾ pint)

Ice cubes (optional)

Combine the sugar and 250ml/8 fl oz of water in a small saucepan. Bring to the boil and cook for 5 minutes. Remove from the heat and add the mint, celery, cinnamon and half of the lemon and orange slices. Let steep for at least 30 minutes.

Strain into a jug and add the wine, remaining lemon and orange slices and peach slices. Dilute to taste with sparkling water. Serve in tall glasses, with ice if desired. Garnish with mint sprigs.

—Pero, dígame, señor—dijo Sancho—por el siglo
de lo que más quiere, ¿este vino es de Ciudad Real?

—¡Brabo mojón!—respondió el del Bosque—; en verdad que no
es de otra parte, y que tiene algunos años de ancianidad.

—¿No será bueno, señor escudero, que tenga yo un instinto tan
grande y tan natural en esto de conocer vinos, que en dándome
a oler cualquiera, acierto la patria, el linaje, el sabor y la dura
y las vueltas que ha de dar, con todas las circunstancias al
vino atañaderas? Pero no hay de qué maravillarse, si tuve en
mi linaje, por parte de mi padre, los dos más excelentes
mojones que en luengos años conoció La Mancha. . . .

'But, tell me, sir,' said Sancho, 'by the world you so love,
isn't this wine from Ciudad Real?'

'Good call, man'! replied the Squire of the Forest. 'To
tell the truth it's from nowhere else, and it's got a few
years of ageing too.'

'And why do you suppose, sir squire, that I shouldn't
have a great natural instinct for knowing wines?' said
Sancho. 'Give me a sniff of any wine and I can tell you
the vineyard it came from, its vintage, grape and age,
how many turns the barrel had, and just about any other
detail concerning wine. But you shouldn't be so
surprised, for on my father's side of the family were two
of the foremost wine tasters ever known in La Mancha.'

Sancho Panza, drinking with the
Knight of the Forest's squire

VENDIMIA LUNCH
WITH THE MARQUÉS

On a bright September morning on the first day of the *vendimia,* grape harvest, Carlos Falcó, the Marqués of Griñón, arrives early at his vineyards of Dominio de Valdepusa to keep an eye on things. A grandee of Spain whose name crops up in society and gossip columns, Don Carlos looks right at home in country clothes as he walks through the vineyards, talking with the workers.

He picks a cluster of the deep purple, almost black grapes and tastes one.

'This is how we know when to pick the grapes,' he says. 'We taste them. We do the chemical analysis too, but I don't have to wait for the lab tests. You can taste the sugars. These are fully ripened grapes. We start tomorrow with the Syrah.'

The grape vines are trained high on wires. Don Carlos explains that this kind of canopy management – once unknown in most Spanish vineyards – allows more sunlight to reach leaves and the ripening fruit.

'That allows greater yield and better wine,' he says.

Most of the clusters are at waist level, meaning the pickers don't have to stoop and bend to cut them. They heap the fruit into crates, which are loaded on a flatbed truck and hauled to the *bodega,* winery, only two hundred yards from the vineyards. The vinification process begins before the dew is hardly dried on the grapes.

This is at the heart of the making of *vino de pago,* single-estate wine.

'*Pago* means "domain"', explains Don Carlos. 'It is the same as terroir.'

Dominio de Valdepusa, where Don Carlos planted his experimental vineyards back in 1974, became, in 2004, the first ever single estate in Spain, like the French *grands crus*, to be granted its own Denomination of Origin. The lands are west of Toledo, at Malpica de Tajo, situated on a plateau overlooking the broad valley of the River Pusa, a tributary of the Tajo. The property, which has been in the family since 1292, lies just outside the old, established wine denomination of Méntrida, one of eight denominations in Castilla–La Mancha.

'They invited us to join the Méntrida denomination,' says Don Carlos. 'But we preferred to stay out. We wanted to do something revolutionary.'

Back in 1974, planting Cabernet Sauvignon, a 'foreign' grape, in native Tempranillo and Garnacha country was revolutionary. It was actually prohibited by the denominations that established which grape varietals could be used in the region's wines. He also set up drip irrigation in the vineyards – also prohibited by the governing wine boards.

Carlos Falcó, studied agriculture at a Belgian university, then studied at the University of California at Davis, where he met Dr Maynard Amerine, the late professor and wine guru.

'He introduced me to Cabernet Sauvignon, and it changed my life,' says Don Carlos. The going wisdom was that you couldn't make good Cab in a hot climate such as in central Spain. But Dr. Amerine encouraged him to give it a try. New winery technology allowing temperature controls during fermentation, use of antioxidants such as ascorbic acid to allow wines to age gently, and cooling of cellars would make it possible.

'Then they told me I couldn't do this in Spain. I lost ten years wrangling with the authorities. Finally I decided to go ahead anyway'. He smuggled in the outlaw vine cuttings in a truckload of apple trees.

'I never looked back.'

Don Carlos was the first in Spain to plant Syrah (1991), a variety he considers especially suitable for Spain's hot zones, and Petit Verdot (1992), producing the first single varietal Petit Verdot wine in the world. He pioneered the use of Australian vineyard consultant Richard Smart's systems of vine pruning and canopy management as well as sophisticated computer-managed watering systems that measure stress levels in the vineyards.

Don Carlos makes three single-varietal wines with the Dominio de Valdepusa label – Cabernet Sauvignon, Syrah and Petit Verdot – plus Emeritus and Svmma Varietalis, both blends of all three, aged in French oak barrels from eleven to twenty-two months. He does not make Tempranillo.

'We're very famous in the wine world,' he chuckles, 'because anyone who wants to taste Petit Verdot can find it only here. In Bordeaux, where it is used in top-growth wines like Château Margaux, you can't taste it unless you go into the cellar and taste from the barrel.'

What happens to Cabernet Sauvignon or other French grapes when they are planted in La Mancha?

'It takes four elements to make wine,' says Don Carlos, 'soil, climate, grape and the person who makes the wine. The soil is Spanish, the climate is Spanish and I am Spanish. Only the grape is not. That's three out of four, so it is a very Spanish wine.' He adds that Jancis Robinson, well-known wine critic, even claimed, perhaps tongue-in-cheek, that Syrah wines from Spain finish tasting like Tempranillo.

If once he appeared a raving renegade, in retrospect Don Carlos looks like the prophet who pointed the way to restructuring of vineyards and winemaking and, most important, marketing wines internationally. The principal wine regions of Castilla–La Mancha now allow plantations of Cabernet Sauvignon, Syrah, Merlot and Petit Verdot.

On the Dominio de Valdepusa estate are two rambling eighteenth-century buildings. The old *casa de labor,* or farm building, houses the winery's receiving centre, offices, tasting rooms and barrel room. The ochre *casa de vacas,* cow keeper's house, is used for family gatherings and entertaining guests (Carlos Falcó and his family live near Madrid).

Lunch is laid on the terrace overlooking a walled garden. With a twinkle, Don Carlos uncorks a white wine to sip as an aperitif.

'This wine is made by a friend of mine, in the Montes de Toledo,' he says as he pours. 'It is a Viognier, very fragrant.' Viognier! Another surprise. Can this really be La Mancha? He passes a plate of *cecina de ciervo,* venison 'ham', also from the Montes de Toledo. It is sliced paper-thin, drizzled with extra virgin olive oil (the marqués's title also appears on olive oil produced on a nearby estate) and sprinkled with thyme.

Lunch begins with *ajo blanco,* a cold garlic-almond soup with the surprise of sweet melon. The main course, *tórtola,* wild dove, braised in a wine sauce, is the perfect foil for savouring the clean, bright flavours of Emeritus, Don Carlos's unique blend of Cabernet Sauvignon, Syrah and Petit Verdot. It is silky, herbaceous, with a hint of liquorice and toffee.

It is a lovely finish to a day in the terroir of Dominio de Valdepusa.

RED WINE SANGRÍA

Sangría

This classic party drink has many variations. Tourist restaurants often serve sangría syrupy sweet, while Spaniards enjoy it fairly dry, with a double punch of brandy or liqueur. Use any young red wine with no oak, preferably a Tempranillo from La Mancha. In Spain, sangría is diluted with *gaseoso,* lightly sweetened, slightly lemony fizzy water.

Use any combination of fruit in the sangría. Strawberries, oranges, melon, apples, pears, bananas, grapes and peaches, sliced or chopped, are some of the best. Apples float, oranges sink. Serve the sangría in a pitcher with a long-handled spoon for ladling out the fruit. Pour into wide-mouthed juice glasses or goblets. Ice is optional – it dilutes the sangría as it melts.

Sangría goes nicely with some tapas and canapés but is too sweet to serve with a meal. I like it for summer entertaining al fresco, on the patio or poolside.

SERVES **8** TO **10**

50g sugar (4 tablespoons)

1 strip orange zest

Chopped or sliced fruit, enough to fill a pint glass

4 tablespoons brandy or liqueur such as Cointreau

One (750ml) bottle red wine, chilled

400–700ml / ¾–1¼ pints chilled sparkling water

Combine the sugar with the zest and 250ml/8 fl oz water in a small saucepan. Bring to the boil and simmer for 2 minutes. Allow the sugar syrup to cool. Strain it into a 2 litre jug. Discard the orange zest.

Add the fruit and brandy to the jug. The fruit can macerate, refrigerated, for up to 2 hours. Add the chilled red wine. Immediately before serving, add chilled sparkling water to taste.

WATERMELON SANGRÍA

Sangría de Sandía

This makes a fun party drink. It can be prepared in advance and chilled. Or, if preferred, serve it over ice cubes.

SERVES 8

3 tablespoons sugar

1 strip orange zest

900g ripe watermelon

3 tablespoons Cointreau or Triple Sec

One (750ml) bottle dry white wine, well chilled

A few strawberries

Fresh mint sprigs for garnish

Combine the sugar and zest with 120ml/4 fl oz water in a small saucepan. Bring to the boil and stir to dissolve the sugar. Remove from the heat and cool. Discard the orange zest.

Remove the seeds and green rind from the watermelon. Save a few chunks of flesh for garnish. Purée the flesh in a blender or food processor. Strain the purée and place in a jug with the sugar syrup, Cointreau and white wine. Chill the sangría for 1 hour.

Serve the sangría, over ice if desired, garnished with the reserved cubes of watermelon, whole strawberries and mint sprigs.

SWEET SPICED WINE

Mistela

In bygone times in the vineyards it was customary to make this sweet wine with unfermented grape must. The addition of distilled alcohol stopped the fermentation of the sugars in the juice. It was allowed to steep for forty days, then filtered.

This recipe is an adaptation, using grape juice in place of must. Use any clear spirit, such as *aguardiente de orujo*, grappa, vodka or gin. Serve it well chilled, in tiny liqueur glasses with cakes and biscuits. Or turn it into a tall drink by diluting it with sparkling water and pouring it over ice.

❧ MAKES 1½ LITRES / 2½ PINTS

1 strip orange zest

1 strip lemon zest

1 teaspoon aniseeds

One 2½cm/1in cinnamon stick

50g sugar

1 litre / about 1½ pints white grape juice

450ml / ¾ pint vodka or other clear spirit

Combine the strips of zest, aniseeds, cinnamon, sugar, and 250ml/8 fl oz water in a small saucepan. Bring to the boil and simmer for 3 minutes. Remove from the heat and allow to cool. Strain the sugar syrup and discard the solids.

Combine the sugar syrup, grape juice and vodka in a container with a tightly fitting cap (jar, bottle, flask). Refrigerate until chilled.

LATE-NIGHT LIQUEUR

Licor de Trasnochá

Use your best cut-glass decanter to serve this liqueur. It is sweet, but not insipid, and aromatic with orange and spices – a fine after-dinner drink sipped neat. Mix it with sparkling water and ice for a tall drink or concoct a Spanish cocktail with it.

Remove the orange zest with a vegetable peeler in as few strips as possible, being sure to leave behind all the white pith. Leave the strips of zest to dry for several days. Once the orange-spice mixture is combined with the spirits (vodka or grappa), the liqueur infuses for 2 weeks before being strained. Take care to use very clean utensils, jars and bottles.

MAKES 1.2 LITRES/2 PINTS

Zest of 2 oranges	2 cloves
375g sugar	1 tablespoon fresh lemon verbena (optional)
1 tablespoon aniseeds, coarsely crushed	3 fresh mint sprigs
1½ teaspoons coriander seeds, coarsely crushed	1 litre vodka or grappa

Allow the orange zest to dry for about 4 days.

Combine the sugar with 350ml/12 fl oz of water in a saucepan. Bring to the boil and stir to dissolve the sugar. Add the orange zest, aniseeds, coriander seeds and cloves. Cook gently for 5 minutes. Remove from the heat and add the lemon verbena, if you're using it, and mint. Allow to cool for 20 minutes.

Place the sugar syrup with the orange zest and spices in a clean glass jar (divide between 2 jars if necessary). Add the vodka. Cover tightly and leave in a cool, dark place for 2 weeks.

Strain the liqueur into a jug and discard the solids. Fit a filter paper into a coffee filter. Pour 300ml/½ pint of boiling water through it. Discard the water. Place the filter over a bottle or decanter and pour in the liqueur. It will filter through very slowly. Continue adding liqueur until it has all been filtered. Again, use 2 bottles if necessary. Cap or stopper the bottles tightly. The liqueur is ready to drink but can be kept in a cool, dark place for up to 1 year.

COFFEE *and* SPICE LIQUEUR

Resolí

This delightful liqueur is traditional in the enchanting town of Cuenca, where 'hanging houses' cling to sheer canyon walls high above the river valley. An Italian monk supposedly introduced the liqueur at the end of the fifteenth century. Although the name, *resolí*, is quite similar to Sicilian *rosolio*, a liqueur made with rose petals, the Spanish version contains coffee and spices, no roses.

In Cuenca the liqueur is made with distilled grape spirits, *aguardiente de orujo*. Any clear spirits – orujo, grappa, marc or vodka – can be used.

❧ MAKES ABOUT 2 LITRES / 3 ½ PINTS

4 tablepoons finely ground dark-roast coffee	5 cloves
60g dried figs, washed	1 teaspoon aniseeds
Zest of 1 orange	375g sugar
One 7cm / 3in cinnamon stick	1.2 litres / 2 pints vodka

Brew the coffee with 250ml / 3 fl oz water.

Combine the figs, orange zest, cinnamon, cloves, aniseeds and 350ml / 12 fl oz water in a saucepan. Bring to the boil and simmer for 2 minutes.

Place the sugar in a heavy saucepan over medium heat. Melt the sugar until it is golden and most of the lumps are dissolved, 6 minutes. Remove from the heat and stir until all the sugar is melted.

Very carefully pour the coffee into the melted sugar. The sugar will bubble up. Stir it with a wooden spoon until the coffee is absorbed. Add the liquid in which the figs cooked. Place the pan over low heat and stir until the sugar is completely dissolved in the liquid. Remove from heat and add the figs, zest and spices to the sugar syrup. Cool.

Place the sugar syrup with spices in a clean 2 litre jar (or divide between 1 litre jars and/or 450–500ml / ¾–1 pint jars). Add the vodka. Cover the jar tightly and allow to steep for 2 weeks.

Strain the liqueur into a jug, discarding all the solids. Line a coffee filter with filter paper. Pour 300ml/½ pint boiling water through the filter, discarding the water. Place the filter over a clean jug and gradually pour the liqueur through it. It will filter very slowly and may take up to 20 minutes.

After filtering, pour the liqueur into clean bottles or decanters. Stopper tightly and store in a dark place. The liqueur is ready to drink after 2 weeks. It keeps well for up to 1 year.

COFFEE WITH MILK
CAFÉ CON LECHE

In Spain, the café, where business is transacted and social engagements take place, is as basic to everyday life as the tapa bar. In fact, sometimes it is the same establishment – serving coffee with snacks in the morning and late afternoon, wine and tapas in the evening, and coffee and brandy in the late, after-dinner hour.

The most typical bar coffee is *torrefacto,* beans dark-roasted with sugar, giving a bittersweet caramel taste, and very finely ground (see Sources). Made in an espresso machine and served with frothy steam-heated milk, it is sort of like a latte, but better. Coffee begins the day at breakfast, served half and half with hot milk. It ends the day as strong espresso served black, *solo,* in tiny cups. In between are many degrees of tonality: a *sombra,* 'shade', is more milk than coffee, but a *nube,* 'cloud', is mostly hot milk with a touch of coffee; a *cortado,* 'cut', is coffee with just a tinge of milk.

Coffee brewed at home may be made in an electric coffee maker, an espresso pot or with a simple paper filter.

HOT CHOCOLATE

Chocolate a la Taza

Hot chocolate so thick it's almost a pudding is a favourite treat for the finale of late-night fiestas, served up at street stalls and accompanied by *churros*, fritters, for dunking. At home, hot chocolate is special for winter mornings during the Christmas season and for family Sunday breakfasts.

In Spain you buy a bar of *chocolate a la taza*, drinking chocolate, which already contains sugar and rice flour to thicken the brew. The chocolate is chopped and melted with water or milk. An American friend of mind, who was mad about Spanish hot chocolate when he lived in Spain, discovered that the packaged mix for chocolate pudding and pie filling which is so common in the United States will, made with extra milk, produce a reasonable substitute for thick Spanish drinking chocolate. My recipe uses real chocolate plus cornflour to thicken it. Want to serve it as a dessert? Pour into shallow soup bowls and add a *buñuelo*, fritter (page 314) and a swirl of whipped cream.

SERVES 4

170g bittersweet chocolate (at least 58 per ent cacao)	450ml / ¾ pint milk
	4 tablespoons cornflour
4 tablepoons sugar	¼ teaspoon vanilla extract

Chop the chocolate and place in a heavy saucepan with the sugar, milk and 450ml/¾ pint of water. Heat the chocolate over medium heat, whisking frequently, until the chocolate is melted.

Stir the cornflour into 250ml/8 fl oz of cold water until smooth. Whisk the cornflour mixture into the chocolate. Cook, whisking constantly, until the chocolate begins to bubble. Reduce the heat and cook for 2 minutes, whisking.

Remove the chocolate from the heat and stir in the vanilla.

Serve the chocolate hot in mugs or large cups.

GLOSSARY

Spanish words and expressions are scattered throughout this book and in many instances the author explains their meaning or origin. But what if, after you've closed the book, you want to go back and find again the meaning of *meloso* or *pago*? This glossary will help you find them again. The Spanish words and terms are listed here alphabetically, followed by their English translation or recipe title. Where it would be helpful, the page number on which the word(s) appears is given in brackets at the end.

The brief definitions given here simply recap the meanings of these words as used by Janet Mendel in *Cooking from the Heart of Spain* – they do not comprehensively define these words.

accidentado rough (as in rough terrain) [page 6]

aceitunas olives

   aceitunas con aliño de tomillo thyme-marinated olives [page 15]

   aceitunero olive picker

acelga chard [page 74]

adobar to marinate

agridulce bittersweet [page 8]

aguardiente a clear, strong spirit made from distilled wine, usually flavoured with aniseed [pages 46, 155, 349, 361, 363]

ajiaceite garlic sauce, also known as *alioli* [page 115]

ajillo a small amount of garlic [page 240]

ajo garlic

   ajo de espárragos garlicky asparagus and eggs [page 61]

   ajo morado purple garlic [page 105]

alajú Cuenca-style honey-almond nougat [page 334]

albóndiga meatball

   albóndigas de bacalao codfish balls with walnuts [page 145]

alboronía meat braised with onions and aubergine [page 153]

alcachofas artichokes [page 53]

alcaravea caraway [page 261]

aleta de ternera rellena stuffed veal roll [page 204]

aliño dressing [page 15]

alitas de pollo chicken wings [page 170]

almeja clam

   almejas a la marinera clams, mariner's style [page 149]

almendras almonds

almirez a small brass mortar for grinding spices [page 8]

alubias beans [page 37]

andrajos 'rags', a kind of pasta

añejo well cured, aged [page 119]

anguila eel

arrope a syrup made from boiled-down grape must [page 332]

   arrope con boniatos sweet potatoes candied in grape syrup [page 332]

arroz rice

   arroz a la quintería farmhouse rice with fish and greens [page 142]

   arroz al cazador hunter's rice with rabbit [page 191]

asadillo roasted

   asadillo de la huerta flame-roasted garden vegetables [page 246]

asado roast

atascaburras literally 'to choke a donkey'; a thick purée of salt cod and garlicky potatoes [page 29]

atún tuna [page 17]

azafrán saffron [page 134]

bacalao salt cod [page 10]

    bacalao a la manchega salt cod with roasted peppers, Manchegan style [page 147]

berenjena aubergine [page 67]

    berenjena a la parrilla con aliño char-grilled aubergines with lemon dressing [page 264]

    berenjena con miel fried aubergine with a drizzle of honey [page 263]

    berenjenas con queso al horno baked aubergines with cheese [page 262]

    berenjenas de Almagro pickled aubergine, Almagro style [page 280]

    berenjena guisada con alcaravea aubergines with tomato and caraway [page 261]

    berenjenas rellenas meat-stuffed aubergines spiced with nutmeg [page 212]

besugo sea bream

    besugo al horno con patatas roasted bream on a bed of potatoes [page 138]

bizcocho sponge cake

    bizcochos borrachos sponge cake soaked in wine-laced syrup (drunken cakes) [page 296]

    bizcochá con flan de queso manchego moulded Manchego cheese custard with caramel sauce [page 322]

    bizcocho de Toledo sandwich cake with apricots and marzipan, Toledo style [page 296]

blanca, blanco white

bocado mouthful, bite

    bocaditos de jamón y queso crisp ham and cheese sandwiches [page 86]

boda wedding

bodega wine cellar, winery [pages 352, 356]

bolos con ajiaceite beans with garlic sauce [page 115]

bombones de higos con chocolate chocolate-fig bonbons [page 336]

boniato sweet potato

borracho, borracha drunk [pages 296, 304]

    borrachos various sweets that have wine or spirits in their dough or else are soaked in wine syrup [page 304]

brócoli broccoli

buñuelos doughnut, also fritter [page 19]

    buñuelitos de higos figgy fritters [page 315]

    buñuelos de viento fritters (puffs of wind) [page 314]

cabrito kid

    cabrito asado herb-roasted kid [page 233]

cacerías smart hunts [page 152]

café coffee

    café con leche coffee with milk [page 364]

    café cortado coffee served with just a hint of milk [page 364]

    café nube mostly hot milk served with a touch of coffee [page 364]

    café solo strong espresso served black [page 364]

    café sombra coffee served with more milk than coffee [page 364]

    café torrefacto coffee beans, dark-roasted with sugar and very finely ground [page 364]

calabaza pumpkin [page 99]

caldereta cast iron casserole

    caldereta de cordero braised lamb with chillies [page 236]

caldillo de codorniz y setas consommé of quail and wild mushrooms [page 89]

caldo stock [page 88]

    caldo de pescado simple fish stock [page 135]

    caldo sencillo simple chicken stock [page 94]

caldoso soupy – in reference to paella [page 9]

campesino, campesina country, rural

cañamones hemp seeds [page 16]

canela cinnamon

carcamusas hearty beef stew with sausage [page 208]

carne meat [page 38]

casa house

    casa de labor farm building [page 358]

    casa de vacas cow keeper's house [page 358]

castaña chestnut

    castañas pilongas dried chestnuts [page 112]

castellana Castilian

cava sparkling wine, also wine cellar [page 348]

cazador hunter

cazuela earthenware casserole [page 7]

    cazuela de cordero lamb stew in cazuela [page 235]

    cazuela de gambas prawns in cazuela [page 150]

    cazuela de habas broad beans with escarole (broad-leaved endive) and mint [page 257]

    cazuela de pollo con arroz a la campesina country chicken casserole with rice [page 176]

cazuelitas earthenware ramekins, for serving *tapas de cocina* [pages 21, 27, 244]

cebolla onion

cebolletas spring onion
 cebolletas escarlatas scarlet-pickled onions [page 282]
cecina de ciervo venison 'ham' [page 358]
Cencibel in La Mancha, another name for the Tempranillo grape [page 349]
cerdo pig, pork
chocolate a la taza hot chocolate [page 365]
chorizo Spanish sausage [page 7]
chucherías kiddies' sweets, the sorts you'd see in Pik 'n' Mix selections [page 259]
chuletas chops, escalopes
 chuletas de cerdo al ajo manchego pork chops in garlicky sauce [page 215]
 chuletas de cerdo al horno baked pork chops with lemon marinade [page 216]
 chuletas de cordero al ajillo lamb chops sizzled with garlic [page 240]
churros fritters [page 365]
ciervo deer
clarete wine made by mixing white wine with enough red wine to colour it [page 348]
cochifrito a type of lamb stew [page 236]
cocido one-pot meal in which the broth is served first, followed by the meat and vegetables from the pot [pages 88, 120]
 cocido relleno para Días de Fiesta one-pot feast [page 120]
coco coconut
 cocos coconut biscuits [page 293]
codornices quails
 codornices con fundas quail in 'slipcovers' of red peppers [page 189]
codorniz quail [page 89]
col cabbage
 coles salteadas pan-sautéed cabbage with cumin [page 253]
coliflor cauliflower [page 95]
 coliflor o brócoli con ajo dorado y almendras cauliflower or broccoli with golden garlic and almonds [page 255]
 coliflor rebosada batter-fried cauliflower [page 254]
collejas a type of wild spring greens [page 142]
comida de mediodía midday meal [page 110]
conejo rabbit
 conejo con higos al estilo mudéjar rabbit with figs and Mudéjar *spices* [page 193]

conservas preserves, tinned foods
convivencia peaceful co-existence [page 4]
corazón heart
 corazones hearts made of marzipan with an egg yolk cream filling [page 287]
cordero lamb
 cordero asado con relleno roast lamb with spinach and breadcrumb stuffing [page 229]
 cordero en rustidera con patatas lamb roasted with saffron potatoes [page 227]
 cordero estofado con alubias lamb shanks braised with beans [page 239]
corral farmyard [page 152]
costrada manchega baked eggs with cheese (*costra*, crust) [page 65]
crema cream
 crema de calabaza pumpkin soup [page 99]
crianza slightly aged (referring to wine) [page 351]
croquetas croquettes
 croquetas de queso cheese and potato croquettes [page 22]
cuajado timbale (vegetarian)
 cuajado de berenjenas aubergine timbale [page 67]
cuajo rennet (a curdling agent) [page 71]
cuarto de hora quarter hour, fish soup [101]
cuerva the Albacete name for white wine cooler [page 354]

dehesas rough pastureland [page 11]
delicia delight
 delicias rounds of marzipan paste folded over an egg yolk filling [page 288]
Denominación de Origen (DO) 'DO' on a label guarantees a particular food or wine to be from the location listed and of a particular quality, equivalent to the French *appellation contrôlée* [pages 7 and 348–353]
desayuno breakfast [pages 58, 67]
desayuno molinero miller's breakfast – in this particular case, an olive miller's breakfast [page 58]
Días de Fiesta holidays, celebrations [page 120]
DO, see *Denominación de Origen*; for information on DO Almansa, DO Jumilla, DO La Mancha, DO Manchuela, DO Méntrida, DO Mondéjar, DO Ribera del Júcar and DO Valdepeñas, see pages 249–351.
dorado golden
duelos toils and travails, or grief

duelos y quebrantos in *Don Quixote*, the name for 'Saturday eggs and bacon' [page 60]

dulce sweet [page 8]
  dulce de membrillo quince jelly [page 329]

empanada pie, pastie
  empanadas rellenas con pollo pasties filled with spicy chicken [page 76]

empanadillas pasties, turnovers [page 17]
  empanadillas de nueces walnut turnovers with honey glaze [page 302]

ensalada salad
  ensalada a la manchega Manchegan salad, with cheese [page 45]
  ensalada con escabeche a salad of pickled partridge or chicken [page 43]
  ensalada de alubias con taquillos do chorizo bean salad with chorizo [page 37]
  ensalada de esquileo sheepshearers' salad, with rice, ham and cheese [page 42]
  ensalada de judías verdes con uvas green bean salad with grapes and anise [page 46]
  ensalada de limones con gambas lemon salad with prawns [page 41]

ensaladilla rusa Russian salad [page 44]

escabeche pickling marinade
  escabeche de alitas de pollo chicken wings in escabeche [page 170]

escalfados poached [page 63]

escarlata scarlet

espalda back
  a la espalda on its back (when referring to grilling fish) [page 136]

espárragos asparagus

espinaca spinach [page 64]
  espinacas a la Iniestense spinach with garlic, Iniesta style [page 252]

esquileo sheepshearer [page 42]

estilo style

estofado stew

filetes fillets, escalopes
  filetes de ciervo en adobo beef or venison escalopes in adobo [page 206]
  filetes de lenguado con uvas fillets of sole with white wine sauce [page 140]

flan baked custard

flan de queso con jamón baked cheese custard with ham [page 69]

flores flowers; also the name of a popular type of fried pastry [page 309]

fresca, fresco fresh

frito, frita fried

frutas de la sartén a type of sweet fritter referred to by Cervantes, typically found in La Mancha and Andalucía (fruits of the frying pan) [page 309]

frutos secos dried fruits and nuts [page 259]

gachas porridge; the recipe for *gachas* on page 277 is for a garlicky chickpea porridge
  gachasmigas manchegas polenta and crunchy croûtons [page 279]

gallina hen
  gallina en pepitoria chicken braised in an almond-saffron sauce [pages 161, 163]

gambas prawns [page 19]

garbanzos chickpeas [pages 108, 116]

gaseoso lightly sweetened, slightly lemony fizzy water (similar to British lemonade) [page 359]

gazpacho Andalusian cold soup [page 196]

gazpachos a game stew with unleavened bread [page 196]
  gazpachos de pastor shepherd's stew with game or turkey [page 196]

gran reserva well aged (referring to wine) [page 351]

granizado iced drink, granita
  granizado de naranja orange ice [page 345]
  granizado de vino tinto red wine granita [page 344]

gratinado gratin
  gratinado de alcachofas con queso cheesy artichoke gratin [page 248]

guardamonte forest ranger and game warden [page 130]

guindillas chilli peppers [page 7]

guirlache praline

guisado stew; *guiso* cooked dish
  guisado de setas y patatas mushroom and potato stew [page 268]
  guiso de boda wedding stew [page 161]
  guiso de bodas de Camacho wedding stew with chicken and meatballs [page 163]

guisantes peas

gusano worm; *gusanillo* little worm

haba broad bean

habitas small broad beans

harina flour

> *harina de almorta* flour made from the legume vetch; Manchegan gachas are made with this flour [pages 277, 279]

hartatunos hash brown potato cake (fill the rascals up) [page 272]

helado, helada frozen, icy, cold; *helado* ice cream, ice milk

> *helado de miel de espliegas* lavender honey ice milk [page 338]
>
> *helado de azafrán con guirlache de piñones y sirope de chocolate* saffron ice cream with pine nut praline and chocolate syrup [page 339]

hierbas herbs

higos figs

> *higos con jarabe de vanilla* figs poached in vanilla syrup [page 327]

hojarascas de calabaza cinnamon pumpkin slices [page 328]

hojuelas crispy leaves: a type of crisp fried pastry [page 309]

hornazos de romería picnic rolls with pork, sausage and egg [page 82]

horno oven

huerta market garden

huevos eggs

> *huevos dobles* double eggs [page 24]
>
> *huevos en nidos de espinacas* eggs baked in spinach nests [page 64]
>
> *huevos escalfados en puré de tomate con queso* eggs poached in puréed tomatoes with cheese [page 63]
>
> *huevos estrellados* crackly fried eggs [page 55]
>
> *huevos mal educados* badly behaved eggs – in the recipe for *revuelto de huevos y patatas con ajo*, the eggs are broken into the already-frying potatoes and garlic [page 58]

jamón ham

> *jamón ibérico* Iberico ham [page 11]
>
> *jamón serrano* serrano ham [page 10]

jarabe syrup

> *jarabe de naranjas* orange syrup [page 326]

jóven young, also refers to young red wines [page 351]

judía bean

> *judías con perdiz* partridge with beans [page 185]

judías verdes green beans [page 46]

> *judías verdes a la Castellana* Castilian green beans with red peppers [page 250]

judío, judía Jewish

lechal milk-fed (as in *ternera lechal*, veal) [page 201]

leche milk

> *leche frita* 'fried milk' [page 324]

lenguado sole

lentejas lentils

> *lentejas con chorizo* lentils with sausage [page 110]
>
> *lentejas para viernes* Don Quixote's Friday lentils [page 112]

licor de trasnochá late-night liqueur [page 362]

liebre hare

> *liebre a la cazadora* hunter's stew with hare [page 195]

limones lemons [page 41]

lira lyre – in this case the lyre is a mechanical arm that breaks up the curds of cheese during cheesemaking [page 72]

lomo loin

> *lomo de bacalao* salt cod 'loins' or centre cut [page 147]
>
> *lomo de cerdo* pork loin
>
> *lomo de la orza* spiced pork loin in confit [page 217]

lubina sea bass

> *lubina con ajillo de piñones* sea bass with garlic, pine nuts and chilli [page 136]

lugar place

macarrones macaroni

> *macarrones con chorizo* macaroni with chorizo sausage [page 221]

maduración curing, ripening of cheeses [page 72]

madurar to mature, to ripen

manos hands, trotters

> *manos de cerdo estofadas* slow-cooked pig's trotters [page 225]

mantecados orange-scented lard biscuits [page 294]

manto blanket [page 160]

masa dough

> *masa para pan* basic bread dough [page 80]

matanza annual pig slaughter [page 200]

matar to slaughter

matar el gusanillo kill the little 'worm' of hunger [page 155]

mazapán marzipan [page 287]

melindres almond rings [page 286]

meloso juicy – in reference to paella [page 9]

membrillo quince paste

mercadillo street market [page 259]

merluza hake

    merluza al azafrán poached hake with saffron sauce [page 134]

meseta high plateau land [page 2]

miel honey

migas fried breadcrumbs

    migas del pastor shepherds' garlic-fried breadcrumbs [page 275]

miguelitos flaky pastries with cream filling [page 284]

    miguelitos con crema de calabaza 'Little Mickeys': pastry squares with pumpkin cream filling [page 300]

místela sweet spiced wine [page 361]

moje dunk – also, another name for *pipirrana* [page 40]

mojete a vegetable stew served with bread for dunking [page 260]

    mojete de acelgas chard sauté [page 251]

mondeo the act of extracting the three filaments of the stigma from each saffron crocus

    mondaderas women who perform *mondeo* [page 160]

morcilla Spanish black pudding (blood sausage) [page 20]

    morcilla con pasas y piñones morcilla with raisins and pine nuts [page 224]

morcilla blanca white pudding (bloodless black pudding) [page 222]

mortero mortar

    morteruelo de Cuenca liver and game paté, made Cuenca style [page 35]

mostachos de nuez chewy walnut biscuits [page 291]

mostillo Moorish delight, a sweet made from grape must, similar to Turkish delight pages 284 and 330]

mosto grape juice [page 330]

movida the 'scene' [page 20]

Mudéjar meaning 'permitted to remain', referring to the Muslim Moors who opted to remain in Toledo after the Christians wrested control from them [page 193]

mustachudos a walnut sweet found in Sephardic cooking [page 291]

nabos turnips

    nabos guisados al pimentón braised turnips with pimentón [page 267]

naranjas oranges

nata cream [page 72]

natillas custard pudding with meringue topping [page 320]

navajas folding pocket knives [page 213]

Navidad Christmas

nidos nests [page 64]

Nochebuena Christmas Eve [page 289]

ñora dried peppers

nuez walnut

obrador workshop, confectionery [pages 3, 288]

ojeadores beaters, who thrash bushes [more on partridge shoots, page 181]

olla large pan in which stew is cooked [pages 38, 88]

    olla podrida rotten stew [page 118]

olleta hearty vegetable soup with beans and sausage [page 107]

orar y trabajar pray and work [page 287]

orejones dried apricots (little ears) [page259]

orza earthenware jug or amphora in which whole pork loins are marinated in a spiced, salty marinade [page 217]

pago estate, domain, chateau [pages 350, 356]

palacio mansion

palotes garlic scrapes [page 270]

    palotes con patatas potatoes mashed with green garlic [page 270]

pan bread

    pan dulce sweet bread roll [page 304]

panza belly [page 50]

pardina [lentils] tiny, dark brown lentils, similar to puy lentils [page 110]

parrilla grill

pasas raisins

paseo a walk, a stroll [page 20]

pasta paste, pastry dough
    pasta quebrada flaky pastry dough [page 79]
pastel, cake, pie
    pastel de viernes 'Friday pie', with fish [page 66]
pastelero confectioner [page 288]
pastor shepherd
pata negra black foot (another name for Iberico ham) [page 11]
patatas potatoes
paté de perdiz y pollo partridge and chicken pâté [page 33]
pato duck
    pato al vino tinto duck braised in red wine [page 178]
pechuga breast
    pechuga de pollo con arroz y verduras frescas chicken breast with crunchy vegetables and rice [page 158]
    pechuga de pollo empanada con salsa de membrillo crispy, cheesy chicken breast with quince sauce [page 156]
pelusas lemon biscuits [page 290]
perdiz partridge [page 33]
    perdiz estofada a la Toledana braised partridge, Toledo style [page 183]
perol deep two-handled frying pan with flared sides [page 191]
pescado fish [page 126]
    pescado en escabeche fish in a tangy marinade [page 132]
picante spicy-hot [page 8]
pichón young pigeon
    pichones rellenos squabs stuffed with raisins, apricots and walnuts [page 187]
piel de sapo a type of melon ('toad skin') grown in La Mancha [page 260]
pierna leg
    pierna de cordero asado con hierbas leg of lamb roasted with Mediterranean herbs [page 229]
pimentón Spanish paprika [page 8]
pimientos peppers, pimentos
    pimientos rellenos con salsa de tomate beef-stuffed peppers with chunky tomato sauce [page 210]
pinchos savoury snacks [pages 20-21]
pinchos de albondiguillas cocktail meatballs [page 31]
piñón pine nut
pipas sunflower seeds

pipirrana a soupy salad served with chunks of bread for scooping it up [page 40]
pisto vegetable medley [pages 2, 153, 245]
    pisto con pollo Toledano chicken with peppers and tomatoes, Toledo style [page 153]
    pisto manchego medley of summer vegetables [pages 244, 245]
plancha griddle [page 21]
poderida powerful [page 119]
podrida, podrido rotten [page 118]
pollero poultryman [page 182]
pollo chicken [pages 33, 76]
    pollo al agraz chicken braised in spiced verjuice [page 166]
    pollo asado relleno con hierbas roast chicken stuffed with liver and spring herbs [page 174]
    pollo con andrajos chicken with pinto beans and pasta rags [page 172]
    pollo con setas y trufas cuando hayan chicken with wild mushrooms and possibly truffles [page 168]
    pollo manchego con aguardiente Manchego chicken with anisette [page 155]
potaje potage – hearty stew with pulses [page 88]
    potaje de carillas con sofrito black-eyed beans with tomato sofrito [page 114]
    potaje de garbanzos y espinacas con rellenos chickpeas and spinach with cod dumplings [page 116]
pote aceitunero olive pickers' cod and potato stew [page 143]
puestos hides (occupied by game hunters) [page 181]
puré purée
    puré de garbanzos con pan frito chickpea purée with crisp croûtons [page 108]
    puré de tomate tomato purée [page 63]
quebrada broken
quebrantos afflictions, cracked [page 60]
queso cheese [page 22]
queso fresco fresh white cheese [pages 74 and 343]
quintería farm, smallholding [page 142]

ración a larger tapa portion, suitable for sharing [page 21]
rebosado batter-fried or breadcrumbed and fried [page 254]
recolección harvesting [page 273]

relleno, rellena stuffed

    relleno stuffing

    rellenos are also a cross between fritters and dumplings [page 116]

    rellenos dulces con canela sweet cinnamon dumplings in caramel sauce [page 317]

requesón cottage cheese [page 72]

reserva aged (referring to wine), [page 351]

resolí coffee and spice liqueur [page 363]

revueltos scrambled eggs [page 168]

    revuelto con habas scrambled eggs with broad beans [page 59]

    revuelto de huevos y patatas con ajo scrambled eggs with potatoes and garlic [page 58]

rey king

rollo roll

    rollo de cordero con acelga lamb roll wrapped in chard leaves [page 241]

romería pilgrimage [page 82]

rosado rosé [pages 350, 352]

rosas roses, saffron flowers

    roseras women who extract the three filaments of the stigma (saffron) from each crocus [page 160]

rosca ring-shaped roll or pastry

    roscos de vino cinnamon-wine rings [page 285]

roscón de reyes cake, served on January 6 for the Feast of the Three Kings (Epiphany, Twelfth Night) [page 304]

rosquillas anise-flavoured doughnuts [page 311]

rubia blonde

    rubia castellana the most common type of lentil in Castilla–La Mancha, sold in England as 'green lentils' [page 110]

rustidera a shallow roasting pan, big enough to hold a whole baby lamb, jointed [page 227]

salpicón hash made from chopped meat and vegetables from a leftover stew, dressed with vinaigrette [page 38]

    salpicón de carne beef and ham salad [page 38]

salsa sauce, gravy

    salsa de caramelo caramel sauce [page 318]

    salsa de tomate frito tomato sauce (literally: sauce of fried tomatoes) [page 26]

salteado sautéed

    salteado de alcachofas artichoke sauté [page 247]

    salteado de guisantes con zanahorias sauté of fresh peas and carrots [page 258]

sandía watermelon [page 360]

sangría red wine sangría [page 359]

    sangría de sandía watermelon sangría [page 360]

seca, seco dry

    secadero drying room where cheese is stacked and turned [page 72]

secretario person who spots and recovers downed birds on a shoot [page 181]

sencillo simple

serrano mountain [page 10]

setas mushrooms [pages 89, 268]

    setas en escabeche pickled mushrooms [page 281]

sin muerte; in referring to fishing, 'catch and release' [page 130]

sirope syrup

solomillo sirloin, fillet

    solomillos de cerdo con cebolletas glaseadas pork fillets with glazed onions [page 219]

sopa soup

    sopa al cuarto de hora fifteen-minute soup [page 101]

    sopa de ajo garlic soup [page 102]

    sopa de ajo emparejado double garlic soup [page 104]

    sopa de almendras para Navidad Christmas almond soup [page 319]

    sopa de tomate con bacón tomato soup with bacon [page 97]

    sopa de vigilia con coliflor y flan de queso cauliflower-potato soup with moulded cheese custard [page 95]

    sopa manchega con espárragos Manchegan soup with asparagus [page 92]

    sopa verde green pea soup [page 100]

sorbete sorbet, iced fruit drink

    sorbete de membrillo quince sorbet [page 343]

surtido de ibérico an assortment of Iberico ham, cured loin, and sausages [page 21]

tapas a variety of bar foods served in small portions [20-21]

tapas de cocina hot, cooked dishes served as tapas [page 21]

tapeo a pub crawl with friends to eat tapas [page 20]

tarta helada de higos frozen fig mousse [page 341]

tasajo sheep or goat jerky [page 60]

tasca pub [page 21]

taza cup

ternera young beef from a yearling steer [page 201]

   ternera lechal veal [page 201]

   ternera mechada con aceitunas y tocino braised veal larded with olives and salt pork [page 201]

tinajas earthenware vats in which grape must used to be fermented [page 348]

tiznao blackened, as in charred from grilling; also a La Mancha dish of roasted peppers, onions and cod [pages 27, 260]

tocino salt pork fat, also fat from *serrano* ham, also bacon [pages 11, 119]

tojunto (*todo junto*) 'altogether' veal or beef stew [page 207]

tomate tomato [page 26]

   tomates rellenos con ensaladilla rusa tomatoes stuffed with potato-caper salad [page 44]

tomatillas sun-dried tomatoes [page 260]

tomatón toast with grated tomatoes on top, known elsewhere as 'Catalan toast' [page 85]

tomillo thyme [page 15]

torno grilled window from where cloistered nuns sell their confections [pages 284, 287]

torrijas sweet toasts, similar to eggy bread [page 316]

torta cake, pie

   torta de acelgas con queso chard and cheese pie [page 74]

   torta de espárragos asparagus tart [page 77]

   torta de nueces walnut cake [page 295]

tortas cakes

   tortas de Alcázar de San Juan bigger-than-sponge fingers [page 292]

   tortas de boniato sweet potato buns [page 307]

tortilla omelette

   tortilla capuchina a thick potato and asparagus omelette [page 55]

   tortilla de alcachofas a thick artichoke and ham omelette [page 53]

   tortilla de patatas a thick potato omelette [pages 21, 51]

tortillitas de almendras almond fritters [page 313]

tórtola wild dove [page 358]

tostada toast with olive oil [page 85]

tostaditas crujientes thin toast crisps [page 30]

trucha trout

   trucha a la judía trout, Jewish style [page 129]

   trucha con setas en cazuela, al estilo de Guadalajara trout and mushrooms in cazuela, Guadalajara style [page 128]

   truchas rellenas con jamón y setas trout stuffed with ham and mushrooms [page 127]

trufas truffles

turrón a honey-almond nougat, a speciality of Toledo and Jijona (Alicante) [page 334]

uvas grapes [pages 46, 140]

vanguadistas [page 2]

vendimia grape harvest [pages 3, 275, 330, 356]

verde green [page 100]

verduras greens, vegetables

   verduras a la parrilla pan-grilled vegetables [page 265]

viento wind

Viernes Santo Good Friday [page 116]

vigilia abstinence, a meatless meal [page 95]

vino wine

   vino blanco white wine

   vino de pago single-estate wine [page 356]

   vino tinto red wine

   Vinos de La Tierra de Castilla wines made within Castilla–La Mancha [page 350]

   vinos de pago single-estate wines [page 350]

viudas widowed [page 112]

yema yolk; also, candied egg cream mixed with marzipan [page 288]

zanahoria carrot

   zanahorias con hierbabuena minted carrots [page 256]

zarajos lamb tripe twisted round grapevine skewers and roasted [page 20]

zurra manchega Manchegan white wine cooler [page 354]

Sources

Many foods from Spain, such as extra virgin olive oil, Manchego cheese and saffron, dried chorizo and serrano ham are now widely available in supermarkets. However, if there are Spanish ingredients you can't find in your local supermarket or delicatessen, one of these sources should be able to help.

PEPPERS BY POST

For fresh chillies

www.peppersbypost.biz

Michael and Joy Michaud

Sea Spring Farm

West Bexington

Dorchester

Dorset DT2 9DD

tel: 01308 897766

fax: 01308 897735

email: info@peppersbypost.biz

COOL CHILE COMPANY

For dried chillies, chocolate and other Spanish and Mexican ingredients

www.coolchile.co.uk

Unit 7, Buspace Studios

Conlan Street

London

W10 5AP

tel: 0870 9021145

fax: 0870 1623923

email: dodie@coolchile.co.uk

R. GARCIA & SONS

For all sorts of Spanish ingredients

(a Spanish delicatessen near Ladbroke Grove tube station, London)

248–250 Portobello Road

London

W11 1LL

tel: 0207 721 6119

THE PAELLA COMPANY

For all sorts of Spanish ingredients, mail order

www.thepaellacompany.co.uk

Unit 1, Lodge Farm

Hook Road

North Warnborough

Hampshire RG29 1HA

tel: 0845 3550559

fax: 01256 703086

email: info@thepaellacompany.co.uk

PURE SPAIN

For all sorts of Spanish ingredients, mail order

www.purespain.co.uk

Unit 202, 80 High Street

Winchester

Hampshire SO23 9AT

tel: 01962 774942

fax: 01962 774822

email: info@purespain.co.uk

BIBLIOGRAPHY

Aguilera Pleguezuelo, José. *Las cocinas árabe y judía y la cocina española*. Málaga: Editorial Arguval, 2002.

Alimentos de Castilla–La Mancha. Bimonthly magazine. Ciudad Real: Periodistas Asociados.

Alimentos de Castilla–La Mancha. ECOS CLM, Consejería de Agricultura y Medio Ambiente, 2002.

Álvarez Cobelas, M., and Cirujano, S. *Las Tablas de Daimiel*. Ecología Acuática y Sociedad. ICONA, 2002. Excerpts from accounts of Julio Escuderos.

Aradillas, Antonio. *Las Rutas del Quijote*. Madrid: Libro-Hobby-Club, 2004.

Ashtor, Eliyahu. *Jews of Moslem Spain,* volumes 2 and 3. Philadelphia: Jewish Publication Society, 1992.

Calduch, Enrique, and Gómez, Roberto. *Los Ajos de Castilla–La Mancha*. Madrid: Junta de Comunidades de Castilla–La Mancha, 2002.

Cervantes, Miguel de. *Don Quijote de la Mancha*. Barcelona: Editorial Ramón Sopena, 1978.

CLM Castilla–La Mancha – La Tierra del Quijote. Bi-monthly magazine. Ciudad Real: Periodistas Asociados.

Cuéllar Tórtola, Javier, and Pardo Domingo, Pedro. *La Cocina Tradicional de la Manchuela*. Iniesta (Cuenca): Centro de Estudios de La Manchuela, 2004.

Díaz, Lorenzo. *La Cocina del Quijote*. Madrid: Alianza Editorial, 1997.

Falcó, Carlos, Marqués de Griñón. *Entender de Vino*. Madrid: Ediciones Martínez Roca, 2004.

García, L. Jacinto. *Carlos V a la mesa. Cocina y alimentación en la España renacentista*. Toledo: Ediciones Bremen, 2000.

García del Cerro, Carlos, and Alonso Madero, Francisco Javier. *La Mancha y el Queso Manchego*. Consejería de Agricultura, Junta de Comunidades de Castilla–La Mancha, 1986.

García Moreno, Enrique, and Agentes Femeninos del Servicio de Extensión Agraria de la Conserjería de Agricultura. *Recetario Gastronómico de Castilla–La Mancha*. Junta de Comunidades de Castilla–La Mancha, 1985. Book is out of print, but recipe database is online at *castillalamancha.es/turismo/SP/contenidos/Gastronomia*.

González Muñoz, Domingo. *La Cocina Tradicional en la Provincia de Toledo*. Diputación de Toledo, 1999.

Gregorio Arriaga, Carmen de. *Costumbres y Cocina Manchega*. Ciudad Real: Biblioteca de Autores Manchegos de la Diputación de Ciudad Real, 2002.

Macías Kapón, Uriel, and Benarroch de Bensadon, Ana. *La Cocina Judía, Leyes, costumbres, y algunas recetas sefardíes*. Girona: Red de Juderías de España, 2003.

Osa, Manuel de la. *Cocina Castellano–Manchega*. León: Editorial Everest, 2001.

Racionero Page, Joaquín. *Guisos, Viandas y Otras Pócimas*. Avila: J. Noticias, 2000.

Repostería Monacal de las Hermanas Clarisas. San Sebastián: Ardatz, 1999.

Rivka Cohen, A. *Los Placeres de mi Cocina Judía*. Barcelona: Parsifal Ediciones, 2003.

Sanjuán Vicens, Gloria. *Ollas, Sartenes y Fogones del Quijote*. Madrid: Libro-Hobby-Club, 2004.

Shaul, Moshe, Aldina Quintana Rodríguez, Zelda Ovadia. *El Gizado Sefardí*. Zaragoza: Ibercaja, 1995.

Useros, Carmina. *Mil Recetas de Cocina de Albacete y Su Provincia*. Albacete: Carmina Useros, 2001.

INDEX